Hollywood Raises Political Consciousness

Political Messages in Feature Films

Edited by Michael Haas

PETER LANG
New York • Washington, D.C./Baltimore • Bern
Frankfurt • Berlin • Brussels • Vienna • Oxford

Library of Congress Cataloging-in-Publication Data

Hollywood raises political consciousness: political messages in feature films /
edited by Michael Haas.
pages cm
Includes bibliographical references and index.
1. Motion pictures—Political aspects—United States. 2. Politics in motion pictures.
3. United States—Politics and government—21st century.
4. United States—Politics and government—20th century.
I. Haas, Michael, editor of compilation.
PN1995.9.P6H65   791.43'6581—dc23   2014013727
ISBN 978-1-4331-2661-1 (hardcover)
ISBN 978-1-4331-2660-4 (paperback)
ISBN 978-1-4539-1372-7 (e-book)

Bibliographic information published by **Die Deutsche Nationalbibliothek**.
Die Deutsche Nationalbibliothek lists this publication in the "Deutsche
Nationalbibliografie"; detailed bibliographic data are available
on the Internet at http://dnb.d-nb.de/.

Hollywood Raises
Political Consciousness

To Brian
Dear find a colleague

[signature]

Dec 2014

This book is part of the Peter Lang Media and Communication list.
Every volume is peer reviewed and meets
the highest quality standards for content and production.

PETER LANG
New York • Washington, D.C./Baltimore • Bern
Frankfurt • Berlin • Brussels • Vienna • Oxford

Table of Contents

Tables

Preface

My first interest in films was the reward for walking down Warren Boulevard in Detroit, quarter in hand, to attend the cartoons, documentaries, B-films (mostly Westerns), and then the A films (I recall only *The Fountainhead* in 1949) at the Alger Theatre every Saturday, beginning at noon.

In 1950, my parents moved to Hollywood, and soon my interest was jolted by a direct association with some movie personalities and their children. Among those whom I met were Bob Hope, Art Linkletter, Ann Sheridan, and fellow classmate Ricky Nelson. My father, a radio station executive, often handled public relations with the film industry. From the students of celebrities at schools and in college, I learned of the Hollywood Ten, the film industry's work ban (the blacklist) on those who had leftist ties, and subpoenas of moviemakers by the House Un-American Activities Committee.

My interest in film receded when I went off to college in the mid-1950s, where I majored in political science. A few films were featured on the Stanford campus on Sunday nights, and friends noticed afterward that I was still caught up in the drama. Due to the blacklist, few feature films had political or social content in the 1950s and early 1960s. When I accepted employment at the University of Hawai'i, I discovered that films exhibited in Honolulu also were mostly devoid of political content. Few of my colleagues had any interest in films, whereas I was the first to use documentaries in class.

With the release of *Reds* (1981), *The Killing Fields* (1984), and *Platoon* (1986), I realized that the time had come to form an organization to reward Hollywood for providing political messages to the public again. I then founded the Political Film Society (PFS). I explain more about PFS within the introductory chapter.

As papers on political films were presented at academic political science conventions, I collected them as *Working Papers*, offering them for sale from on the PFS website, which was created in 1998. I also collected syllabi for courses on film from various scholars, making them available at a nominal cost. Membership grew over the years along with interest in the publications. Although interest continued in the *Working Papers Series* and *Syllabus Series*, the task of making photocopies for each request has remained burdensome because most of the material was written before articles could be filed on computers. Accordingly, I decided in early 2013 that some of the *Working Papers* should be collected in book form for easier distribution.

Most of the following chapters have their origins as a PFS *Working Paper*, though they have been updated. Chapter 6, by Elizabeth Haas, has never appeared as a *Working Paper* and thus appears for the first time herein. The book is intended not only for courses on political film but also as a commentary that should intrigue the film industry.

Most chapters were originally papers at academic conferences. Chapter 1 was presented at the 2004 convention of the Western Political Science Association. Chapters 2, 3, and 4 were first presented at the annual convention of the American Political Science Association during August 1995. Chapter 5 was originally presented as a paper at a conference of the Western Political Science Association during March 2001. Chapter 7 was originally presented at the 1996 annual convention of the American Political Science Association. Most authors have updated their papers to serve as chapters herein.

The authors of Chapters 2–5 and 7–8 granted permission for their distribution in the *Working Paper Series* of the Political Film Society. Chapters 1 and 6 are the only essays not previously available in the *Working Paper Series* of the Political Film Society; instead, the essays debut herein. (Incidentally, I am not related to or Elizabeth Haas, who is the sister of Peter J. Haas, who has written extensively on political films.) Chapter 8 conjoins and updates two of my essays written expressly for the Political Film Society *Working Paper Series* in 2001 and 2002; similar to the other chapters, the content is updated.

Chapter 3, as revised from the original *Working Paper Series* version, was published in Ernest D. Giglio, *Here's Looking at You: Hollywood, Film & Politics,* 4th edn., New York: Peter Lang, 2014, and is herein reprinted, including some updated passages, with the kind permission of the present publisher.

An appendix listing films nominated for Political Film Society awards is provided for those who might want to view films that focus on democracy, cinejournalistic exposés, human rights, and peace. The Political Film Society awards are known as Stanley Awards after the late Stanley Mark Castillo, who was the first vice president of Political Film Society, Inc.

Michael Haas
President, Political Film Society

Introduction
Michael Haas

Members of the film industry are quite conscious of politics. Although the industry is perceived as liberal or leftist, chapters in this volume argue otherwise for several reasons. Hollywood films are not nonprofit ventures but primarily rely on box office receipts. Second, most films portray the status quo. Third, the liberal reliance on government is at odds with the recurrent theme that government is corrupt and incompetent. Fourth, success of Hollywood films abroad requires sensitivity to conservative cultural elements.

Nowadays, the number of feature films with explicit political content fluctuates from year to year. Recently, Oliver Stone–type blockbusters have not been standard fare in contemporary America, though films produced abroad are less timorous. Yet politics pervades everyday life and is always somewhere on screen, providing images that subtly impress the minds of filmviewers. That's why a reading of chapters in the present volume is so important: The essays provide tools with which to analyze messaging in films as a clue to how the public may subliminally perceive political reality through otherwise entertaining feature films. Both students in political film classes and members of the film industry, I believe, should enjoy what the present book provides and will marvel at the lively legacy that films are leaving for the better understanding of social problems and political life.

Part I consists of three essays that try to define "political film." The Political Film Society has offered no such definition but instead identifies four categories in which films might be placed for purposes of an award. Chapters 1–3 try a more formal approach to the definitional question. The authors disagree with one another and with my definition above, leaving the question for the reader to ponder.

Chapter 1, which I wrote, provides a controversial thesis—that all films have political elements. Next, I offer a short history of political film, including the formation of the Political Film Society. Next, I present a step-by-step tracing of phases in film production where political themes could be inserted or deleted. Similar to other chapters in the book, the narrative is peppered with examples.

In Chapter 2 (Art and Politics: The Political Film as a Pedagogical Tool), Michael Genovese asks how films might create optimal conditions for political change. The author points out that films are the most accessible and popular art form in the contemporary world, so there is something in that artistry that can be used to motivate audiences beyond the need for entertainment and escape. To do so, films must overcome four barriers—the desire of those who go to the movies for light entertainment, the fast pace of public issues, resistance to overly preachy dialog, and the fear of producers that political films will not do well at the box office. There is no single formula for success, so political films must seek acceptance by clever artistic innovation.

In Chapter 3 (Searching for the Political Film), Ernest D. Giglio begins with *The Birth of a Nation* (1915) and traces four purposes served by political films—ideology, propaganda, history, and acting as an agent of change. He also identifies films that support as well as question the status quo. But to be a "political film," he insists on two elements—that the producer, filmmaker, or studio must consciously want to make a political statement, and that audiences must perceive the film as conveying a political message. His definition, offered after a careful review of writings on politics and film, is more stringent than that presented in the previous chapter.

Part II (Chapters 4–8) reverses the previous question, asking how "politics" is defined or portrayed within films. Films create stereotypes, sometimes favorably and sometimes maliciously. In this section, the focus is on the depiction of elections, civil society, ethnic groups, disasters, and foreign countries. The ideal essence of democracy is to have free elections after intelligent campaigns, respect for diversity in the public, and the indispensability of groups to mediate between government and the individual. But films do not always realistically portray what they depict.

In Chapter 4 (Real Oliver North Loses: The Reel Bob Robert Wins), John W. Williams argues that films are social constructions of reality. He contrasts four candidates for the U.S. Senate—two fictional and two real. Employing cultivation analysis, the author analyzes images in media content from two films and television's social construction of two actual candidates running for office. He finds that both types of media exhibit very similar techniques in creating images of politics—focus on everyday topics, cultural or literary allusions, exaggerated traits of the candidates, and background in the form of timely events, issues, and personalities. He also contrasts themes that differ from decade to decade.

Chapter 5 (Escape from the Bowling Alley: Traditional Associations as the Antagonist in Popular Film) by Hans Noel tests Robert Putnam's influential view that Americans do not socialize together as in the past, thereby undermining civil society (Putnam 1995, 2000). He provides the background within which six memorable films are analyzed. In all cases, the younger generation (those most likely to watch the six films) rebels against the generation of their parents, thus rejecting traditional associations as inappropriate for their more diverse lives. Indeed, the youth appear more than ready for the later development of social media. The six films serve not only as a critique of Putnam's thesis but also of old-fashioned civil society groups that must either adapt to the opportunities provided by social media or become ossified and irrelevant.

Chapter 6 (The Politics of Disaster Films) by Elizabeth Haas reports that many films of the twenty-first century have responded with a steady stream of disasters, more real than imagined—from Y2K to 9/11, hurricanes, oil spills, economic meltdowns, and political crises. The chapter analyses disaster films, including documentaries, as reactions to tragic events. Whereas documentaries provide facts, feature films exploit fears to demonstrate that individual heroism is possible, while governments are portrayed as ineffective. Thus, there is some continuity with how disaster films have been portrayed from the mid-twentieth century to the present.

One important focus is on the ethnic groups portrayed in films. Analyses have already focused on African Americans (e.g., Guerrero 1993), Arabs (Shaheen 2009), Hispanics (Reyes and Rubie 1994), and Native Americans (Kilpatrick 1999), but relatively few on Asian Americans (e.g., Feng 2002). Most writing on the subject identifies ethnic stereotyping, but Chapter 7 (The Blending of a Kaleidoscopic Culture: Films on Asian Americans) by Andrew L. Aoki discusses a more political theme—how films of Asian Americans fit into expectations by some in the United States that they should assimilate and act in a manner similar to Europeans who have more easily become Americanized (cf. Ignatiev 1995). But, since Asian cultures have many excellent characteristics, which I for one would not want to see abandoned, a certain tension is felt acutely by Americans of Chinese, Filipino, Japanese, and Korean ancestry, many of whom trace their origins in the United States back more generations than some European Americans. The essay carefully distinguishes between various alternatives to assimilationist thinking and then analyzes the implicit classifications applied to Asian characters in popular films in order to determine which images are being presented to the general filmviewer. Aoki concludes that amalgamationism, wherein one can both be American and retain the various Asian identities, is the answer to assimilationists who fear a balkanization of America into separate ethnic groups.

Chapter 8 (Films about Thailand and Vietnam), which I wrote, focuses on how Thailand and Vietnam are portrayed in film. Analyses of movies made in various countries around the world usually describe the major film-producing countries of Britain, France, Germany, India, Italy, and Japan (Leach 2004; Hayward and Vincendeau 2000; Brockman 2010; Ganti 2012; Landy 2000; Nornes and Gerow 2009). Instead, I decided to examine two countries that have not received as much attention, and thus may be victims of stereotyping, by comparing films made outside with those inside both countries. Thailand has a favorable image around the world as a place with smiling people calmly going about their lives in a bejeweled tourist destination spot that has a verdant countryside. Films made in the Thai film industry, which show considerable diversity, contrast with those made elsewhere, which often portray cardboard characters and sometimes offend Thai government sensibilities. In sum, the films do not provide much understanding about the country but do captivate audiences about the beauty and charm of the people. Films about Vietnam, in contrast, are half as numerous as those about Thailand. Over time, they have changed from love triangle themes to confront the reality of war. Today, with the exception of France, there is nearly an absence of interest in Vietnam within the West. Meanwhile, Vietnamese-made films have focused on the difficulties of survival after the end of a devastating war, a matter that is underappreciated outside Vietnam.

Other genres and themes may be presented in future volumes. Meanwhile, the reader is directed to the PFS website (*www.polfilms.com*), which reviews the latest films with political content approximately twice monthly. It is from the best of those films, as determined by PFS members, that directors are given awards each year.

All essays pose a fundamental question: How can filmmakers project political messages onto filmviewers. According to reception theory (Jauss 1982; Holub 1984), there are two basic elements. One is what political ideas are in the minds of filmmakers, consciously or otherwise. The other is how sophisticated filmviewers are before and after they are exposed to film content. The essays to follow focus more on the former than the latter, and indeed members of Congress have often responded quickly, as their staff personnel report what they view, whereas most moviegoers prefer unalloyed entertainment.

For observations about the general public, there are only a few experiments on filmviewers, using control groups. Two such studies found that filmviewers were swayed by outlandish conspiracy theories in two different films (Butler, Koopman, Zimbardo 1999; Mulligan and Habel 2012). In time, the gap in knowledge about political effects of film on filmviewers will be filled by a new generation of film scholars willing to engage in experimental research. For the present, the volume decodes the political messages that are present in films that may be the public's only conception of political reality.

Part I
Defining the "Political Film"

1
Films Contain Political Messages
Michael Haas

Films Impact Politics

Films can deeply shape human consciousness. To what extent do they impact political life? That question, asked as early as 1947 by scholar Franklin Fearing, continues to beguile filmmakers, filmviewers, and film analysts.

As pure entertainment, movies can amuse, provide excitement on the screen that enables escape from ordinary life, and offer role models. Much has been made of the impact of films on subsequent behavior of filmviewers, particularly on the youth. By observing how actors and actresses respond to personal and social problems, young persons accumulate a set of programs, called scripts, for dealing with issues in their lives (Bushman, Jamieson, Weitz, Romer 2013). Similarly, puzzles about how to deal with political and societal problems are often solved on the screen in ways that filmviewers may believe can be applied outside the moviehouse.

Psychologists have concluded that there is a definite link between aggressive behavior and film violence (Media Violence Commission 2012). Various studies link film portrayals with alcohol use (Wills, Sargent, Gibbons, Gerard, Stoolmiller 2009), sexual behavior (Brown et al. 2006), and smoking (Dal, Stoolmiller, Sargent 2012). In regard to attitudes, studies on the socialization impact of television, using cultivation analysis, find that fictional media tend to mainstream audiences—that is, tend to bring about a consensus in views—much moreso than those who rarely view fictional television (cf. Miller 1990). In contrast, films appear to shock audiences with unusual portrayals.

Any linkage between film content and contemporary political behavior is difficult to predict and assess. There are four avenues to explore: (1) Filmviewers must perceive political content, which may not be the case if the content is too remote from the individual's daily life. (2) For a film to make an impact, there must be a change or modification in an attitude (a predisposition or a tendency to respond positively or negatively towards a certain idea, object, person, or situation). (3) Members of film audiences might act out their views in various forms. (4) But, as Steven Ross (2011) has pointed out, film stars have used film and their notoriety to promote their own political agendas, outside their own films, including Ronald Reagan, Jane Fonda, Arnold Schwartzenegger, and many others. What they have accomplished is to raise political consciousness by dramatizing issues, often mobilizing non-voters (ibid., pp. 409–18).

An excellent example is the film *The Killing Fields* (1984). The emotional impact of films on the politics of actors is often overlooked. Sam Waterston, lead actor in *The Killing Fields* (1994) has confessed that the project "changed the lives of every single person involved in making it" (King 2014); he went on to support Refugees International and other advocacy organizations. Director Roland Joffé co-founded the Cambodia Trust, which finances the making of artificial limbs.

Thus, films directly or indirectly impact politics. "If you've got a message, call Western Union," an epigram falsely attributed to Samuel Goldwyn, was commonly understood in the industry as a norm to discourage film writers from writing scripts to lecture the public. Authors in the present volume have very different answers to the question. Michael Genovese, for example, interprets the fact that explicit political questions are seldom raised in feature films to mean that the movie industry is by default supporting the status quo. For Michael Medved (1992), the film industry propagandizes leftist views; Ben Shapiro (2011) echoes his judgment about television. Steven Ross (2011) has identified how financial contributions from Hollywood have influenced officeseekers and officeholders. From time to time, a film will bring something to light that will galvanize a politician to call for an investigation, as noted by Elizabeth Haas in Chapter 6. Messages are inevitable as long as screen actors are viewed as role models with identifiable personas and quotable lines, such as Clint Eastwood's "Make my day!" Insofar as films pretend to portray fantasy or reality in the past, present, or future, filmviewers will inevitably engage in autocritiques—that is, social comparison with their own lives, possibly producing profound changes to their everyday lives (Lefebvre 1947).

In 1999, I interviewed two of my high school classmates who had become movie stars, asking them whether their political views helped or hurt them in their careers. Mike Farrell, who holds very progressive views, answered that on balance his opinions resonated with most in the film industry; he has enjoyed prominence in two popular television series, *M*A*S*H* (1972–1983) and *Providence* (1999–2002). Chris Robinson, a conservative supporter of Ronald Reagan, felt the opposite: He believed that he was isolated within the industry as a result, though he has 93 film credits to his name, more than Farrell's 87. Whereas Hollywood is still perceived as a liberal bastion, biographies of the major film industry activists provided by Steven Ross (2011) indicate that about half supported Democrats, half Republicans.

The film industry is clearly aware that movies affect the public. But any pretence in Hollywood that films are strictly for entertainment and lack political themes should occasion laughter.

For example, film critic David Denby, in a review of Spike Lee's *Do the Right Thing* (1989), wrote that "the movie is going to create an uproar," and he felt that Lee would be responsible "if some audiences go wild" (quoted in Zeitchik 2013). Yet no riot resulted. The film critic evidently missed the avowed effort by Spike Lee to portray multicultural cooperation. *Zero Dark Thirty* (2012) received considerable negative policy from prominent members of Congress for implying that torture was useful in extracting information from a terrorist that led to the capture of Osama bin Laden (Horn 2014).

A Short History of Political Film

The impact of the film *The Birth of a Nation* (1915) is undeniable. There were many protests over the racist treatment of African Americans, and the movie was banned in several American cities. Film director D. W. Griffith responded by releasing *Intolerance* (1916) as an antidote. Nevertheless, the Ku Klux Klan turned the film into a cult classic and has used the film as a recruiting tool (Stokes 2007).

Some of the earliest films, shot in black and white, were highly political albeit not professional in terms of today's standards (Sloan 1988). Before World War I, such films as the Russell Sage Foundation's *The Usurer's Grip* (1912) were made as propaganda films. What then happened is that labor unions boycotted films that they did not like, and businesses did likewise in response to leftist films. The Federal Bureau of Investigation even decided to monitor the leftists (Ross 2011:3).

The lesson for the burgeoning film industry, not yet centered in Hollywood, was that overtly political films would not maximize profits. As the costs of production increased, box office criteria loomed larger in the calculations of which films to release, and political content was watered down.

One way to increase attendance is to portray sex, and Mae West was eager to do so. But moralistic America condemned such themes so loudly that several states and many municipalities began to ban films that they deemed offensive. In *Mutual Film Corporation v. Industrial Commission of Ohio*, the Supreme Court in 1915 ruled that film content was not constitutionally protected speech. In 1934, as pressures mounted to counter Mae West films, the Motion Picture Producers and Distributors of America capitulated, establishing the Production Code Administration to enforce a censorship code that ultimately stopped or modified production of several films with overt political content (Black 1989), as with *The President Vanishes* (1934), a film suggesting that war is primarily in the interest of munitions manufacturers, capitalist barons, and radical anti-fascist trade unions.

Nevertheless, Charlie Chaplin's popularity assured success for such films as *The Little Dictator* (1940), and the subtler political overtones of *Citizen Kane* (1941) slipped through. With the advance of Nazi Germany, directors from Europe with definite political agendas arrived in Hollywood (May 2000), but their voices were blocked until the code was abandoned some twenty years later, when the Supreme Court reversed the 1915 case in *Burstyn v. Wilson* (1952). Nevertheless, box office caution has continued to prevail.

After World War II, as armies of the Soviet Union gained control in Eastern Europe, there was a belief in some quarters that Communist-sympathizing traitors in Washington bore some responsibility. The House Un-American Activities Committee (HUAC) was formed by a Democratic-controlled Congress. Soon, an investigation of malign political influences descended on Hollywood, which was bullied to clean up its miscreants who had attended suspect meetings or had communist-leaning friends. HUAC began hearings in 1940, postponed them during World War II, and resumed again in 1947, subpoenaing prominent members of the film industry to testify. Some members of the film industry complied, fearing that there might be film boycotts (Sklar 1994:266), and a blacklist was developed; some 200 persons banned from participation in films (cf. Belton 1994; Buhle 2001). During hearings, ten members of the film industry refused to testify despite Congressional subpoenas. They became known as the Hollywood Ten (Dick 1989).

During the 1950s, following HUAC's crusade, films that questioned traditional values or provided alternative lifestyles were discouraged (Quart and Auster 1991). *Quo Vadis?* (1951) and *Viva Zapata!* (1952), two popular films, portrayed the evils of dictatorships consistent with the Cold War narrative of the West. Yet the decade also portrayed neurotic anti-heroes in *East of Eden* (1955), *Rebel Without a Cause* (1955), and *Giant* (1956), which suggested angst as a response to pressures for cultural conformity perhaps better expressed by Allen Ginsberg's poem *Howl* (1956).

Attacks and defenses of HUAC appeared allegorically during the 1950s (Belton 1994). *High Noon* (1952), *Johnny Guitar* (1954), *A King in New York* (1957) attacked HUAC. *Big Jim McLain* (1952) mercilessly attacked Communists. *On the Waterfront* (1954) whose director, Elia Kazan, had exposed some of his colleagues to HUAC, supported the anti-Communist crusade, and *The Bridge on the River Kwai* (1957) attacked those who would collaborate with the enemy. *The Salt of the Earth* (1954) was sympathetic to an earlier strike by Mexican-American zinc miners, but immigration officials deported the Mexican star, anti-Communist film workers refused to process the film, and the American Legion threatened to boycott any screening; as a result, few saw the movie. As a further rejoinder to HUAC, Joseph Welch, who asked HUAC's Senator Joseph McCarthy, "Have you no decency?" in 1954, was given a prominent role in *Anatomy of a Murder* (1959).

After the Supreme Court banned segregation in 1954, *Edge of the City* (1957), *Island in the Sun* (1957), and *The Defiant Ones* (1958) emerged, protesting racial injustice. *Twelve Angry Men* (1957), which exposed discrimination against a Puerto Rican, could have been viewed as a paradigm of prejudice against all minorities. *Guess Who's Coming to Dinner?* (1967) made the case for miscegenation ten years later.

Major films in the 1960s were largely bland. Movie box office proceeds collapsed in the competition with television (Sklar 1994:ch16), which seized upon the public's interest in major film genres and on the popular desire to rebuild traditional families after the wars.

Spartacus (1960) portrayed a slave revolt in Rome, a story that might have resonated with the burgeoning civil rights movement, but that theme was much more clearly evident in *To Kill a Mockingbird* (1962). *West Side Story* (1961) brought problems of Puerto Ricans to the screen again, albeit mildly. The films *Hawaii* (1966), *The Hawaiians* (1970), and *Little Big Man* (1970) might have been perceived as portrayals of ethnocide, but that theme was muted by playing up exotic elements.

The Manchurian Candidate (1962) and *Dr. Strangelove* (1964) dealt with the Cold War. The former warned of Communist brainwashing, the latter posed a serious challenge to the policy of stockpiling nuclear weapons, as had *On the Beach* (1959). Similarly, a critique of nuclear mutual assured destruction was implied in *Planet of the Apes* (1968).

According to Jonathan Kirshner (2012), the civil rights turmoil of the late 1960s, opened the door to a "golden age." *Easy Rider* (1969) paraded a countercultural pursuit as an answer to various forms of mindless conformity, as politics was discounted as a lost arena for political change. Then overt political themes began to emerge in the mid-1970s with *Chinatown* (1974), *Nashville* (1975), and *One Flew over the Cuckoo's Nest* (1975). *Chinatown* exposed the way capitalists might do almost anything for a buck. *Nashville* featured a presidential candidate of the Replacement Party, which sought to ban lawyers from Congress and re-write the national anthem. *One Flew*

Over, which questioned why so many odd persons were locked up as "insane," served to fuel a successful movement to stop unjust incarcerations.

A decade after the pro-war *The Green Berets* (1968) came a spate of films about America's tragic role in the Vietnamese civil war. After Americans evacuated the country in 1975, *The Deer Hunter* (1978) and *Apocalypse Now* (1979) were ambiguous about the war. Such films as *Coming Home* (1978) portrayed the sad fate of veterans of the war. But *Go Tell the Spartans* (1978) thoughtfully raised the same questions as the prophetic *The Ugly American* (1963), namely, that Americans were hopelessly naïve about the country's ability to impose solutions on other countries. The younger generation, accustomed to protest on college campuses when drafting young men to serve in Vietnam might mean death for an irrational cause, was now providing a market for political films. Film courses at colleges and universities began to emerge at that time (Sklar 1994:301–2).

Hollywood gossip says that Warren Beatty settled a lawsuit with a film production company when the latter agreed to finance any film he wanted. His choice was *Reds* (1981), a portrayal of the way the American Communist Party was suppressed during World War I. He had completed a draft of the screenplay in 1969 and was interviewing witnesses to the events during the 1970s. Now he could set the record straight while fusing the political aspects with a love story. When I saw the film in Honolulu, all seats were packed. Clearly, the political film genre had been reborn.

But that was only the beginning of the revival of the unabashed political film. In 1984, *The Killing Fields* emerged as possibly the most influential political film of all time. Although the horrors of the Pol Pot regime in Cambodia had been reported in print, the depth of the inhumanity was largely unappreciated until the film provided a portrayal unparalleled in the history of film—a person fearing for his life every second at the hands of ideological thugs who supervised backbreaking manual labor that led to deaths of thousands by exhaustion. Although Hollywood film producers ordered a cut of the scene when Cambodians in Phnom Penh cheered the victorious Khmer Rouge as they entered town, Washington was also suppressing information that the administration of Ronald Reagan, in order to "bleed Vietnam," was then bankrolling the same Khmer Rouge, which was seeking to retake possession of the country, as Hanoi had an army occupying Cambodia until the newly established government in Phnom Penh could defend itself (Haas 1991a, 1991b, 2012a). Judging from the reaction of reporters who kept posing questions to the Reagan and later George H. W. Bush administrations, the film had aroused their emotions to keep Washington on the defensive until Cambodia could be left alone, at peace.

After seeing *The Killing Fields*, I realized that I must form an organization linking film and politics, if only to reward the courage of filmmakers to again express political themes in their products. Then in 1986, a legion of films with profound political content was released. Featured that year were the following:

- *Agnes of God* (nun tried for killing her baby)
- *Back to the Future* (a time machine goes from 1985 to 1955 and back)
- *Brazil* (Freudian-type analysis of how industrial society produces insanity)
- *Colonel Redl* (blackmailing of gay Austrian military officer)
- *The Color Purple* (problems faced by African Americans in the early 1900s)
- *Jagged Edge* (unfairness in a trial of an innocent for murder)
- *Kiss of the Spider Woman* (torture in a Brazilian prison)
- *The Official Story* (events of Argentina's "Dirty War")
- *Out of Africa* (Danes learn about African culture)
- *Ran* (end of feudalism in Japan)
- *Return to Oz* (adaptation of Frank Baum's satirical novel)
- *Sweet Dreams* (husband jealous of successful wife)
- *Top Gun* (American Navy pilots train to defeat Soviet counterparts)
- *White Nights* (Russian ballet defectors)
- *Witness* (protecting an Amish girl who witnesses murder).

And Oliver Stone was perhaps the first contemporary director to make films with overtly political film themes (cf. Sklar 1994:360–65). His *Salvador* (1986) was a trial balloon of sorts, preparing the way for *Platoon* (1986), for which he had written a script one decade earlier that overcautious film producers held up from release. Whereas *Salvador* questioned American foreign policy when Democrats were opposing secret aid from the Reagan administration to topple the Nicaraguan government, *Platoon* opened a dialog about absurdities of the intervention in Vietnam in which too many Americans lost their lives—and their sanity. *Platoon* was celebrated by Vietnam veterans for telling the real story and by Hollywood movie producers for being the first political film to be a smashing box office success.

Thus, I realized that the era of problem-oriented political films had definitely returned to Hollywood. The era of the blacklist was definitely over. The floodgates had opened for Spike Lee, even more from Oliver Stone, and for more political films by other directors (Sklar 1994:365–72). Cinemas in the United States also were less reluctant to run foreign films with political themes. Now the question was how institutionally to advance the goal of films that would raise political consciousness.

Founding of the Political Film Society (PFS)

In 1970, historians John E. O'Connor and Martin A. Jackson founded the Historians Film Committee, which then began publication of the journal *Film & History* the following year and has ever since sponsored annual conferences. Both invite papers on films and their relation to history. The journal also publishes reviews of books on films. Political themes are often the focus of attention, and I have even presented a paper at one of the conferences in recent years.

But in 1986, when my colleague Ted Becker returned from a leave of absence to chair the Department of Political Science, I asked him to permit formation of the Hawai'i Political Studies Association. I then founded the Political Film Society as a project of the Association. PFS thereby became the first such organization in the world focused on the politics embedded in film. Lifetime membership is offered for the nominal flat fee of $5.00.

The reason for starting the Political Film Society was to recognize outstanding achievements of feature films for raising political consciousness. Before, film directors were discouraged from becoming associated with "political films," which often had little box office appeal, but the Political Film Society was determined to give awards as a way to encourage the film industry to make the public more aware of political realities. The PFS constitution was closely modeled on the basic document of the American Academy of Arts and Sciences, which sponsors the "Academy Awards" each year.

The PFS focus on feature films and exclusion of documentaries from consideration for awards is because documentaries usually preach to those already in agreement with the thesis and tend to be quickly out of date. But feature films are artistic productions that depict a theme much more abstractly yet seductively, are seen by more filmviewers, and are most likely to shape political consciousness of the ideologically uncommitted. (A carefully written contrast between the two forms appears in Chapter 8 in the present collection.)

Rather than granting awards to all kinds of films, the Political Film Society permits members to nominate films that promote political consciousness in four topical categories—democracy, exposé, human rights, and peace. Early each year, members of the Society vote to determine the top nominated films of the prior year in the following four categories:

- A film that wins the *democracy* category is the one that best raises political consciousness of filmviewers on the superiority of democratic methods of governance over authoritarian rule. The first winner, *The Milagro Beanfield War* (1988), showed how a group of farmers combined forces to defeat developers from driving them out of business. Robert Redford directed the film. Steven Spielberg's *Lincoln* won the same award in 2012.

- The *exposé* category is for films that bring deliberately suppressed facts to the attention of the public. Fred Schepisi's *A Cry in the Dark* (1988), the first chosen for an award in that category, presented the story of an Australian woman who was accused of killing her baby because nobody would believe that a dingo had done so instead. Ben Affleck's *Argo*, the story of how some American diplomats were smuggled out of Iran, won in 2012.

- The *human rights* category, which has had more nominees than the other three, was first awarded to *Matewan* (1987), a story about the massacre of American coal miners who sought to join a union. The director was John Sayles. For 2012, the best human rights film was *West of Thunder*, in which directors Steve Russell and Jody Marriott Bar-Lev demonstrated the injustices suffered by the Lakotas.

- *Peace* films, which were originally the most numerous, have slumped in recent years. Oliver Stone's *Platoon* (1986), the first winner, depicted the horrors of war experienced by battlefield soldiers. Because the Lakotas' response to their injustices was to disavow a violent if well-meaning defender of their cause, preferring nonviolence, *West of Thunder* won in the peace category as well for 2012.

Although the only movies allowed for awards are feature films, not documentaries, *Roger & Me* (1989) posed a challenge to such a rigid dichotomy. Since docudramas (films attempting to duplicate events dramatically) were permitted, the Michael Moore semi-documentary was considered in effect to be a docudrama rather than the canned presentation of past video footage that is spliced together in a documentary. Thus, the focus of the Political Film Society remains on identifying the political content within films that have original dramatic action and will be viewed by the general public without a specific narrative presented in the form of a voiceover.

In 1989, Becker's successor as department chair discontinued the Association, but I continued to operate the Political Film Society as an independent body. I recruited new members at meetings of the American Political Science Association (APSA), particularly with the help of Ernest Giglio, and sponsored panels on film at conventions of APSA and even the Western Political Science Association. In 1991, the editor of an APSA journal, *P.S.: Political Science and Politics*, asked me to write about PFS in an article that they titled "Why a Political Film Society?" (Haas 1991c). Later, I edited *The Political Film Today* (1998), reprinting 11 short essays for assignment in a course on film and politics.

At the APSA convention in Chicago during 1995, again with Giglio's kind assistance, the Political Film Society was accorded the status of a Related Group. PFS was allowed to sponsor one panel, and the Political Transformation Section co-sponsored a second panel. PFS held a business meeting and a cocktail reception at that convention. After the convention, PFS issued its first newsletter, started to collect conference papers for the *Working Paper Series*, and solicited syllabi for courses on political films for the *Syllabus Series*.

For a time, the Political Film Society was a Related Group within the Association. But membership did not reach the required minimum of 200 members to become a Section, primarily because many members are not political scientists, so in 1997 the new Politics and Literature Section agreed to a merger, which then became the Politics, Literature, and Film Section. That Section currently has 271 members, about as many as the Political Film Society.

Back in 1989, I attended a screening of *Romero*, an exposé of the life and assassination of Archbishop Óscar Romero of El Salvador, after attending an academic conference held in Los Angeles. Upon my return to Honolulu, I was eager to tell my friends about the film. But the film never arrived in Honolulu. The die was cast that I would ultimately retire to the city where I had graduated from Hollywood High School.

When I did so in 1998, I incorporated the Political Film Society as a nonprofit corporation in California. I also launched a website (*www-.polfilms.com*), which has more information about the Society. For five years (1999–2004), I produced a five-minute feature program for radio station KCLA in which one film was reviewed each week. Accordingly, the number of reviews on the website, which I call *Political Film Review*, peaks in those years. I also cross-post my reviews on the International Movie Data Base website (*www.imdb.com*).

Three Conundrums

A list of films nominated by the Political Film Society, including the winners each year, is appended to the present publication. What filmviewers will note is that about half are not from Hollywood but instead from a variety of countries around the world. Three conundrums result (cf. Wasser 1995). One is why American films avoid politics. Another is whether there is any political impact of films made outside the United States, which only are screened in American cities with large populations or in art theaters within college towns. A second puzzle is whether Hollywood films impact other parts of the world politically.

The first question is repeatedly answered by many contributors to the present volume. The consensus is that political films are rarely financially successful. A film attacked for an ideological slant may gain supporters from among those with definite political leanings, so there is a tendency to kill controversial films with silence until they become popular.

Regarding non-American films exhibited in the United States, the 2011 Korean film *Silenced* (*Do-ga-ni*) was screened at a cinema in Koreatown, Los Angeles. Following the movie, I was present when Koreans took up a collection for the unfortunate deaf children who had been abused at a school in Korea. A similar appeal appears in titles at the end of the film *A River Changes Course* (2013), in which Cambodians demonstrate and speak of how they live on the edge of starvation.

A more sensational political impact occurs whenever a film made outside the United States is banned in the United States. The 1967 Swedish film *I Am Curious (Yellow)* was banned as pornographic in Massachusetts until a court lifted the ban. Another example is *The Tin Drum* (1979), a German film in which oral sex involving a boy and a woman is displayed; though banned in Oklahoma, the film won an Oscar for best foreign language film that year. Even Monty Python's *Life of Brian* (1979), a British film, was banned: Censors in some small towns attacked the movie for mocking Christianity.

Hollywood films impact the rest of the world in several ways. One is to display an ideal version of middle-class America, fueling a desire by many individuals to immigrate. During the Cold War, the Soviet Union banned American films for that very reason (anon. 2012). Nevertheless, millions of persons around the world are in awe of American films, which often serve to combat anti-Americanism without trying to do so (Wellemeyer 2006).

Of course, some American films are banned abroad (McNally 2012). The most famous is *Anna and the King of Siam* (1946) and *Anna and the King* (1999), which portray the monarch of Thailand in a manner deemed undignified in that country. Similar objections to American films are made because of negative portrayals of people in other countries, such as Islamic countries. Ireland interpreted the Marx Brothers' *Monkey Business* (1931) as promoting anarchism, but lifted the ban seventy years later. Nazi Germany would not allow *The Bohemian Girl* (1936) because Roma (gypsies) were portrayed. Iran banned *Zoolander* (2001) because of the positive portrayal of gays.

Political reasons also contribute to adverse reactions. *The Simpsons Movie* (2007) was banned in Burma because of the prominence of the color yellow, which activists wear to display their opposition to the regime. China pulled *Avatar* (2010) because the forced removal of the Na'vi was too similar to the plight of Chinese who were facing eviction from their own homes. Otherwise, Beijing bans films involving "fantasy, time-travel, random compilations of mythical stories, bizarre plots, absurd techniques, even propagating feudal superstitions, fatalism and reincarnation, ambiguous moral lessons, and even a lack of positive thinking" (quoted in Wellemeyer 2006). Objections to the pro-torture slant of *Zero Dark Thirty*, as mentioned above, served to deprive the film of coveted Academy Awards (Horn 2014). Given the threat from drones in the Middle East and the example of torture at Abu Ghraib and Guantánamo, current American films tend to portray Americans as feisty and overly aggressive (Fleishman 2014).

However, some American films may not create a favorable impression. Such noir films as *Force of Evil* (1948) or *Drive* (2011), where dark or sinister characters prevail, are unlikely to persuade persons outside the United States that life in America is idyllic. Islamic fundamentalists who believe that the United States is the Great Satan have perhaps no better recruitment film than the *The Wolf of Wall Street* (2013), in which there is an excess of drug addiction, commercial greed and mendacity, as well as libertinistic sex that seems to have been scripted from parties hosted by Hugh Hefner.

The analysis of Hollywood's political impact in Steven Ross's brilliant *Hollywood Left and Right* (2011) is restricted to what the subtitle says—*How Movie Stars Shaped American Politics*. Yet the impact on public opinion remains largely unanalyzed systematically. Nevertheless, students of American politics ignore the world of movies and their political messages at their peril.

In Chapter 6, Elizabeth Haas demonstrates how some films have had direct political impact. *Contagion* (2011), a film about a hypothetical epidemic caused by a virus, was produced when "Tea Party" Republicans were contemplating cuts in the budget of the Centers for Disease Control; because of the film, no such cuts were made.

Where Can Political Messages Be Inserted into Films?

Contributors to this volume identify the substance of political messages, so it is important to dissect how and where such themes can be introduced or stopped. Below I list elements in the making of films, from conception of the idea for a film to screenings in cinemas. At each stage in the process of filmmaking, a political message could be inserted or deleted:[1]

Conception. The idea for a film, known as "Conception," comes from two main sources. The origin of small-budget films is from creative individuals. Large-budget films, such as sequel to films that have box office success, can be the product of ideas from producers, directors, and many writers. Small-budget films are more likely to have political messages.

Production. The person who gives the go-ahead for a film after funds are raised is the "producer." The producer is responsible for calculating costs and raising funds. A budget is drawn up based on the amount of funds committed to all persons involved before and behind the camera, both those credited at the end of the film and those uncredited. Materials, electricity, publicity, and payments to studios or persons controlling off-studio locations are also included in the budget. As Phillip Gianos (1995:1) reminds us, "films are produced to make money . . . it is essential to understand that that films are a commodity intended to make money to understanding their relationship to politics and of politics' relationship to film." Producers are supposed to ensure that actual costs do not exceed estimates. "He or she supervises the budgeting process, approves major expenses, and answers to the studio or production company when there are problems" (anon. n.d.). Anything too political can be edited out under orders from the producer, often to the dismay of a director, who may later get approval to release a "director's cut" version of the film.

Politics affects the source of funds to finance films in several ways. Big studios try to raise funds with a promise of a percentage of the profits, and clusters of films have been pooled into stocks sold on the open market, though investors tend to be wary of political controversy. Independent film producers who push a political agenda have sought funds from those who support the same cause. In addition, state and local governments are now allowing tax incentives for films made in their locales. About $1.5 billion in tax credits, rebates, and grants were doled out or approved by forty states during 2013, compared to $2 million a decade ago (Verrier 2013). Wealthy persons can secure up to a 15 percent reduction in their tax bills as a result. Yet raising funds for films in Cuba will run afoul of the embargo by the United States (Burnett 2014).

William Randolph Hearst, eager to have a president take decisive action to stop the economic meltdown of the Great Depression, not only had his newspapers support Franklin Delano Roosevelt for president but also financed *Gabriel over the White House* (1933) to build public support for a strong leader who would take unprecedented measures (Goldberg 2014). Today, the major producer of political films is Participant Media, founded by Jeff Skoll, who has raised funds for and produced more movies with deliberate political messages than any film production company in history. Many have been box office successes. Perhaps the most famous are *An Inconvenient Truth* (2006) and *Lincoln* (2012). Instead, of raising funds from business-oriented investors, the company solicits from nonprofit organizations concerned with the environment, health care, human rights, institutional responsibility, peace and tolerance, and social and economic justice (Solomon 2008).

Screenplay and story. The most important method for dissemination of a political message, however, is through the explicit words spoken during a film to tell a story. Original screenplays and film adaptations from novels and other sources serve as the basic texts for movies until they are altered by producers or directors. An illustration of the struggle between a writer hoping to preserve the original meaning and the adaption of the story by screenwriters is presented in *Saving Mr. Banks* (2013).

From 1930 to 1968, the Motion Picture Hollywood Production Code was the moral standard for what could be contained within films, so vulgarity and similar vices were not allowed, though moreso earlier than later (Freedman 2013:112). Interestingly, in developing the story for *Gabriel over the White House*, the script was referred to Franklin Roosevelt, who liked the plot but suggested changes that were incorporated into the rewrite (Goldberg 2014).

As Gianos (1995:3) observes, "the conventional wisdom of the industry is that political subjects are to be avoided [because of the view that] politics is neither interesting nor important." Some observers believe that there is a film genre known as the "political film" alongside other recognizable classes of films, such as cops-and-robbers films, horror films, musicals, noir films, romance films, science fiction films, situation comedies, and Westerns. But political themes can often be found within most film genres. The Western drama, often viewed by filmviewers as a portrayal of good (law and order) versus evil (lawlessness), might seem quintessentially political because of the favorable role assigned to the government law enforcement officer. Yet *High Noon* (1952), which appeared on the surface to be within that framework, had a subtext in which the protagonist was upholding American constitutional law against those who were subverting the law by persecuting film industry personnel for their beliefs. Whereas many Westerns portrayed Native Americans as uncivilized, the story in *Lone Ranger* (2011) was more sympathetic to Native Americans. *High Noon* was a box office success, whereas *Lone Ranger* was a box office flop.

Movie convention. When a film intends to convey a political message, there are four ways to cover up the message by focusing the story on elements that are likely to please filmviewers (Gianos (1995:8):

- *Personalization.* One way to distract filmviewers away from political content is to provide interesting and sympathetic protagonists and their friends. *The Hurt Locker* (2009), for example, avoided asking the question about the legitimacy of the Iraq War of 2003 by focusing on heroism of soldiers.

- *Sugar-coating.* The love story in *Reds* (1981), directs filmviewers from a plot that is decidedly sympathetic to the Communist Revolution in Russia during 1917. Leaving out inconvenient facts is why director Danny Boyle once said, "It may not be factual, but it's truthful," referring to his 2010 film *127 Hours* (cf. Horn (2014).

- *"The unlabeled bottle."* Few movies provide labels of political parties. Jonathan Lynn's *The Distinguished Gentlemen* (1992) painted all politicians as crooks. *The Butler* (2013) showed the perseverance of an African American refusing to make partisan comment while working for a succession of Democratic and Republican presidents until his son finally persuaded him to take a stand on an issue.

- *Ambivalence.* Gianos notes that director Spike Lee's *Do the Right Thing* (1989) presents a case both for violence and non-violence in racial conflict. Similarly, *The Iron Lady* (2011), a biography of Margaret Thatcher, presents several sides of her personality. One could imagine supporting her initially and opposing her toward the end of her career as prime minister, all as footnotes to her final battle against a debilitating mental disease.

Direction. Throughout the first half of the twentieth century, films were handled democratically, with input from many participants in a project. Today, a movie's director is responsible not only for ensuring that actors play their parts accurately and convincingly but also for the choice of shots, camera angles, lighting, light filters, composition, editing, costume selection, and set designs (Giannetti 1996:293).

There are two major approaches to direction—realism and formalism. Directors who choose *realism* are trying to reproduce reality; they do so by filming in locations that represent where a story is supposed to have taken place. *Formalism*, on the other hand, stresses the esthetics and symbolism of a story with contrived set designs. Realist films involve little film editing, but formalist films often involve considerable editing to achieve a specific appearance or mood. Either approach may be used in sending a political message. In *2001: A Space Odyssey* (1968), director Stanley Kubrick used strange sounds and classical music to make a film warning that machines might supersede humans. Angelina Jolie's *In the Land of Blood and Honey* (2011) used a realistic approach to achieve an anti-war message.

During the 1950s, French film theorists espoused the "auteur theory," insisting that directors create a work of art and thus should be given wide latitude to make films:

> The greatest movies are dominated by the personal vision of the director. A filmmaker's signature can be perceived through an examination of his or her total output, which is characterized by a unity of theme and style. The [screen] writer's contribution is less important than the director's, because subject matter is artistically neutral. The director dominates the treatment, provided he or she is a strong director or auteur. (Giannetti 1996:445)

Some directors are accorded artistic license to make films their way because they have a political following. Examples are Spike Lee, John Sayles, and Oliver Stone. Nevertheless, a director might direct a politically interesting film once in a while, revert to a nonpolitical film the next time around, and thus prove that they seek good scripts, rather than good politics. And the political persuasions of directors may change over time. According to Peter Biskind (1983:5), "Particular directors are often able to put their stamp on their work, intentionally insert messages into their movies. But these are exceptions, and it often happens that the films of an individual director, even one with a strong directorial personality, convey different ideologies."

At least five aspects of direction could be used to send a political message:

- *Titles*. A film's title is the least subtle indication that a film is "political." Such titles as *JFK* (1991) and *Nixon* (1995) were destined to have political commentary, even if filmviewers did not know that Oliver Stone was the director. The film *Blood Done Sign My Name* (2010) provided drama even before racism becomes center stage.

- *Sound/dialog.* The sound of the lash made the evils of slavery more realistic in *12 Years a Slave* (2013). A clutter of voices may indicate anarchy, as in Robert Altman's *Nashville* (1975). The music at the end of *Nashville* is also intended to provoke thought.

- *Music.* A director may hire a composer to develop an original score or choose a sound track (existing music). The riveting sound in *The Killing Fields* (1984) conveyed a realistic sense of panic as the Khmer Rouge triumphantly entered the capital of Cambodia. *Lincoln* (2012) mixed the song "The Battle Cry of Freedom" with Beethoven, Gounod, and Mozart.[2] Robert Altman's choice of the song "It Don't Worry Me" for the climax in *Nashville* (1975) has been described as *"a hymn to apathy and alienation"* (Quart 2005).

- *Editing/montage.* Europeans use the term "montage" to refer to film editing, which is crucial in providing quick and dynamic changes of scene ("jump cutting"), slow-moving plots that give filmviewers time to think about the story, or other coloration. Some films begin with a montage of film cuts to set the mood or to establish the context in time and place. The controversial insertion of the sound of torture in *Zero Dark Thirty* (2012), which could have been edited out as gratuitous, was left in the film because of the director's political agenda.

- *Composition/mise-en-scène.* The unfamiliar term "mise-en-scène" is used in Europe to refer how cameras frame people and objects (Giannetti 1996:83–84). When sexual acts are presented, the focus could fall on a number of elements, highlighting dominance (just one person's face) or mutual satisfaction, (both faces) depending on where the camera is placed; the effect is a profound statement about the power distribution between two characters. "Cinematography," the word used to refer to photography in movies, refers to three elements used to produce story-linked effects. Once again, the director makes the selection:

- *Lighting/color.* Natural lighting can make an environmental statement. Inside scenes can use bright lamps, rely on shadows, or use filters to distort images. In *All the President's Men* (1976), the brightly lit pressroom symbolized truth seeking, whereas the dark, foreboding parking garage inhabited by "Deep Throat" served to convey a sinister image (Derry 1995:130). Thanks to an innovation by Steven Spielberg, flashbacks are often filmed in black-and-white to contrast with full color in the present. *Pleasantville* (1998), for example, implied that the 1950s were dull compared to the liberated 1990s. *Traffic* (2013) contrasted scenes in México saturated with yellow, while blue dominated scenes in the United States. The darkened picture of the 2013 version of *Great Expectations* alerts filmviewers to the seriousness of the story.

- *Camera angles and placement.* An extreme camera angle can be used for emphasis. In *Citizen Kane* (1941), Orson Welles is shot from below, thereby enabling filmviewers to spy on the secret life of a legendary person, namely, William Randolph Hearst (Gianos 1995: 38). The satellite residence of the rich in *Elysium* (2012), similarly, provides much larger-than-life images than would be realistically possible.

- *Sets, props, and special effects.* "In the best movies," according to Louis Giannetti (1996:297), "settings are not merely backdrops for the action, but symbolic extensions of the theme." Oliver Stone's *Natural Born Killers* (1994) achieves both "technical virtuosity and dark commentary on the modern American landscape" (Blaise 1994). Those who tour Universal City will recognize sets consistent with various times and places. Several films replicate the White House as a set, but the messages have ranged from the political biography *Nixon* (1995) to such political thrillers as *White House Down* (2013).

Acting. At least three elements in film production refer to the role of actors:

- *Casting.* According to James Monaco (1981:220–21), the existence of film celebrities—stars—means that movies have impacted the public's values. In the earliest films, the actors and actresses came from the more prestigious stage theater, so they did not want to discredit themselves as mere film actors. But filmviewers away from Broadway began to idolize them as they reappeared in movies, production companies promoted their names, and fan magazines were formed to provide gossip about them: "Stars [are] the creation of the public: political and psychological models who demonstrate some quality that we admire" (ibid., p. 222).

Casting, the selection of actors and actresses to play particular parts, became "type casting"—that is, appearance of an actor or actress in a film is associated with a stereotypic role, such as the patriotic hero, the villain, or the sex symbol. Jimmy Stewart, for example, became "everyman." His contemporary successor, Tom Hanks, has appeared in the same types of roles, including the recent *Captain Phillips* (2013), who heroically saved his men from death at the hands of terrorists.

Film reviewers, then, are quick to identify stars who are cast "against type"—that is, not in accordance with their traditional roles. An example for Hanks is his role in *Road to Perdition* (2002). According to Giannetti (1996:516), there are two types of actors and actresses: (1) Those who "fit a preconceived public image" are called "personality stars." (2) Stars, on the other hand, "play roles of greater range and variety." For Giannetti, the "star system" serves as a clue to a film's political leanings. Whereas Robert DeNiro plays a variety of roles throughout his career, Willem Dafoe is cast as a clever bad guy in film after film. When films are made about particular persons, an effort is made to find lookalikes or those whose physical features can be modified to resemble the person.

Casting also involves selecting unknowns as "extras" or even in starring roles. Haing Ngor, for example, was chosen by casting director Pat Golden in *The Killing Fields* after being spotted at a Cambodian wedding in Long Beach, California. Although Ngor was not eager to play the role, the film's producer David Putnam appealed to him in the following terms: "You have to do it for your country" (King 2014). Ngor went on to win the Academy Award for best supporting actor.

As Steven Ross (2011) has pointed out, well-known actors can use their fame to support political causes. If they run for office, as did Ronald Reagan and Arnold Schwarzenegger, they might even repeat lines from their films in their campaign oratory. Meanwhile, politicians might seek to emulate famous scenes from films, as when President George W. Bush appeared on an aircraft carrier in 2003, announcing "Mission Accomplished" to trumpet victory in the Iraq War, a scene scripted from *Independence Day* (1996), where the hero saves the world from aliens.

- *Characters*. Gianos (1995: 29) notes that political figures are often "male, white, at least middle-aged, overweight, self-important, not terribly bright, not terribly well-informed, and with a cigar." As in *The Distinguished Gentleman* (1998), filmviewers have become accustomed to the view that politics and politicians should be eschewed. Another type, the "underdog," fights against the powers-that-be or speaks truth to power. Michelle Yeoh's dignified portrayal of Burmese democratic leader Aung San Suu Kyi in *The Lady* (2011) was in sharp contrast with the stiff Burmese male military leaders. Counterculture white male protagonists, such as Andy Richlbaum and Mike Bonanno in *The Yes Men* (2007) and *The Yes Men Fix the World* (2010), appeal as role models for younger filmviewers. Minorities often play distinctive roles. Blacks, bumbling idiots in silent films, are now given more positive roles, such as judges or, such as Morgan Freeman as Nelson Mandela in *Invictus* (2009).

- *Names*. Gianos (1995:28) believes that names of film characters can also give clues about political statements. Jimmy Stewart's political message was easier to fathom when he played the title role in *Mr. Smith Goes to Washington* (1939). The name of the lead character in *Bulworth* (1998) was a hint that politicians are worthless because they are full of bull. Gianos cleverly decodes the evil computer's name "HAL" in *2001: A Space Odyssey* (1968) as one letter removed from "IBM," which then was the foremost manufacturer of computers. *The Iron Lady* (2011) was already the nickname of Margaret Thatcher.

Previewing. Film studios are often cautious about any untoward messages in films that they may not detect. Producers and other executives want to know what they are paying for and demand to see a film before release. The purpose of film festivals, which are heavily attended by film critics, is to determine which films are worthy of general release, art cinemas, or perhaps will not be picked up by any moviehouse.

In addition, film studios invite the general public to attend preliminary screenings in which they pass out questionnaires and form focus groups to determine what is liked and disliked in a film. In *Changing Lanes* (2002), the conflict between Ben Affleck and Samuel L. Jackson was trivialized in the initial cut, but a very different ending was provided in the final version of the film.

Distribution and promotion. Blockbuster movies are so costly to make that the film industry has increasingly been dominated by a few conglomerate corporations:

> To those who champion film as an art form, the coming of media conglomerates has meant that corporate chieftains prefer safe, formulaic films to even the most elementary experimentation. To those who look to film to help with ideological struggle, media conglomerates have effectively strangled the marketplace and kept alternative means of expression marginalized. (Gomery 1994:73)

Therefore, publicity drives home nonpolitical messages so that a movie will be seen in "general release." Independent films, especially those with explicit political themes, are likely to be viewed only at film festivals or in art cinemas of larger American cities. A fascinating example is *Cider House Rules* (1999), a film that dealt with the problem of abortion: Nowhere in any publicity was there mention of such a controversial subject, and even film reviewers provided no clues. As a result, the Political Film Society did not nominate the movie for an award at the time; when the word finally got out, the film received a special award in a later year.

Distribution is thwarted politically when cities or countries ban films. Most recently, China and many Islamic countries have blocked *Noah* (2014) for religious reasons (Makinen and Horn 2104).

Viewing. Phillip Gianos (1995:25) observers that moviegoing serves many social purposes. Since one or more persons must take the effort to leave home and join a community of strangers fixated on a screen, films impact audiences in ways that television cannot. Initial film screenings in Los Angeles, for example, often receive audience applause. The special features of films in DVD and Blu-Ray format fall between home and theater in potential influence.

Although some observers believe that Hollywood films are biased in a leftist direction, film critic Michael Medved, in *Hollywood vs. America*, writes: "Americans are passionately patriotic, and consider themselves enormously lucky to live here; but Hollywood conveys a view of the nation's history, future, and major institutions that is dark, cynical, and often nightmarish" (1992:10). What he means is that movies are critical of religion, tolerate swearing, glorify violence, approve extramarital sex, and often "bash America." As he eloquently states in the next chapter, Michael Genovese believes that most films simply accept the status quo. Whichever slant is present, audiences make the final interpretive judgments.

The most profound statement about how movies generally impact politics has been written by James Combs:

> [M]ovies have been a central aspect of the American popular experience. They have expanded and enriched the popular imagination while deriving much of what they

depicted from that imagination. The relationship between the movies and us is truly transactional, an interplay of the influence between moviemakers and movie audiences (as well as the larger population and power structure) that takes subtle twists and turns in the relationship as time goes by. The imagination of moviemakers extends popular experience, and the experience of moviewatching extends the popular imagination. Although no one shall never know for sure, it seems reasonable to conclude that the movie experiences have made a difference in the shaping of our national imagination, in other words, that we would not be who we are, nor do what we do, without the movies. (Combs 1990:iv)

Recognizing the difficulty of making a desired political impact, Participant Media raised funds in 2005 for special screenings of *Gandhi* (1982) in Israel, Jordan, Lebanon, Palestine, and Syria (Harris 2005), with the aim of promoting peaceful conflict resolution. That same year, Participant Media negotiated a contract with Paramount Classics, distributor of *An Inconvenient Truth*, providing that 5 percent of box-office receipts in the United States would be donated to the Alliance for Climate Protection (McNary 2006).

Themes

Political science differs from economics and other social sciences by focusing attention on power, which pervades all life. Everywhere, in families as well as governments, there is a power structure consisting of those who vie to make controlling decisions and those who are controlled by decisions. Accordingly, I believe that every film has "political" content insofar as an audience can observe decisions, sometimes after conflict over which decision to make amid various pressures. Many films depict those in a story who deal with decisions made in accordance with or against their interests. However, not all films are topical, focused on a particular social or political issue.

For example, *Lion King* (1994) depicts a decision about naming a successor to a king in accordance with royalist principles without any consultation with the people. Such a film falls within the category of raising political consciousness about democracy by the very antithesis of such a consideration. A second example, *The Life of Pi* (2012), features a shipwrecked boy seeking to impose his power over a tiger in the remaining vessel; the two are the only survivors. Pi wins the power struggle, but the topical lesson that can be applied to politics (how to deter the instinct for violence, using carrots rather than sticks) is far more subtle than in *Lion King*.

Both films make a common political statement: They emphasize the single hero as the proper basis for resolving conflict. During World War II, the emphasis in films was on individual sacrifice and group cooperation. Growing up during the era, I was fortunate to discover that same culture during my thirty-five years in Hawai'i as did Barack Obama when he grew up in Honolulu (Haas 2011). But the "star" system that has arisen now emphasizes conflict resolution by a charismatic leader who eschews informal and formal political processes and instead undertakes bold, sometimes illegal, action to overcome obstacles. The impact of such a culture on public perceptions has been profound, fueling gridlock among prima donnas in Congress and clouding the perception of Obama, whose declared effort to build consensus is a mismatch with current American hyperindividualism (Haas 2012b). Although Obama won elections thanks in part to celebrity endorsements, particularly that of Oprah Winfrey (Ross 2011:410–11), he could not convince Republicans who had assimilated the anti-government ideology of former film star Ronald Reagan, the "Great Communicator."

Nevertheless, authors in Part I of the present volume want to be very precise in defining "political film." In so doing, they document many fascinating ways in which the stories in films have political content.

Part II, in contrast, seeks to review film genres that are overtly or subliminally political. They focus on the electoral process, associative behavioral forms, generations of Americans with ancestry outside Europe, tragic circumstances, and lives of persons living in Asia. In so doing, they prove that almost any film genre can have political implications. Among many other film genres, perhaps the most attracting analysis that could be construed as political is the "film noir," which portrays the dark side of human existence in which no political solutions seem possible, as if government is powerless to deal with the human condition (cf. Muller 1998; Hirsch 2008). Many other genres could also have been analyzed herein (e.g., action, coming-of-age, comedy, gay, historical, horror, musical, romance, science fiction, and about 200 more that are identified by Wikipedia), and indeed some may be the subject of future books.

Readers will learn in the chapters below the nuances of politics within films. One aim is to assist filmviewers in decoding the intended or unintended biases of films. Another aim is to appreciate how films persuade. But the most ambitious goal of the book is to demonstrate that films can serve as stimuli for action within political systems.

A final word of caution. The meaning of films is in the eye of the beholder. What one filmviewer may find highly political, another may not. The point of the award-winning *Rashomon* (1951) is that the same scene in a movie or in real life can be interpreted (socially constructed) is many different ways depending on the bias of the viewer.

Notes

1. The following section is based in part on "Film Production Techniques and Political Messages," which appears within Chapter 2 in *Projecting Politics: Political Messages in American Film* (2014) by Terry Christiansen and Peter J. Haas.

2. As an aside, when Dmitri Tiomkin accepted his Academy Award for the musical score for the *The High and the* Mighty (1954), he thanked "Johannes Brahms, Johann Strauss, Richard Strauss, Beethoven, Mozart, George Gershwin, Jerome Kern, Wagner, Tschaikovsky, Rimsky-Korsakov," but he failed to acknowledge that he had nearly copied a passage from the music of Jan Sibelius, almost note for note. Until this footnote, nobody has ever contradicted him.

2
Art and Politics: The Political Film as a Pedagogical Tool
Michael A. Genovese

Art hath an enemy called ignorance.—Ben Johnson

The Political Lens of Film

What garlic is to salad, insanity is to art.—Augustus Saint-Gaudens

Movies are a truly modern art form. With roughly 100 years of movie history to draw from, film can be looked upon as the infant art. But the rise of film in America and around the world has been phenomenal. Worldwide, more people see movies than any other art form.

Film has been viewed and discussed almost exclusively as art, business, or entertainment. Precious little has been done on film as a social or political medium. Movies develop many themes—views of life and society, politics and people, power and importance, dominance and submission, revolution and stability. The audience enters the theater voluntarily (even pays to get in), sits in darkness and near silence, and waits attentively to be entertained. But more than entertainment occurs. The audience is exposed to social and political ideas, and it seems very likely that these ideas will—to a degree—influence the audience. Thus, it is important to view film from a political perspective as well as viewing film as art, business, or entertainment.

Audiences may fall victim (willing victims) to the social and political influences contained in movies. Filmviewers are being influenced, perhaps propagandized, without really being aware of what is happening to us.

The Artist Confronts Society

If art reflects life, it does so with special mirrors.—Bertolt Brecht

Throughout history, one can see a link between politics and art—the paintings of Goya, the plays of Shaw, the comedies of Aristophanes, the poetry of Milton, the works of Swift—all represent the use of art forms to make political statements. In modern times, the movie has developed into one of our more potent and universal art forms, and writers and directors in Europe,

America, and elsewhere have turned to the cinema—in the tradition of their artistic forefathers—to make statements about politics.

Primarily, movies are entertainment. But they are more than entertainment—they are also an art form, a social force, and a propaganda device. Films reveal conscious and unconscious wants, goals and needs. They reveal aspects of a country's character and embody its culture.

As various forms of the media become more widespread, studies of their impact will become more important. Movies have quickly become a universal form of art. Accordingly, studies of the impact of film on our emotional and intellectual makeup have begun (cf. Bergman 1979; Sklar 1994). One attempt can be seen in the analysis of films from Germany. Several studies examine the relationship between the films of pre-Nazi and Nazi Germany and public attitudes (Kracauer 1947; Leiser 1974; Hull 1973; cf. Genovese 1984). To the Nazi regime, films were an important part of their propaganda efforts.

Films do something to audiences. They affect, amuse, shape, entertain, and influence those who watch. They are tools of socialization. Those who enter the theater blind to the power of cinema will become its victims. Films do what they want, leaving filmviewers unable to control the effects. This chapter seeks to make more explicit some of the political influences at work in the cinema. If you, the viewer, are more aware of the political messages contained in films, you can be more discriminating in the ideas and messages to accept or reject.

Society has many agents of socialization—family, church, school, etc., —and the media are an increasingly important socializing agent. The public, in part, learns through the media about itself, how to behave, and what to think—in short, proper forms of behavior in society. From James Bond movies, one can learn how to be suave. From *Father Knows Best* (1954–1960), one can learn of family roles, relations and moral codes. From *Dirty Harry* (1971), for example, we may be encouraged to take the law into our own hands. Film serves as one of society's most powerful sources of role models, and its ability to socialize is growing every day. As producer Cecil B. de Mille said somewhat sarcastically in 1935: "So the Mickey Mousians of today will be the New Dealers of tomorrow, whereas the Popeyesian will breed a race of fascists" (De Mille 1935).

Films that were most popular may have the widest potential for influence. The more one form of behavior is glorified on the screen (e.g., war and violence, or peace and brotherhood), the more filmviewers are apt (consciously or subconsciously) to (1) accept it, (2) embrace it, and (3) emulate it. Constantly presented images and role models cannot help but influence filmviewers. Be it John Wayne, the Fonz, Forrest Gump, or the *Terminator*, audiences can become—in part—what they see.

Even the movies considered as "escapist" or "fantasy" films contain social messages. For example, *Star Wars* (1977), an immensely popular film, celebrated simple (even simplistic) values by creating a wholesome fantasy which, in the words of critic Charles Champlin "sweeps away the cynicism that has in recent years obscured the concepts of valor, dedication and honor" (quoted in Wood 1980).

In the aftermath of Vietnam and Watergate, the public seemed to be searching for a morality play that simplified the conflict between the good guys and the bad guys. The moral climate of *Star Wars* was, to George Lucas, an attempt to provide young audiences with "a moral anchor" and to give a "psychological tool that children can use to understand the world better and their place in it and how to adjust to that" (ibid.).

Star Wars was a fantasy in the old-time-Western good-guy/bad-guy tradition. And like its Western forefathers, *Star Wars* was a lesson in morality. It was not the simple, innocent fantasy some made it out to be. The film drew an enormous audience which was being influenced by moral principles in fairy tale clothes. On the surface, *Star Wars* was fantasy, but it was also persuasion. It gave us clues as to how to behave and what to think.

What Makes a Film "Political"?

The aim of art is to represent not the outward appearance of things, but their inward significance. —Aristotle

In exploring the relationship between film and politics, "What is a 'political' film?" In a very real sense, all films are political. All films present social and/or political views and positions either implicitly or explicitly. Portrayals of views of life, relations, good and bad, etc., all have important political implications. But to say that all films are political takes us no farther in our understanding of the political impact of the movies.

Dwight MacDonald writes that for a film to be considered political, it must be a "vehicle for international propaganda or with the intention of bringing about political change" (quoted in Udoff 1964:37). This definition is useful on two levels. First a "vehicle for international propaganda" includes such explicitly political films as Nazi Germany's *Triumph of the Will* (1935), the Soviet Union's *The Battleship Potemkin* (1925), and the United States' *I Was a Communist for the FBI* (1951).

The second part of MacDonald's definition, films with the "intention of bringing about political change," is useful for the less explicit forms of political film. This category, much larger than the first, includes some films not ordinarily viewed as political. If we view the second part of MacDonald's definition loosely, bringing about political change need not mean simply changing a particular law or supporting a particular candidate or cause. It should mean supporting or glorifying a particular social, political or economic arrangement. Thus defined, such movies as *It's a Wonderful Life* (1946), *Citizen Kane* (1940), *Dr. Strangelove* (1963), and *12 Years a Slave* (2013) all have important political overtones.

I would, however, add a third part to make MacDonald's definition more complete. Often, the political film serves as an ideological/cultural support for the status quo. Due to the economic factors involved in making films as well as the political considerations, most films support and glorify the status quo. In terms of the political and economic system, moral climate, social relationships, etc., most films glorify "what is" at the expense of "what might be" or "what ought to be."

Art and Audience

> Any authentic work of art must start an argument between the artist and his audience.—Dame Rebecca West

In order to understand the political role of films, they must be analyzed in relation to their audiences. The political film, while seeking to entertain, also attempts to do other things—to get the viewer to think, act, or change. But the moviemaker, to be effective, must never lose sight of the audience. Every viewer brings intellectual/political/cultural prejudices to the viewing of films. As director Konstantinos Gavras (Costa-Gavras) has said: "A movie is like a Spanish Inn—you can eat only what you bring with you" (Camera Three 1976). Each member of an audience sees a movie with the culture, information, and the character brought into the cinema.

The view that the filmmaker must never lose touch with the audience (or potential audience) has caused some controversy between those who feel that for a political film to be effective it must be watered down and made into an entertainment film, and those who feel that a political film must be "intellectually pure." These differences can be seen by contrasting the views of George Bernard Shaw and Bertolt Brecht. Shaw felt that if he wanted the audience to swallow his political view, he had to "sugar-coat the pill . . . provide an audience with enough of the pleasures they were used to getting from the dramatic experience so that they would be open to the play of ideas as well" (quoted in Monaco 1976).

One could contrast Shaw's view with Brecht's opinion that it is "paramount not to involve the audience but to separate it from the experience (the so-called *Verfremdungseffekt*) . . . not to win over an audience by propaganda (which uses all the forces of the medium to manipulate viewers) but on the contrary to set up the dialectic of a political situation, objectively, on the theory that then the attraction of the logic would involve the audience intellectually rather than emotionally" (ibid.).

The truth probably rests somewhere between these two views. Shaw's sugar-coating is, in part, necessary because for a political film to spread its message, it must attract a wide audience. Conversely, if the message itself is so muted by the demands of excitement and entertainment, then the political film loses possible social and political impact. The truly successful political film marches a middle ground between entertainment and intellect, between the sugar-coating required to get the audience into the theatre and the dialectic process required to convey a message.

To persuade or move an audience, the filmmaker must attract a wide audience. But for a film to be considered "political," it must do more than become popular—it must get the audience to think, to question. Thus, to Brecht, the artist must unfold the structural layers of an argument, thereby allowing the audience to see, in as objective a light as possible, the intellectual components of the political argument. The important action takes place after the film, when the viewer has a chance to digest the arguments and when the dialectic intellectually unfolds.

A filmmaker like Frank Capra might fall into Shaw's "sugar-coating" category (e.g., *Mr. Smith Goes to Washington*, 1939; *Mr. Deeds Goes to Town*, 1936; *Meet John Doe*, 1941), while Rainer Werner Fassbinder *(Berlin Alexanderplatz*, 1980, *Satan's Brew*, 1976, *Despair*, 1978) might fit into Brecht's model. But can either style of political film "teach"? Teaching and learning require time, thought, attention, whereas films may not be able to offer these things. Films tend to offer brief glimpses and not deep exploration. Films are best at portraying human relations and emotions, but are somewhat weaker at exploring ideas.

Seeing the Political

Anyone who sees and paints a sky green and pastures blue ought to be sterilized.
—*Adolf Hitler*

Ultimately, all films are political, either in their content or in their omissions. They portray our fantasies and failings, our aspirations and our artifices. The screwball comedies of the 1920s may have been explicitly political, but they also served the escapist desires of much of the populace. The movies of the late 1960s consciously avoided mention of the war in Vietnam, yet this absence was significant in itself. Even escapist movies tell us about ourselves. On a conscious or a subconscious level, movies reveal a great deal about both the national character and individual goals and desires.

"Films," wrote Marshall Flaum (1978:xi), "are mirrors of our lives and times." During the course of this century, our evolving attitudes and concerns—our history—in fact have been reflected in our films, perhaps less explicitly in features than in documentaries, but no less emphatically. Even the distortions and lies often found in that celluloid mirror reveal inescapable truths not only about those who create the falsity, but about those who demanded and avidly paid for it at the box office. As such, the motion picture is fit study for the historian and the sociologist as much as it is for the film student (ibid.). Movies capture more than just the entertainment tastes of the public. Movies go below the surface realities and tap parts of the national character that may not seem obvious on first inspection.

Primarily, political films support the powers that be. Very few political films call for the overthrow of governments or the radical revision of society. The enormous cost of making, distributing, and publicizing films makes radical content unlikely. Why would the wealthy finance the making of films designed to overthrow the system which protects their wealth?

Occasionally, however, a film answers both the demands of the movie industry for "profit" and the requirements of subversion. While such efforts are infrequent, they must nonetheless be explored and their consequences examined. Such films may take very subtle forms. Manipulation by a skilled director may go unnoticed, but its power is enthralling. Andrew Sarris (1978:6) notes the subtle but powerful abilities of the director to manipulate the audience when he writes:

> The late Andre Bazin revolutionized film aesthetics by suggesting deep focus was more "democratic" than cross-cutting. A whole generation of film critics grew up with the revisionist credo that montage was manipulative. Consequently, a filmmaker could preach liberation in content, and yet practice repression in form. Jean-Luc Godard once stated that there could be a moral issue in the choice between a cut and a camera movement.

Thus, politics can be seen in even the most seemingly technical aspects of films. Since films are not usually thought of as political documents, one must reorient one's thinking to see beyond the entertainment content of films and move to the social content. Moviegoers are sponges to the social content of films unless they can understand how films affect them. If that can be accomplished, rational and thinking individuals can decide whether to accept or reject the messages contained in films. If freedom means, in part, the ability to control one's own life, then true freedom means to be in control of the ideas that one embraces. In this respect, one who views films must be able to determine how the film attempts to influence the viewer. As the visual media becomes more pervasive in our society, the need to recognize and control its influence on the individual becomes all the more important. Thus, film and other forms of media must be examined in an effort to determine their impact upon those who are exposed to the messages provided (Ross 2011).

The Artistic Sensibility

> *Film is the greatest teacher, because it teaches not only through the brain, but through the whole body. —Vsevolod Pudovkin*

The scene is unforgettable. Charlie Chaplin in *The Great Dictator* (1940) plays Adenoid Hynkel, a Führer-figure, modeled comically after Adolf Hitler. Hynkel, alone in a large room, wanders over to a globe, picks it up, and begins to playfully bounce the world into the air, buoyantly kicking and tapping the globe into the air like his little toy balloon. Suddenly, the balloon explodes.

The comical image is powerful. He is Chaplin, the Little Tramp, holding Hitler up to ridicule, mocking his desires to do with the real world what Hynkel does with the globe. Chaplin makes a forceful political statement through his comic talents. In this brief scene, Hitler's power-hungry drives are conveyed to the audience while Hitler is being ridiculed at the same time.

There are many ways to make political statements. Speeches, statistics, songs, books, and articles are all used as conveyors of political statements. Through the dramatic or comical presentation of ideas and events, filmmakers can—and often do—present political issues to the public. To be effective, these messages must also be entertaining, but within this context, political issues can be presented.

In *Duck Soup* (1933), the Marx Brothers are not only very funny, they are also making statements about the absurdity of war and diplomacy. In *Citizen Kane* (1941), Orson Welles is not only presenting the story of a personal tragedy, he is also making statements about power and influence in America. In *Ninotchka* (1939), Ernst Lubitsch is not only presenting an endearing romantic comedy, he is also reinforcing the predominant prejudices concerning life in the Soviet Union versus life in Western culture. All these movies are entertaining; all are political.

Even *The Wizard of Oz* (1939), that favorite of grown-ups and children alike, is much more than entertainment (cf. Genovese 1988). The story was originally designed as a political allegory of the Populist movement in America. The Tin Woodsman represented industrial workers, the Scarecrow was the farmer, the Cowardly Lion was William Jennings Bryan, Dorothy was Everyman, and the Wizard was, of course, the president (powerful as long as the curtain allows him to fool his people). The journey down the "yellow brick road" (the gold standard) only led to disappointment. The people were misled by their leaders; they were manipulated by industrialists and politicians.

Through the expansion of the communications media, the world is quickly becoming, in Marshall McLuhan's terms, a "global village." People in disparate geographical areas, speaking different languages, with different customs, can be brought closer together through the common experiences found in a shared cinematic experience. What will this new tribalism bring? Will it bring people closer together? Will it have the power to wither away national boundaries? Will it decrease differences between people? Increase understanding? Increase the sense of "universal community?"

It could do all these things. Or it could increase jealousy (with developing nations resenting the prosperity of the West). It could usher in a new totalitarianism, with the power over communications being despotically held by one man or a political movement. It could destroy the cultural differences that make ethnic variations so interesting. It could make the world so homogeneous and so much alike that life would be dull.

Movies have the capability of transcending national boundaries. People all over the world learn through movies not necessarily what America, for example, is like, but what movies make America look like. Movie stars are more recognizable than most political leaders, and more people attend movies than political rallies and meetings. Movies are all around, affecting everyone. Movies impart common experiences: The same stimuli are shared. They have the capacity to bring about what William Hocking (1956:52) calls "civilization in the singular." Film causes exposure to a single, common "attention frame" that may have a common effect upon filmviewers.

The significance of these common shared experiences is yet to be fully determined, and there are some conflicts in the images presented (some liberal, some conservative), but the exposure is to many common forms of stimulation, and these shared experiences do something. As historian Arthur M. Schlesinger, Jr., writes:

> The American movie has provided a common dream life, a common fund of reference and fantasy, to a society divided by ethnic distinctions and economic disparities. At the same time, it may well have excited and even incited the oppressed by displaying the abundance presumably available to their masters. One may guess that movies have generated as much discontent as they have acquiescence (1979:xii).

And Max Lerner has written in his study *America as a Civilization* (1957:820):

> Never in history has so great an industry as the movies been so nakedly and directly built out of the dreams of a people. Any hour of the day or the evening you can go into a darkened theater . . . and as the figures move across the screen you sail off on storm-tossed seas of sex, action, and violence, crime and death. . . . When you come home to sleep, your dreams are woven around the symbols which themselves have been woven out of your dreams, for the movies are the stuff American dreams are made of.

Escaping Reality

The artist is the seismograph of his age.—Robert W. Corrigan

Movies can extend the experiences of those who watch, who can see and even feel things seemingly withdrawn from daily lives. Filmviewers may vicariously take part in any number of human activities. Through movies, members of an audience can "escape" into other worlds, other experiences, other lifestyles. While "escape" is often viewed as a derogatory activity, it is not necessarily a bad thing. As Hortense Powdermaker (1950:12–13) writes:

> Escape per se, is neither good nor bad. All forms of art offer some kind of escape, and it may well be that escape is a necessary part of living. The real question is the quality of what one escapes into. One can escape into a world of imagination and come from it refreshed and with new understanding. One can expand limited experiences into broad ones. One can escape into saccharine sentimentality or into fantasies which exaggerate existing fears. Hollywood provides ready-made fantasies or daydreams; the problem is whether these are productive or nonproductive; whether the audience is psychologically enriched or impoverished.

Indeed, the question is the quality of the escape. Do movies enrich or impoverish? Do the political messages contained in a film help to make audiences slaves to the state or do they help to liberate? Do they educate and enlighten or do they numb one's senses? Films can be influential in both a positive and a negative way.

The way "reality" is portrayed in film may have an effect upon the way the world is viewed. Thus, the images on the screen may help to shape perceptions of the world. If films tend to portray certain types of people in consistent and repeated ways, this image may become one's view of reality. In this respect, the way political ideas and politicians are portrayed in films can be quite important. For example, Hollywood films have never been very kind in portraying politicians. Rarely are they pictured as decent, honorable men intent on doing good. Rather, as Rob Edelman (1976:531) writes, "through its brief history, Hollywood has consistently depicted politicians as either ruthless, gutless scoundrels or pompous, bumbling idiots concerned not with serving their constituents but with mouthing meaningless rhetoric, making deals to get elected or obtaining the fast buck."

Films that deal with political issues are commonly referred to as "problem films." While many in the movie industry have shied away from dealings with controversial topics ("movies are entertainment" . . . "If you have a message, call Western Union"), such issues cannot long be ignored. Matters of consequence cannot help but creep into films. Most criticism of the lack of meaning in film content has come from the left, with suggestions that films avoid dealing squarely with such issues as racism, fascism, imperialism, etc., but even though their criticisms have merit, they are only partially correct. Films avoid more issues than they confront; but, on occasion, they do confront serious and controversial issues. For example, during the 1920s, it was unusual to find films attacking the "American Dream." Yet, such early films as Erik Von Stroheim's *Greed* (1923), Chaplin's *The Gold Rush* (1925), and King Vidor's *The Crowd* (1928) did indeed attack aspects of the American Dream.

Those who say that a movie is no place for a political statement suggest that a theater is a place for "dreaming, not learning." Maybe so, but dreams reveal a good deal about oneself—our wants and wishes. Dreams reveal a truth which is important. Movies cannot long avoid presenting matters of social significance, for such matters are at the core of drama and human existence.

Certainly there have been periods in which the major issues of the day were avoided: The years of the Great Depression offered escape more than illumination, and the 1950s saw Hollywood running with fear in the face of Communist investigations by the House Un-American Activities Committee. But in spite of momentary lapses, films express many of the social conflicts at work in society. The record is not admirable, but it may be defensible. For even in the escape offered by Hollywood and films from around the world, hopes and dreams are being offered to people.

Richard MacCann (1969:58) notes three major problems that producers confront when making a film of social consequence. First, most people prefer "lighter" films—musicals, spectacles, comedies, etc. Consequently, the potential audience is perceived (mistakenly, I think) to be somewhat small. Second, public issues may not remain in the public's mind for very long; thus, an issue may be a thing of the past before the movie can be completed. Finally, there is the problem of dramatic treatment: How to present a topic in an entertaining and convincing way?

To these three, I would add a fourth reason—money. Studios and individuals with the amount of money needed to finance the production and distribution of movies are generally not interested in stirring up the hearts and minds of the general public. Better to keep them in a state of mindless bliss than present political ideas that might ultimately be used to arouse the public to action—action that might be directed against those with wealth and power.

Making problem films, thus, is a difficult matter. One wonders about their effect on public attitudes. The escapist films of the 1930s were thought to relieve some of the tension brought on by the Great Depression. But have the problem films brought about social change? Dore Schary (1955), the producer of a number of problem films has said that:

> movies seldom lead public opinion; they merely reflect public opinion and perhaps occasionally accelerate it. . . . No motion picture ever started a trend of public opinion or thinking. Pictures merely dramatize these trends and keep them going.

Whether films change people's minds, reinforce already held beliefs, or numb people's senses is uncertain. Film content is a mixed bag of images and ideas aimed at a variety of audiences with a variety of purposes.

Democratic or Elitist Art?

A true artist takes no notice of the public. The public to him are nonexistent.
He leaves that to the popular novelist. —Oscar Wilde

In the political film, art and politics come together. But whose art, whose politics? Artists and politicians tend to produce the art and politics (respectively) that society compels them to produce. Thus, we must ask of art and politics: Who governs? Is society—and with it, its art and politics—elitist or democratic? And should art be elitist or democratic?

Is the role of art to attempt to elevate the masses to elite tastes, or should art reflect the democratic tastes of the masses? In film, the most popular and mass-based of the arts, this dilemma is played out daily. While there is enough pluralism in film to allow for elements of both "high" and mass culture (art films coexist with the action-adventure blockbusters), such pluralism masks the deeper conflict inherent in art's relationship to society.

One representative of the "film as democratic art" school is noted critic Pauline Kael, who wrote film criticism for the *New Yorker* magazine, and whose film reviews were compiled in book form several times (Kael 1965, 1969, 1976, 1982). Kael believed film should "represent us" and therefore had no difficulty accepting escapist entertainment. She saw movies as "a great popular democratic art form." (Cynics suggest that there are several internal contradictions in that short phrase.)

Kael grew up at the movies, mesmerized by the imagery and drama. She felt herself moved and shaped by movies. They spoke to her, and she in turn attempted to celebrate popular filmmaking in her reviews and commentaries.

Film critic John Simon (1981) believes that our films should reflect the very best in high art and not pander to mass tastes. He believes that film should elevate the public. Art, he writes "leaves us with insights, epiphanies, a climate of elation in which it is easier to breathe in the perennial problems, more possible to live with them according to our individual lights." "Tastefully designed bauble(s)," Simon's term for mass entertainment, leave little behind. But "art makes demands," for true art is "a place of comic or tragic insight available fully only to an enlightened perception" (Wood 1982).

Film as a Political Document

If that's art, I'm a Hottentot!—Harry S. Truman

To a public accustomed to thinking of movies almost exclusively as a form of entertainment, it may be difficult to reorient thinking toward the social and political content of film. But since film and television have become more and more a part of our lives, understanding their effects upon the public will take on increasing importance. As the public continues to absorb the input from the media without discriminating between the worthwhile and the worthless, the true and the untrue, they fall victim to whatever messages are conveyed. Therefore, if the viewer is to rationally decide on the value of film content, there must be awareness of the ways in which film influences attitudes and behavior. To do so, messages contained in films should be made more explicit.

Movies are entertainment, art, and politics. They contain social and political messages that the viewer receives, either consciously or unconsciously. In this sense, movies can be considered as "hidden persuaders" (cf. Packard 1957). They convey messages, but not always (or even usually) in an obvious way. Movies normally convey messages in a subtle way. This is why it is important to be aware of the political role of movies.

Thinking about movies is thinking about oneself. What films say and how they are interpreted is a window to one's value systems and philosophical preferences. Films are political documents, and humans are political animals. If film is, as Bruno Bettelheim says, the "ruling art" in America (cf. Nelson 1981), then it has a responsibility to do more than entertain us. It must also enlighten, enliven, and elevate us.

I do not wish to suggest that film is or will soon become the primary source of influence in society. Films do inspire thought (or non-thought) about things in certain ways, but there is a limit to what film—as a source of influence—can do. Trying to explain the difficulty the visual media has in educating, Paul Robinson (1978:14) writes:

> There is no great mystery here. It's a simple matter of time. Learning requires one kind of time, visual media are bound to another. In learning one must be able to freeze the absorption of fact or proposition at any moment in order to make mental comparisons, to test the fact or proposition against known facts and propositions, to measure it against the formal rules of logic and evidence—in short, to carry on a mental debate.

Perhaps films can't "educate," but they can help to shape the terms of debate or highlight (and ignore) certain issues. Look at the influence that *Roots* (1977) had when it was first aired on television or the impact of *Citizen Kane* (1941) on thousands upon thousands of moviegoers. Movies can, and do, influence us. And as technological advances continue, films will become more important as hidden persuaders, informers, and propagandizers. It is likely that in the future, films will have a greater and greater impact on our lives.

When considering the political role played by movies, it is always good to remember that, whenever possible, Hollywood tries to avoid controversial issues. Playing it safe is the way Hollywood normally views its sense of social responsibility. Controversy makes enemies, and why alienate the paying public? As Michael Wood (1975:127–28) writes, "Hollywood . . . often looked like a veritable school of evasion, teaching directors how to raise questions they were not raising at all, and how to take on burning questions that were so safe that not even the Daughters of the American Revolution could worry about them."

But political ideas—if not the controversial issues of the day—do get into movies, and there is often concern with the quality and ideological direction of those ideas. While action, sex, and violence "sell," films with powerful social and political messages **can** be made—with or without the action, sex, or violence. The *Godfather* films (1972, 1974, 1990), while very violent, are an excellent example because they show that a film can be very popular and also contain significant messages.

But there are few *Godfathers* in the movie industry, and most films are simplistic, superficial, and insulting to the intelligence. It need not be this way. Hollywood *can* make films that are more thought-provoking, truthful, and humane than they now produce. The Hollywood dilemma seems to be—in Hollywood's eyes—"either make meaningful films, or make money."

They have opted for the money. Mark Rosenberg commented on this notion when he said:

> In Hollywood, it's not a question of radical vs. liberal vs. conservative movies. It's a question of cartoon-like movies with cardboard characters vs. more honest pictures in which people are portrayed in a fairly sophisticated way. It's a question of Woody Allen's *Annie Hall* [1977] vs. Mel Brooks' *Blazing Saddles* [1974]. *Annie Hall* is simply a much richer film than any of Mel Brooks' comedies because it examines human experience and talks about personal relationships in sensitive and insightful ways. I mean I liked *Blazing Saddles*, I laughed a lot. But I would never go back to see it again. It just doesn't have the resonance that *Annie Hall* does. Now *Annie Hall* will not make as much money as *Blazing Saddles* because it's not as broad a film—it's geared to the educated, urban population. But I hope the industry makes more movies like it. I'd rather see movies which confront reality, which tap something inside you—that's my personal taste (quoted in Talbot and Zheutlin 1978:289).

It is always difficult for filmmakers to get the backing to make quality political films. Perhaps the formula which must be followed was the model for the film *Reds* (1981): Make a film with strong political content, but have a love story take center stage (or screen). This is what Warren Beatty did with *Reds*, and he was able to attract a wide audience and also receive critical acclaim for this film. Another film which followed a similar formula was Costa-Gavras's *Missing* (1980), a political film that concentrated on a personal tragedy—a father trying to locate his missing son. Even a film like *Gandhi* (1982) focused more on the man than on his politics. The key may be to *personalize* politics.

But it is unlikely that the quality of the political films coming out of Hollywood will improve in the near future. In fact, many critics (among them Pauline Kael and James Monaco) suggest that the overall quality of films in general will decline. Why? The conglomeratization of the movie industry!

The movie industry has shifted from the hands of the "industrialists" to the hands of "business executives." The businesses running these new conglomerates are concerned almost exclusively with profit and not product. As long as the product sells or can be sold through advertising blitzes, it will be produced (and imitated *ad nauseam*). Now the conglomerates control the industry (United Artists is owned by MGM, Warner Brothers by Time Warner Communications Inc., Universal by Comcast, and Paramount by Viacom). What has this meant? The effect of increased conglomeratization of the movie industry is that fewer films are now being made (so that higher profits per picture can be made), and more and more money and concern are being invested into marketing rather than production. Formulaic pictures are now being made by the conglomerates (comic book stars and cartoon-fantasy heroes, such as Batman, Terminator, Superman, and in Star Wars, etc.).

The product (movies) becomes a secondary factor. No longer are "movie people" running the movie companies. Now, businesses dominate the industry. It would be foolish, within this atmosphere, to expect better movies, not to mention better political films. Perhaps the growing impact of the cable industry will have a positive effect upon film content. For example, cable companies may follow the lead of the Home Box Office (HBO) and produce their own movies as did HBO with *Sakharov* (1984) and *Game Change* (2012), or as Netflix is now doing.

Conclusion

Art is not an end in itself, but a means of addressing humanity.—Modest P. Mussorgsky

One of the true geniuses of film, Federico Fellini, worried about the future of filmmaking. "Can it survive?" he asked himself. "It seems impossible, but cinema is an impossible realm. It is always having a crisis of some sort, complaining about its aches and woes. Still it has never been in such peril. It is threatened by television, cable television, mounting costs, dwindling audiences, but worse, it is threatened from within" (quoted in Curtiss 1982).

Whether movies get better or worse, more meaningful or less so, one thing seems clear: Movies will continue to capture the imagination of the public. At their best, films can help to expand horizons by enabling filmviewers to see, and even feel, things beyond parochial world and interests. Film can help to create a more global community which sees and understands its surrounding world. Living in a "media culture," it remains to be seen whether the media will be used to liberate or enslave.

Accordingly, filmviewers must become aware of the ways the media might control and/or manipulate. To gain control of one's life, one must understand the social and political messages contained in an explicit and implicit way, in movies as well as other forms of the media. One must become aware of what films do. By succeeding in this venture, filmviewers may become masters of their intellectual lives rather than the victims of manipulation and propaganda.

Movies are political documents that communicate messages to a vast worldwide audience. But the messages are wrapped within the framework of entertainment. As producer Darryl Zanuck once said, "If you have something worthwhile to say, dress it in the glittering robes of entertainment and you will find a ready market" (quoted in Phillips 1976:97).

But how much of an effect can films have over an audience? And how much of an effect should films have? As director Stanley Kramer (*On the*

Beach, 1959; *Guess Who's Coming to Dinner?*, 1967; *The Defiant Ones*, 1958), has said:

> After all these years of making a lot of movies, I don't believe I could revolutionize the world, nor do I want to. Nor do I believe I could change anybody's mind. I think you can plant a seed or have someone say, "I never thought about it that way," but that's the most. I don't think it's required [that] you provide any answers, but I certainly do think you're obligated creatively to ask the questions. (quoted in Davis 1979)

3
Searching for the Political Film
Ernest D. Giglio

In a scene from the film *Casablanca*, Claude Rains, who plays the corrupt Vichy French police chief, Captain Renault, warns Humphrey Bogart, the cynical American owner of Rick's Café:
Renault: "We're going to make an arrest in your cafe."
Rick: "Again?"
Renault: "This is no ordinary arrest, a murderer no less. If you're thinking of warning him, don't put yourself out. He cannot possibly escape."
Rick: "I stick my neck out for nobody."
Renault: "A wise foreign policy."

Does this scene at the beginning of *Casablanca* set up the audience to expect an anti-Nazi, pro-Allies political film? Released in 1942 to take advantage of the Allied invasion of North Africa, this classic film has earned high praise from screen critics and film buffs alike. Once considered by Warner Brothers to be a B-list production with a script crafted by four different writers, often on the day of filming, *Casablanca* has become a Hollywood legend. Ranked second only to *Citizen Kane* (1941) on the American Film Institute's best 100 films list, *Casablanca* has inspired numerous books and articles over the past seventy years.[1] Yet no consensus exists on the question of whether *Casablanca* is essentially a romantic drama, a political film, or both.

What elements are required to make a film "political"? There is no definitive answer despite many attempts to develop a definition of the genre that would appeal to most film scholars. The Library of Congress catalog, for instance, describes political film as "Fictional work centering on the political milieu, often of candidates, elections, and elective or appointive office. Some of the protagonists may be corrupt or dictatorial."[2] That description may satisfy a library catalog, but it is much too narrow for our purposes. Instead, Wikipedia offers one that is generic enough to avoid controversy: "Political cinema in the narrow sense of the term is a cinema which portrays current or historical events or social conditions in a partisan way in order to inform or agitate the spectator. Political cinema exists in different forms such as documentaries, feature films, or even animated and experimental films."[3] Definitions are almost always flawed; but, rather than analyze the above, it is more profitable for us to first examine why the genre drew interest from scholars and how political science and film studies sought to develop a category wherein such films could be placed.

The issue was first raised and debated in the 1970s, when the American Political Science Association published a series of articles on the teaching methodologies of courses that integrated film as part of the curriculum. Historians were utilizing film as a teaching tool since at least World War II, but political scientists were more cautious. Why, they wanted to know, would you examine documentaries and fictional films to explain and understand historical and political events if you could read primary sources instead? What advantages, if any, did visual imagery have over the printed word? How would the use of film in the classroom enhance students' knowledge of the subject matter? Before these questions could be addressed, political scientists and film scholars had to determine whether a separate and distinct genre of "political film" existed and could be readily defined. The effort to identify a distinct genre, however, is so fraught with traps and tricks that scholars and practitioners ought to heed the warning by anthropologist Clifford Geertz (1973:196), who recounted a Javanese folktale of the legendary "Stupid Boy" to his colleagues as a reminder of their obligation to precisely identify the object of their studies: "Stupid Boy," having been counseled by his mother to seek a quiet wife, returns to his village with a corpse.

In identifying the political film, scholars have to provide satisfactory answers to the following questions: What distinguishes a political film from other genres? How does the viewer know when a film contains a political agenda or seeks to promote a particular political ideology? The answers are vital to defining the genre. Unfortunately, the questions are easier to raise than to answer with any degree of certitude. Instead, what has emerged from interdisciplinary efforts has been the identification of various schools of thought regarding political film—the inclusives, the exclusives, the categorization of four subgenres by Peter Haas, the political message approach and my own twofold scheme. I describe each school of thought in the following sections:

The Inclusives

For want of a better descriptive term, I will use the term "inclusives" to refer to those who consider most films to contain some level of political meaning, whether deliberate or inadvertent, brilliant or simple-minded. This group points to a wide range of films that contain a variety of political ideas and concepts, including thematic messages that express the ideas and values that reflect the spirit of the government in power, mirror the national mood at the time, or provide support and reinforcement for the status quo (e.g., Crowdus

1994; Litwak 1994). This category contains a wide divergence of films ranging from serious dramas, action-adventure movies and comedies.

Political scientist Terry Christensen identified 261 political films in *Reel Politics* (1987), including the Errol Flynn swashbuckler *The Sea Hawk* (1940), the film *Country* (1984) about farmers in a struggle with the federal bureaucracy to keep their land, as well as *The Moon Is Blue* (1953), a film featuring two older men in competition to seduce a young virgin. But the expansive nature of the category does not bother the inclusives, who essentially believe that most films contain a political message of some sort, be it to display the opportunities an open society provides for individuals to move up the economic ladder or the freedoms enjoyed by citizens living under a democracy. And in the Introduction to the present volume, Michael Haas claims that all films are political because power is an omnipresent phenomenon, but he does not define "political film," preferring to identify four political subgenres.

Another political scientist, Michael Genovese (see Chapter 2 herein), built on Christensen's work by putting limits around the inclusives' open-ended category. Genovese developed a taxonomy that requires a film to be classified as "political" if it contains at least *one* of the following criteria:

- It serves as a vehicle for international propaganda.
- Its major intention is to bring about political change.
- It is designed to support the existing economic, political, and social systems.

The value of Genovese's classification lies in the development of a discriminating category of films with specific characteristics. It thus provides some shape to Christensen's loose classification. His first criterion is fairly obvious, as those in power or those who wield power use the film medium to serve their own propaganda objectives. Propaganda is a communication tool used by governments, institutions, organizations, and others to promote self-serving ends.

His second requirement, however, is more problematic, as it singles out films that advocate political change, thus seemingly omitting film stories that expose the corruption of political systems or the exploitation of economic systems without mandating their downfall or destruction. Suppose a film scrutinizes the government of the day or the fundamental principles supporting the political system, the unequal distribution of justice within the legal system, the inequality of the social class structure, or the prevailing power relationships without offering a prescription for change? Why should such a film be excluded if it merely discloses wrongs without advocating a political solution? Is it not possible that a film can educate an audience about a social or political issue by bringing it to the attention of the film's viewers and thereby may serve as a catalyst for political change?

Let us take the 1979 film *The China Syndrome* as an example. It does not preach against the use of nuclear power per se, but it nonetheless demonstrates the potential for nuclear disaster and alerts the audience to expect a possible government cover-up should such a catastrophe befall the country. In light of the Three Mile Island nuclear accident outside of Harrisburg, Pennsylvania, which coincidentally happened a few weeks after the film's release, why is it not legitimate to state that the film served a political function by informing the public about the negative side of nuclear power as an energy source—a viewpoint unlikely to be publicized by the nuclear power industry or the U.S. government? Since its theatrical release, Japan, Russia, the United States, and other nations have experienced just such accidents at nuclear power plants.

Genovese's third criterion refers to films that support the status quo. In one sense, a film that supports the status quo says that life is good and change is unnecessary. Genovese's contention is that any film that justifies the government in power or supports the existing justice system or the socioeconomic class structure is inherently political because it works against institutional reform and social change. The assertion is correct, but it fails to be bolder and include films that support the existing political and socioeconomic systems at the expense of disadvantaged and deprived groups. This qualifying adjustment would make the criterion, more useful because it would include a host of politically intended movies, such as *The Grapes of Wrath* (1940), *Salt of the Earth* (1953), *Norma Rae* (1979), *Alamo Bay* (1985), and *Capital* (2013), among others. These films attacked the uneven distribution of goods and rewards while addressing issues of regional poverty, labor exploitation, and racial and ethnic discrimination.

The Exclusives

At the other end of the spectrum are the "exclusives," comprised mostly of film critics and cinema society members, who consider the very phrase "political film genre" an oxymoron. To these cinema purists, a political film is simply a piece of propaganda. This group argues that filmmaking is essentially a collaborative process, from the banks that provide film studios with the finances to support their projects to the editing process that shapes the film's final narrative style. With so many participants in financing, distribution, and production, it is may seem unlikely that the process could ever deliver ideological or political messages. (But see Chapter 1 herein, where the opposite case is made.)

The exclusives are skeptical that an industry devoted almost exclusively to "making money" would turn out a product that offends its audience, insults its leaders, thumbs its nose at deeply held moral beliefs of its populace or advocates radical changes to core values. Moreover, the argument goes, whenever Hollywood tackles an obvious political subject, such as election campaigning, the industry dilutes the political message with comedy, romance, or action to subvert the message by distracting attention from it. Warren Beatty's *Bulworth* (1998) is a good example, wherein the need for campaign finance reform, a worthy subject of scrutiny, is soft-peddled by general silliness, rap music and an implausible plot. Similarly, *The Iron Lady* (2011) focuses on personal characteristics of Margaret Thatcher rather than seeking to explain or justify her policies politically.

In addition, the exclusives maintain that there is little support today for "political films," as measured by box office earnings. Their contention is supported by the financial returns of a half-dozen Hollywood films released in 2011; although flawed, several nonetheless explored contemporary and historical political issues: Robert Redford's film *The Conspirator*, about the trial of Mary Surratt's part in President Lincoln's assassination; *A Better Life*, in which an illegal immigrant is deported to allow his son to remain in the U.S.; George Clooney's *The Ides of March*, about a Pennsylvania governor running for president; Clint Eastwood's psychological drama *J. Edgar*, about J. Edgar Hoover, the head of the Federal Bureau of Investigation (FBI) and the post-9/11 film, *Incredibly Loud and Extremely Close* (2011), in which a son tries to unravel a mystery after his father dies at the World Trade Center. Combined, these five films had a domestic gross of slightly more than $122 million, failing to approach the domestic gross of the 2011 comedy *The Bridesmaids*, which grossed $169 million.[4] Of the 20 top grossing films of 2012, *Lincoln* was the only political film to make the list.[5]

Finally, the exclusives believe that Hollywood is incapable of producing a film with a political theme because the industry reduces the subject to easily recognizable clichés and stereotypes. Hollywood, thus, is viewed as reducing the complexities of political life to personal stories that are most likely to attract the masses. This tendency to dilute political ideas led film critic John Simon (1970:66) to maintain that Hollywood cannot make commercially successful political films because

> the issues are complex and, to some extent, abstract, and have to be embodied in human antagonists to make them come alive. But then in order to make the characters both dramatic and human in a 90- or 100-minute context, the issues usually

have to be foreshortened and oversimplified. In effect, the filmmaker is caught between the Scylla of depersonalization and the Charybdis of oversimplification.

The tendency to dilute political ideas led Simon, relying on classical music
as a reference point, to remind us that "Beethoven will not sound like Beethoven if played on a kazoo" (ibidem.). Moreover, to say that Hollywood only makes entertainment movies for the masses overlooks that small group of
films, ranging in any one year between five to ten percent, which probe serious public policy issues despite modest financial returns. Over the last decade Hollywood has produced a list of quality political films, including more
than a dozen nominated for best picture. The problem that confronts both the
inclusives and the exclusives is not that Hollywood avoids political films altogether but that the industry fails to produce enough of them.

A Third Alternative: A Typology

Both Christensen and Genovese were pioneers in examining the characteristics that rendered a film "political." Another political scientist, Peter Haas,
supports the idea of a political film genre but approaches the subject differently. Since political themes may be conveyed in narratives that are dramatic,
comic or thrilling, political films differ in structure and content from other
genres, since they lack the simplicity of Westerns or science-fiction, where
the forces or good and evil are clearly delineated. By its very nature, politics
is more complicated. Films dealing with political issues are peopled with
more ambiguous characters, flawed individuals who are closer to reality.

Table 3.1. Typology of Film Types

Political Content	Political Intent	
	Low	**High**
Low	Socially Reflective Films *The China Syndrome* (1979) *The Help* (2011)	"Auteur" Political Films *Compliance* (2010) *Go for Sisters* (2013)
High	Politically Reflective Films *Casablanca* (1942) *The Hurt Locker* (2009)	"Pure" Political Films *The Killing Fields* (1984) *Frost/Nixon* (2008)

Source: Christiansen and Haas (2014)

Instead of attempting to define a political film genre, Peter Haas creates
a typology to identify four different kinds of political films (Table 3.1). In
Peter Haas's scheme, the "pure" political films are also the most obvious—
fictional films whose titles often announce their political content.

What Peter Haas identifies as "politically reflective" films are those in
which the political content is used as a plot device but is secondary to the de-

velopment of a non-political major theme. He cites such films as *Independence Day* (1996) and *Air Force One* (1997), which utilize the institution of the presidency as a contrivance for an action thriller in which Bill Pullman and Harrison Ford, respectively, are depicted as invincible heroic presidents.

The third category of "auteur" political films refers to a small group of directors whose films impart political meaning, but without the requisite political references. Francis Ford Coppola's *Godfather* films fit in here, since the American-based mafia is run like an efficient political machine, dispensing rewards and administering punishment.

The last category in Peter Haas's typology, that of "socially reflective" films, is the depository for the vast majority of Hollywood movies that are produced and marketed as entertainment. These films have no political intentions, characters, or events; in some cases, however, they may suggest or infer slight political meanings. The classic and popular *Gone with the Wind* (1939), a romantic drama that takes place during the American Civil War, is a prime example.

A Fourth Gambit: Political Messages

In 2005, Terry Christensen and Peter Haas teamed up to write *Projecting Politics*, a book that attempts to avoid the seemingly insolvable problems inherent in identifying a "political film" genre by concentrating solely on American movies that convey political messages, which the authors define as content "that depicts various aspects of the political system, especially (but not necessarily) political institutions, political actors, and the political system" (ibid., p. 4). Both accept the fact that these messages can be of two kinds—overt or explicit and covert or implicit. Obviously, the overt messages are easier to identify than the covert ones, which are more subtle and may turn up in the film's subtext. However, the authors soon abandon their objective definition in favor of identifying political films in terms of their political and ideological messages, whether understood by audiences or not.

Taking their approach avoids the frustrations involved in reaching agreement on an established "political film" genre, but it nonetheless raises several questions of its own. First, if, as the authors maintain, most Hollywood movies contain political content of one kind or another, then how would audiences be able to sort out the more significant messages from the less important ones? How, for example, would audiences distinguish between the serious explicit messages conveyed in D. W. Griffith's *The Birth of a Nation* (1915) and another silent film of that era, *The Red Kimono* (1925), which detailed the story of a former prostitute who is involved in a sensational murder trial? Race is the issue in the first, the struggle of women for respect in the second. Does the content of both these films qualify them for inclusion as political films? Would Terry Christensen and Peter Haas claim that both contain political messages of equal importance? I cannot speak for them, but film historian Kevin Brownlow (1990:ch2) considers the silent film, *The Red Kimono*, as an early plea for women's rights. Nevertheless, they consider both race and gender are considered in later chapters of their book, now in its second edition.

Another question that the Christensen-Haas approach raises is the issue of how to measure the significance of the political message among other material in the film? Is there a quantity standard for the political material? Is 10 to 20 minutes of political material in a two-hour film sufficient to make that film political? For example, the comedy *Legally Blonde 2: Red, White and Blonde* (2003), Reese Witherspoon's sequel to *Legally Blonde* (2001), has the actress working for a congresswoman intent upon securing legislation to prohibit the testing of cosmetics on animals. While animal rights is a worthy cause, Witherspoon's character is so stupid that she has trouble locating the ladies room. Besides being "dumb," her dog is gay. So here is a plot involving a dumb lawyer with a gay dog fighting for animal rights simply because she meets the committee chair, and their male dogs fall in love. Is this really how legislation gets passed in Congress? Is this a civics lesson to convey to citizens? Additionally, the film exploits the image of the 1939 film *Mr. Smith Goes to Washington* in a scene where Witherspoon goes to the Lincoln Memorial to brood after her animal rights bill fails, reminiscent of the famous Jimmy Stewart scene in the Capra film. Films like *Legally Blonde 2* demonstrate the problem of substituting a political message approach for a definitional approach to political film. In the end, who is better off?

Projecting Politics includes a political filmography that contains almost 500 films (ibid., pp 308–24). Many films, such as *Advise and Consent* (1962), *JFK* (1991), and *The Manchurian Candidate* (2004), are explicitly political. But others, notably *High Noon* (1952) and *A King in New York* (1956), require backstory knowledge of the historical context to decipher their covert political messages. But there are others on the list, such as *Gentlemen Prefer Blondes* (1953), *Attack of the Fifty-Foot Woman* (1958), and *Basic Instinct* (1992), which require more explanatory material to justify their inclusion.

My Contribution to Defining "Political Film"

I believe that there is a political film genre, even though scholars differ over which films belong in its category. Terry Christensen, Michael Genovese,

Michael Haas, and Peter Haas acknowledge the presence of political content in selected Hollywood films, but they differ over the selection criteria.

Because of my background and interest in constitutional issues, I have created a two-tier test to identify political films—their intent and their effect on audiences. Taking my cue from constitutional law scholar Cass Sunstein (1992:304), who defined "political speech" as speech that is "both intended and received as a contribution to public deliberation about some issue," my approach necessitates that both criteria be satisfied before a film qualifies for inclusion in a "political film" category. I now put my scheme to the test:

Criterion one: Intent. At the production level, my definition requires that those involved in the filmmaking process—producer, director, film studio— intend to deliver a political statement and say so either in advertising or media interviews. Unmistakable examples of intended political films are two propaganda films—Leni Riefenstahl's *Triumph of the Will* (1935) and Frank Capra's *Why We Fight* (1942–1945) series. These nonfiction films were made with the support of their respective governments to further a state's interests and to encourage their populations during wartime to make the requisite sacrifices. Two examples drawn from contemporary politics are conservative Dinesh D'Souza documentary *2016: Obama's America*, intended to influence the outcome of the 2012 presidential election, and Michael Moore's documentary, *Fahrenheit 9/11* (2004), which criticizes President George W. Bush's decision to invade Iraq and was intended to sway audiences to vote against the President's re-election. When intentions are so blatantly stated by filmmakers, why would viewers question the motives of such ideologues as Moore and D'Souza?

On the other hand, identifying the intent of commercial films like *Che* (2008) is more problematic because the director's purpose is ambiguous. Was Steven Soderbergh's intent to glorify the revolutionary hero of the 1960s or merely to present an historical portrait? Was it Clint Eastwood's intention to emphasize the personal life of J. Edgar Hoover in *J. Edgar* (2011) rather than the role he played as FBI director during the Red Scare of the 1950s? Eastwood devotes only a small percentage of his film to Hoover's obsession with communism and communist sympathizers—such content would have moved his film closer to the political category.

However, even in contemporary Hollywood, directors often have to fulfill contractual obligations under which the studios exercise final judgment on their work. Under such conditions, filmmakers first must satisfy the demands of the studio before personalizing the film with any political messages. One relevant example from the 1950s is Carl Foreman's script for the

Western film *High Noon*. Was the film a tribute to the rugged individualism and personal courage of the Western law officer or an intended attack on the friendly witnesses, which included major studio heads who testified before House Un-American Activities Committee (HUAC) during the post-World War II Hollywood hearings on communism in the film industry? Many film analysts prefer the latter interpretation (Nimmo 1993:277; Crowdus 1994: 153-54; Christiansen 1987:93). According to screenwriter Carl Foreman, his original script was a parable of individual decency (Marshall Will Kane) versus the forces of evil (Frank Miller's gang) and an indifferent community. Once HUAC subpoenaed Foreman, the script began to reflect his personal opposition to the HUAC hearings and his anger at the capitulation of the studios (Everhart 2002). *High Noon* then became a critique of Hollywood cowardice, as revealed in the documentary *Darkness at High Noon: The Carl Foreman Documents* (2002). Had the studio heads understood it as an attack on them and on the HUAC hearings, the film likely would have been shelved.

On other occasions, the initial intention behind a film may change during the course of production. This is what happened to *Force of Evil* (1949), a film about two Jewish brothers coming to terms with crime and greed in a New York City ethnic ghetto (Brinckmann 1981:369). Director Abraham Polonsky, whose name would subsequently be placed on the blacklist, wanted to make a traditional gangster film, but he was asked to deliver a popular movie that had liberal overtones. During the shooting, the content became more radical as the film reached its conclusion, resulting in a film that challenged the acquisitive and materialistic values of capitalism.

Films like *High Noon* and *Force of Evil* are capable of delivering multiple messages to an audience. Which message the audience receives requires the kind of analysis that is often left to the film critic to decipher. Further complicating the definition of "intentionality" is the fact that filmmaking is a collective enterprise, especially when a film is made under contract for a major studio. Hollywood journalist Peter Biskind (1983:5) explains the problem inherent in the making of any political film, particularly for a major studio:

> A conservative director may work with a liberal writer, or vice versa, and both, even if they are trying to impose their politics on their films . . . may be overruled by the producer who is only trying to make a buck and thus expresses ideology in a different way, not as a personal preference or artistic vision, but as mediated by mainstream institutions like banks and studios, which transmit ideology in the guise of market decisions.

Under these conditions, only established auteurs and independent filmmakers have an opportunity to make a political film with few, if any, strings attached. Another necessary consideration is the capital required to finance film projects. The studios often borrow millions from banks to finance their projects, and banks are notoriously conservative institutions that minimize risks. Even the independents require national distribution if their films are to compete with the major studios at the box office.

Criterion two: Effect. If a film's intent is not always discernible to its viewers, its impact on that audience is even more problematic. How to measure the reception of a film's political text raises additional obstacles in defining the genre. An appropriate measuring instrument would gauge an audience's understanding of the film's political text, which is whether the primary story depicts some aspect of political history, promotes a particular ideology, delivers propagandistic messages, advocates political change or reform, and supports the benefits of a capitalist socioeconomic class system that exploits some and disadvantages others.

Audiences that saw *Abe Lincoln in Illinois* (1940), *Wilson* (1944), or *Milk* (2008), to cite a few examples, are unlikely to mistake these films for a genre other than political biography (biopic). Nor will audiences misconstrue the intent of a film like *Welcome to Sarajevo* (1997), which depicts the plight of two reporters caught up in the Bosnian War. The political nature of the film is reinforced by the inclusion of news reports from Kosovo on the fighting and the ethnic killings.

Hollywood has produced a number of films that have examined American institutions and found them lacking in compassion and human justice. For example, some film studios in the 1930s produced a number of specific social message films: Audiences empathized with the plight of the Okies during the Great Depression as depicted in John Ford's *The Grapes of Wrath* (1940), a sympathetic story of poor farmers struggling to hold on to their land despite adverse weather conditions, callous banks, and an indifferent federal bureaucracy. Reform of the prison system was the message of *I Am a Fugitive from a Chain Gang* (1932). Prejudice against outsiders and minorities depicted in films like *Fury* (1936) and *They Won't Forget* (1937) cautioned against the injustices of mob violence.

In the post–World War II era, films like *Crossfire* (1947) and *Gentleman's Agreement* (1947), spoke out against anti-Semitism. A cycle of movies such as *Intruder in the Dust* (1949) and *No Way Out* (1950) confronted racial prejudice and discrimination at a time when segregation was the law of the land. In the post-Vietnam era of the late 1970s–1980s, audiences watching films like *The Deer Hunter* (1978) and *Apocalypse Now* (1979) viewed the conflict in Southeast Asia with ambiguity as to its merits. And in the twenty-first century, films like *Brokeback Mountain* (2005), *Milk* (2008), and *The Kids Are Alright* (2010) became pleas for tolerance and acceptance of equal rights for gays and lesbians. American audiences could hardly misinterpret the social and political messages expressed in these films.

Film audiences may not always understand or accept the intended messages because these meanings are subject to interpretation. A perfect example was the popular film *Forrest Gump* (1994). Audiences who saw this sentimental film could root for its dim-witted hero as he overcame adversity, while other viewers may have been offended by its celebration of ignorance. *Forrest Gump* is the kind of film Hollywood loves to make because its slick entertainment production offers viewers ambiguous interpretations.

Still another film with an enigmatic message is director Stanley Kramer's *Guess Who's Coming to Dinner?* (1967). The storyline for this Spencer Tracy–Katharine Hepburn film centers on the intended marriage of their white daughter to a black physician (Sidney Poitier). Audiences that viewed the film at face value could accept it as another romantic comedy by the popular Hepburn-Tracy team. But viewers who came to the theater with relevant background information on interracial marriages would view the film as a statement against state anti-miscegenation laws, albeit packaged in a highly entertaining movie.

Cineaste founder and editor Gary Crowdus (1994:235–36) maintains that Kramer's social message pictures were commercial successes because he provided simple-minded solutions to complex problems. In *Guess Who's Coming to Dinner?*, the film suggests that racism can be resolved at the personal level of two families having a friendly discussion over a cup of coffee. Furthermore, Crowdus questions Kramer's political liberalism, since off-screen he deserted friends during the time of McCarthyism and the blacklist.

However, *Casablanca* is open to dual interpretations. Viewed by millions worldwide since its release, *Casablanca* presents audiences with optional interpretations, depending on the knowledge of the audience. For many viewers, the Rick-Ilsa (Bogart–Bergman) romance remains the quintessential love story. But there are individual scenes with dialog that would lead other viewers, cognizant of the pre–World War II political climate, to accept the film's anti-isolationist, pro-democracy message. In this scenario, Rick's neutrality is transformed by his love for Ilsa, a passion so strong that it overcomes his cynicism and persuades him to assist Ilsa's husband, Resistance leader Victor Laszlo, in his escape from Nazi-occupied Morocco. On the other hand, if *Casablanca* is really about world politics, why is Laszlo's anti-Nazi character secondary to the Bogart–Bergman love story? Furthermore, had Warner Brothers intended the film to deliver a pro-interventionist message, why was it not made and released a few years earlier, such as before Pearl Harbor? Then the timing of the film's national distribution, together with Warner Brothers' anti-fascist stand, would have lent credibility to the film's pro-U.S. intervention message. Whether *Casablanca* is a romantic drama or a plea for American intervention in the European War (World War II) is still debated.

Similarly, Charlie Chaplin's *A King in New York* (1957) also can be viewed at face value as one of Chaplin's lesser comedies or, with additional information, as political satire on HUAC and McCarthyism. A viewer seeing the film without the background material is likely to accept it as a comedy, but the viewer who takes the following knowledge into the theater surely will view the film differently: English-born, Chaplin never became an American citizen, so when his loyalty was questioned during the 1950s, Chaplin left the country, eventually residing in Switzerland. Later, when he wanted to return to the United States, he discovered that he was persona non grata and refused re-entry by the Immigration and Naturalization Service. *A King in New York*, therefore, was produced in London but not exhibited in the U.S. for two decades. As scriptwriter, director, and star of *A King in New York*, Chaplin exercised complete control over the film, lending support to the view that he sought to critique America because it questioned his loyalty as it embraced mindless conformity and vacuous cultural values (cf. Chaplin 1964; Robinson 1985).

Likewise, is there a film with greater ambiguity of meaning than *Seabiscuit* (2003)? This 1930s story of an undersized racehorse, which is given little chance of outrunning War Admiral, can be viewed as a tribute to a horse with a bigger heart and spirit than the reigning champion. It is a story that applauds the underdog and, hence, may be interpreted as a tribute to the spirit of the American people and their president, Franklin Delano Roosevelt (FDR), in their desire to overcome the hardships of the Great Depression. To make the parallel between the underdog Seabiscuit and the hard times faced by the American people during the Depression, the film strategically intersects the racehorse story with newsreel footage showing breadlines and unemployed workers. Thus, for the common man, the racehorse Seabiscuit represented a symbol of resilience and courage, the very qualities that the president said were necessary to restart the engine of American capitalism.

The idea that good films contain several layers of meaning is supported by film scholar Don Morlan (1994a, 1994b, 1995), who argues that the popular shorts of the Three Stooges were more than exercises in mindless slapstick, but rather were films of social criticism and pro-World War II interventionism. Morlan discovered that during the period from 1934 to 1958 the

Stooges made a total of 190 shorts for Columbia Pictures, of which 34 portrayed conflicts between the upper and lower classes. These included their signature pie-in-the-face routine. The recipients of these pies were the wealthy and snobbish upper classes who were often the butt of the Stooges's silly antics. Morlan contends that these shorts helped to uplift the morale of the working class during hard economic times. He also insists that the Stooges contributed to pro–World War II propaganda in several shorts released from 1935 to 1941. One short in particular, *You Nazty Spy* (1940), was released to theaters nine months before Chaplin's *The Great Dictator*, leading Morlan to conclude that the Stooges were turning out shorts that, in their slapstick style, warned Americans of the evils of Nazism and fascism before even Chaplin.

For Morlan's thesis to be more than mere speculation, tangible evidence of intent and viewer perception is required. Even if we concede that Jules White, the head of Columbia Pictures Short Subjects Division, was an admitted interventionist, and even if Curly, Larry, and Moe were Popular Front activists (no evidence exists to support this assertion) who abhorred fascism and deliberately poked fun at Adolf Hitler and Benito Mussolini in their films, these assumptions would merely satisfy the first requirement of intent.

But relying on my two-tier definition, political intention alone is not enough. The effective requirement must also be met, and this is where the Morlan thesis about the Three Stooges breaks down. What did the audience at the time think of the Three Stooges and what did the masses make of their films? Were Curly, Larry, and Moe recognizable political activists? Did they appear at public pro-war rallies? Were they outspoken members of the Popular Front movement? The basic question here, which neither Morlan nor I can answer with authority, is whether audiences who viewed the Stooges in the 1930s and early 1940s accepted their shorts as social criticism and a call for U.S. intervention against the forces of fascism.

To state the question differently, did a consensus exist among critics, film scholars, and movie audiences that the Stooges's short films preached revolution, the overthrow of the government, or reform of the political or socioeconomic class system? Unless such a perception existed at the time, it remains problematic what messages, if any, the Three Stooges were communicating in their slapstick routines. Film critic Leonard Maltin (1972) identifies the Stooges as "low comedians" who recycled one basic plot formula in all their films. All their story lines developed from that one premise. Maltin admits that the Stooges made one political film, *Three Dark Horses*, a satire about a crooked presidential campaign. But the public embraced the shorts and ignored the film.

Unlike *The Great Dictator*, which made a statement against anti-Semitism and fascism that angered Hitler and Mussolini, the shorts made by the Three Stooges were generally conceived to be mindless slapstick routines from beginning to end, recycling the same plot in different contexts. If dictators were the patsies in one film, the victims in others were employers, the rich, and the military. In sum, the Stooges's shorts were no more than mass-produced "fillers" to accompany the main feature or to round out a double bill at a Saturday matinee. Political interpretations of these shorts are inconclusive because they do not satisfactorily prove the political intent or the widespread reception of their content as political.

In theory, my two-tier requirement to determine whether a film's content qualifies as political film material demands the kind of empirical proof that satisfies scholars. However, as the above discussion demonstrates, the two-tier definition represents an ideal, since serious practical problems arise in its application. Even in those instances when the intent requirement is met, documentation of the effect criterion involving audience perception is close to impossible to determine in films with multiple levels of meaning. Hence, I realize that my attempt to identify the political film is just as flawed as those attempts described previously in this chapter.

To make the point more emphatic, below is a case study of a recent film about President Franklin Roosevelt that on its surface would lead viewers to believe that it is a political biopic. But they would be mistaken.

Case Study: *Hyde Park on Hudson* (2012)

Hyde Park borders the Hudson River in Dutchess County, New York, about two hours north of Manhattan. It is a largely rural community with a small downtown commercial area that has seen better days. Its primary purpose today is to serve as a tourist attraction for history buffs to visit the homes of Franklin and Eleanor Roosevelt and the FDR museum. It is a place steeped in the history of the 1930s and 1940s, when America struggled with the woes of economic depression and the events leading to World War II. But director Roger Mitchell's film depicts only a narrow view into the more mundane aspects of the 32nd president's private life and neglects his substantial achievements. *Hyde Park on Hudson* focuses on one summer when FDR, disabled by polio that he contracted as a young man, is preparing for the visit of King George VI of England and his wife, Queen Elizabeth (mother of the current reigning monarch).

In the film, Roosevelt (played by Bill Murray) is surrounded by four women—his domineering mother, whose home provides a retreat from Washington politics; his wife, Eleanor, is more guest than First Lady; and two mistresses, his secretary Missy and a distant cousin, Daisy Suckley, who provide him with sexual pleasures to ease his headaches and other ailments. The one sex scene is carefully and discreetly staged, and the few others are mostly implied. Roosevelt's wife Eleanor, who acted as his social conscience and played a major role in his political life, appears in only a few scenes and disappears into the background.

When the film opens, the inhabitants of the Roosevelt home are busily preparing for their royal guests, who are on a diplomatic mission to enlist the assistance and support of FDR in a likely war with Hitler's Germany. Much time is spent on a formal dinner party that goes seriously wrong and an afternoon "hot dog" picnic with the King and Queen that was expected to go wrong but in fact turns out to be unexpectedly right, as the royal couple decide to behave as ordinary people. But these scenes omit even the slightest hint of politics. There is one scene, late at night, when the president and the king retire to Roosevelt's private study, liquor in hand, and engage in small-talk conversation—devoid of any mention of the pending war that looms on the horizon.

It is disappointing that the director, who shot mostly on location, missed a golden opportunity to add to the memory of one of the country's most admired presidents. Instead, this 94-minute film would have the audience believe that all Roosevelt cared about were his stamp collection and fulfilling his sexual needs. The president who gave the United States hope during the Great Depression and guided the country through most of World War II is nowhere in sight.

Factors to Consider in Identifying the Political Film

Several aspects of *Hyde Park on Hudson* and other movies must be considered when trying to identify "political films":

Location. Realtors constantly remind us that in purchasing property the primary consideration should be "location, location, location." This is sound advice in buying real estate, but does it assure audiences that a film set in Washington, D.C., is automatically a political film? A film's location is important because it provides the frame in which the plot is carried out. But can it stand alone in classifying a film as political? Not quite, but it can be a contributing factor in certain films. Two films set in the nation's capital have different effects—Frank Capra's classic, *Mr. Smith Goes to Washington* (1939), and Roger Donaldson's film, *No Way Out* (1987). Capra's film has numerous shots of the Washington monuments; but, more importantly, many scenes of political activities, including a filibuster inside the Senate chamber.

These scenes establish the frame in which the narrative of the story takes place because they depict the struggle of a naïve young Senator using the filibuster as a tool to expose the greedy interests of a corrupt political machine. The Washington background lends authenticity to the story but does not necessarily define it.

On the other hand, in Donaldson's film, Kevin Costner, a naval officer assigned to the Secretary of Defense (Gene Hackman), becomes romantically involved with Hackman's mistress. When the mistress turns up dead, Costner is put in charge of the investigation, which eventually leads back to Hackman. A good many scenes take place inside the 17-mile Pentagon building in Arlington, Virginia, but the narrative focus is on romance and suspense rather than the workings of the Defense Department. In this case, the location provides legitimacy to the story's framework but is unnecessary to the development of a plot that has the Defense Secretary unintentionally kill his mistress and then cover up the accident.

A successful political film, then, takes advantage of location and integrates it into the context of the film. A prime example is the 1996 film *City Hall*, shot in the working offices of the New York City Mayor and the City Council. The plot that involves a besieged mayor (Al Pacino), who is actively engaged in trying to keep racial peace after a black youth is accidentally shot. Pacino's mayor is occupied by politics in virtually every frame. The audience learns little about the mayor's personal life because the focus of the narrative is on his official duties and public activities. Whether the mayor is single or married, a Mets or Yankee fan, is of secondary concern. What is important is how the mayor deals with adversity, makes crucial decisions affecting the city, and cuts deals to further his political agenda.

Major characters. Here again, audiences can be misled into thinking that simply because a film's major characters are political leaders or major players in the world of politics, this fact alone would qualify it as a political film. Not necessarily so. While there is no litmus test based upon screen minutes, it is important for the major characters to be actively engaged in their official public and political duties for a significant amount of time. Take for example the Geena Davis–Michael Keaton film *Speechless* (1994), about two speechwriters for opposing candidates in a race for the U.S. Senate from New Mexico. The political subject is electioneering, with the story's inspiration coming from the real-life romance of two speechwriters in the 1992 Clinton versus Bush, Sr., presidential campaign. While Davis and Keaton supposedly are slaving away, writing exciting speeches for their respective candidates, the audience sees only their romantic life. Except for a few brief scenes of campaigning, *Speechless* could have been about two sportswriters who meet, fall in love, have a misunderstanding, but end happily in a romantic embrace at an Albuquerque minor league baseball game. The audience, meanwhile, learns no more about running a Senatorial campaign than if they had stayed at home.

Or take a look at the 1995 film *The American President*. Audiences could reasonably expect a film with such a title to concern itself with a working president. But this president (played by Michael Douglas) is a lonely widower who spends most of the film romancing his new love interest, an environmental lobbyist (played by Annette Bening). There is one brief five-minute scene when Douglas meets with his Cabinet on a foreign policy matter, but the focus then turns quickly to the appropriateness of the president dating a lobbyist for an environmentalist organization, while he is running for re-election. In the end, the film is a pleasant trifle but hardly one that takes politics seriously.

The 2011 film *J. Edgar* demonstrates what can happen when a filmmaker takes a prominent political figure and concentrates more on the personal aspect of his life than on the political role that he played in American history. Director Clint Eastwood focuses on implied and repressed sexual feelings of J. Edgar Hoover, FBI Director for his Associate Director (Armie Hammer) and his tendency towards transvestism rather than on the misuse of his office to carry out his private political agenda. Hoover led the FBI for 48 years during the turbulent Cold War years, Civil Rights Movement, and Vietnam War, all significant political-historical events. Yet these are treated superficially by Eastwood. Leonardo DiCaprio is a very credible Hoover as a suppressed and closeted homosexual. But it is a distortion of history by omission to make a film about the famous FBI director and underplay his role as an unscrupulous lawman whose obsession with subversives led him to violate individual rights. Eastwood's misplaced emphasis places the film to the fringe of a historical-political film.

Narrative. Finally, an overriding factor in the identification of a political film is its dominant theme and prevailing message. Audiences can ignore the film's location and even its major characters if a movie's dominant theme, considered in its entirety, provides insight and understanding of political events, political actors, political institutions, and the workings of the political process. At least four recent feature films qualify—*Fair Game* (2010), *The Ides of March* (2011), *Red Tails* (2012), and *Zero Dark Thirty* (2012).

Conclusion

Admittedly, I offer a subjective judgment, but that evaluation remains the heart of the problem of trying to gauge audience reaction to a film. In theory, it is possible to measure audience feedback, but it is also impractical. To measure a film's effective qualities requires exit-polling and other strategies to survey viewers immediately upon leaving the theater after a film's showing. But who would take on this task? What government agency or private organization would be willing to commit the time and resources to collect the data? Hollywood can do so in conjunction with "sneak previews" by including specific questions in post-screening questionnaires and focus groups about the film's message, but why would the industry want to do so after a film is released? Both Hollywood and the government have the resources, but neither has the motivation or the interest.

In the final analysis, to assist audiences and create a viable political film genre, my attempt to require both production intention and audience effect as essential characteristics of the political film is as problematic as Terry Christensen's and Peter Haas's effort to utilize political content. This is not a problem for mainstream Hollywood, since the major studios mostly deliver commercial entertainment. But for that small minority of films produced mostly by auteurs and independent filmmakers, where the political message is paramount and takes precedence over commercial success, a clearly defined political film genre would be useful.

Can it be that the task of defining the political film is similar to the law's effort to define "obscenity"? Recall Justice Potter Stewart's famous phrase on obscenity, namely that "I don't know what obscenity is but I know it when I see it."[6] Possibly, political film identification is similar in that we know it when we see it, but we cannot explain the indispensable characteristics of its content.

In the end, both obscenity and the political character of a film may rest in the eye of the beholder rather than any textbook definition. Quite possibly nonfiction film, with its less ambiguous intentions, is a better classification to help us understand the nature of political film, even if its effect on audiences remains problematic.

Notes

1. The literature on *Casablanca* is too large to cite here, but a few noteworthy sources include Harmetz (1992), Koch (1992), and Roberts (2010). If you are interested in what happened to Rick and Cpt. Renault, read Walsh (1998). For a new perspective on the film see Snider (2010).
2. *http://www.loc.gov/rr/mopic/miggen.html#Political* (accessed August 9, 2013).

3. The definition must be understood in the context of the largely collaborative work by the Internet's Wikipedia (2012).
4. The data come from *http://www.boxofficemojo.com/movies/?id=wiigapatow.htm.*
5· *Lincoln* grossed $180 million at home and was ranked 13 among the year's top grossing films. See *http://boxofficemojo.com/movies/?id=lincoln.htm.*
6. *Jacobellis v. Ohio*, 378 U.S. 184 (1964:197).

Part II
How Films Define the Political

4

The Real Oliver North Loses:
The Reel Bob Roberts Wins
John W. Williams

Does Life Imitate Art?

The present chapter is primarily about the elections involving three candidates for the United States Senate—Bill McKay, Bob Roberts, and Oliver North. The first two candidates are fictions of the Hollywood film industry, although they are convincing. The third candidate could have been fiction, an invention of a very creative screenwriter. They ran, respectively, in California in the early 1970s, in Pennsylvania in 1990, and in Virginia in 1994. This chapter is about the reality of their stories. The three stories are supplemented with a brief mention of a fourth candidate, Rick Santorum, who ran successfully for U.S. Senate in Pennsylvania in 1994, was defeated for reelection in 2006, and ran for president in 2012.

Constructing Reality

The theoretical perspective known as "social constructionism" goes beyond the argument that media, in this instance film, informs us of reality. The perspective argues that the experience of consuming media, watching a film in a movie theater for example, is itself a process of constructing reality. Kenneth Boulding (1956:14) argued "for any individual organism or organization, there are no such things as 'facts.' There are only messages filtered through a changeable value system." For Murray Edelman (1988:34), media help "construct a social reality to which people respond." James Anderson and Timothy Meyers (1988:47) expanded this view by suggesting that "meaning is not delivered in the communication process, rather it is constructed in it." They argued that "meanings arise in the intentions of the producer, in the conventions of the content, and in the interpretations of the receiver" (ibid., p. 48).

Within television studies, the social constructionist perspective has led to the cultivation hypothesis (Gerbner 1973; Signorielli and Morgan 1990), which holds that television has acquired such a central place in daily life that it dominates our "symbolic environment," substituting its message, albeit distorted, about reality for personal experience and other means of knowing about the world (cf. Edelman 1985). The central hypothesis is that viewing, particularly television, leads to the adoption of beliefs about the nature of the social world that conform to the stereotyped, distorted, and very selective view of reality as portrayed in a systematic way by television fiction and news . Other research argues that television is "not a window on the world or a reflection of the world but is the world itself" (McQuail 1994:365). According to Nancy Signorielli and Michael Morgan (1990:15),

> Cultivation analysis is the third component of a research paradigm called "Cultural Indicators" that investigates (1) the institutional processes underlying the production of media content, (2) images in media content, and (3) relationships between exposure to television's message and audience beliefs and behaviors.

Suspecting, based primarily on anecdotal reactions of viewers to the two movies under examination herein, that this third component may exist, the present chapter undertakes to explore the second component—images in media content. Two movies about U.S. Senate races, *The Candidate* (1972) and *Bob Roberts* (1992), offer a rich opportunity for comparison with actual Senatorial campaigns, particularly that of Oliver North in Virginia. I chose them because they seem to agree upon a particular paradigm about elections.

Denis McQuail (1994) argues that the media is defective as a source of meaning: "One of the least ambiguous results of revised or alternative paradigms is the conclusion that mass communication [not limited to television] is centrally about the giving and taking of meaning . . . " (ibid., p. 379). He finds "plenty of evidence that audience 'readings' do often follow conventional and predictable lines of interpretation and that familiar media genres such as news and television series are probably read . . . as is intended" (ibid., p. 379). He lists several topics and domains of meaning in which mass media operate for consumers. The domain most relevant to the movies under consideration herein is "Reality and real-life context. The dimension at issue is that of reality versus fantasy, fact versus fiction, truth versus falsehood" (ibidem.). Driving my study is McQuail's assertion "There is a power of the text which it is foolish to ignore" (ibidem.).

I have found that undergraduate students routinely accept fictional feature films as documentation of established facts. The controversy surrounding Oliver Stone's film *JFK* (1991) is a much-touted example. An upper division undergraduate once tried to inform me that the president authorizes CIA covert operations when he decides that there exists "a clear and present danger" to the nation. I asked the student for his source, knowing that the legal standard in CIA oversight legislation is not "clear and present danger." (In fact, the only clear-and-present danger standard, discarded over fifty years ago by the U.S. Supreme Court, pertained to constitutional limitations on free speech and press.) And, I knew the source of the student's "knowledge." He sheepishly agreed that he based his assertion on the Harrison Ford movie, from the Tom Clancy novel, entitled *Clear and Present Danger* (1994). Movies as text would be foolish to ignore.

Some argue that media can change consumers' attitudes, beliefs, and behaviors. Others argue that the effects of media are not so clear. In their extensive review of numerous studies of cultivation, Robert Hawkins and Suzanne Pingree (1983) found indications of a relationship between media consumption and ideas about social reality. However, they found no conclusive proof about the direction of the relationship. They concluded that

> television can teach about social reality and that the relationship between viewing and social reality may be reciprocal: Television viewing causes a social reality to be constructed in a certain way, but this construction of social reality may also direct viewing behavior (ibid., p. 76)

The study of the constructive power of the mass media has not been limited to television. The editorial cartoon found in print media, which often has explicitly political content, has been the subject of several studies (cf. Williams 1995). Anderson and Meyers (1988) have examined editorial cartoons as a process of social construction or "social action." Michael DeSousa and Martin Medhurst (1982:85) have described political cartoons as attempts to tap "the collective consciousness of readers." Except for a sound track, political cartoons share similar communication characteristics with film. As Gail Piepre and Marie Clear (1995:1) have noted, "imagery is stock in trade for anyone visually communicating a message."

Medhurst and DeSousa (1981) have done extensive research on the powerful nature of visual caricature, particularly the political cartoon, and suggest four techniques used by the latter to give power to messages: (1) the "political commonplace," everyday topics in modern politics; (2) allusions, literary or cultural, from folklore, media, literature, and the arts; (3) caricature, personal traits of the message's subject, often in an exaggerated form; and (4) timely events, personalities, or issues occurring contemporaneously with the message. The typology is a useful structure for studying films.

Background of the Candidates

Bill McKay is the name of the character played by Robert Redford in the 1972 film by director Michael Ritchie entitled *The Candidate*. According to movie publicity heard on television,

The polls show he'll lose big. He was told he'd lose—but not that he'd be humiliated. So Bill McKay, California Democratic candidate for U.S. Senate, a man of in-
tegrity and ideals, is about to give in. He's about to let himself be manipulated by
the great American political machine. Because now, he's got to win.

Director Ritchie is generally known for such feature films as *Downhill
Racer* (with Redford) in 1969, *Fletch* (with Chevy Chase) in 1985, and *The
Golden Child* (with Eddie Murphy) in 1986. He has directed feature films
that are biting social commentary, such as *Smile* (1975), about teenage beauty contests. The screenplay for *The Candidate* was written by Jeremy Larner,
who won the Academy Award for his screenplay of *Drive, He Said* (1971).
Larner was a top speechwriter in Eugene McCarthy's 1968 bid for the presidency. While satire, *The Candidate* is listed in movie catalogs and video
stores under "comedy." It was given a PG rating and released on video in
1988. Viewers in California quickly recognized that Bill McKay represented
Pat ("Jerry") Brown, Jr., son of the popular twice-elected governor.

Bob Roberts is the name of the character invented and played by Tim
Robbins in the 1992 film titled, aptly, *Bob Roberts*, which Robbins directed.
The film is represented in television movie publicity as "Bob Roberts, a radical folksinger turned senatorial candidate, in this satirical comedy that blends
his campaign trail with singing and music videos." However, it may be misleading to consider the film "hilarious," as the publicity touts. Some viewers
found its plot and characters quite disturbing. It received an R rating "for
momentary language," and was released on video in 1993.

Oliver North was the "star" of the U.S. Senate investigation into Iran-
Contra, the secret operation in which arms were sold to Iran in 1980 to obtain
the release of hostages within the American Embassy in Tehran, and then
used the profits to supply weapons to the Contras, a group in Honduras that
sought to overthrow the left-leaning Nicaraguan government. He was also
the Republican challenger to incumbent U.S. Senator Charles Robb in the
1994 Virginia race. After a bitterly fought, nationally monitored campaign,
North lost in a three-way struggle to Robb (Robb, 46%; North, 43%; Coleman, 11%).

The stories of these three candidates are remarkably similar. Each was a
fairly young, very attractive challenger of an incumbent U.S. Senator. There
are obvious, though surface, differences among these stories. Bill McKay is
portrayed as a young liberal Democrat who is drawn into a race against an
incumbent Republican Senator. Bob Roberts is a young conservative populist
seeking to replace an old school liberal Democrat, played by novelist Gore
Vidal. The differences may be less important than as a vehicle of the times in
which these two films were made: McKay represented the rise of the liberal,

as heralded during the 1960s. Roberts represented the rise of the conservative, as trumpeted during the 1980s.

Oliver North was a youthful, though ethically tainted, conservative Republican outsider who challenged Robb, a youthful, though ethically-tainted Democratic incumbent. Neither of the filmic candidates was directly challenged by ethical, legal or moral accusations. Roberts's campaign manager, Lucas Hunt, was somehow involved in Iran-Contra and drug smuggling, although Roberts himself ran on a morality and patriotism platform. Neither North nor Robb could run on a morality platform. North's felony convictions over Iran-Contra had been dismissed through technicalities, and Robb was struggling with accusations of backrubs from Miss Virginia and attendance at parties in Virginia Beach at which cocaine was consumed. Both North and Robb had been Marines and commanded troops in Vietnam, unlike McKay who somehow avoided the war and Roberts who was young enough to have just missed military service. North, consistent with his conservatism and portrayal in his Marine uniform at the Iran-Contra hearings, ran on a patriotic platform. Both filmic challengers win, unlike candidate North, who was defeated by incumbent neoconservative Democrat Robb.

The Candidate is the story of a campaign professional, played by Peter Boyle, who, after a campaign season, is scouting for another prospect. He spots youthful, liberal, legal aid attorney McKay, who has name recognition as the son of a former governor. McKay has "the name, the looks, the power," the latter a subtle reference to his sexiness. Boyle persuades McKay to run as a vehicle of promoting greater social consciousness. McKay asks what guarantee he has that the campaign will stick to issues, representing his vision and idealism, and not slip into the glitzy superficiality of the modern campaign. "So you're saying I can say what I want, do what I want, go where I please?" McKay questions. Boyle hands McKay a short note, written on the inside of a matchbook cover, declaring, "You lose." But, as the campaign develops, the professionals slowly and effectively manipulate the campaign into a slick media machine. McKay loses control over his demand for substance and gets swept up in the possibility of winning. When polls are released, showing a dramatic defeat developing, McKay pleads that he thought he would lose but not be humiliated. At this point he concedes, while convincing himself otherwise, to direction by campaign professionals. He wins.

Reviewer Richard Schickel (1972) summed up the movie in the following manner:

> In all fairness, the movie's main concern is not ideology. Writer Jeremy Lamer and
> director Michael Ritchie are more interested in showing how, in the process of being

merchandised, an allegedly idealistic and potentially abrasive candidate is turned into a gasbag no better than his middle-aged opponent—just cuter, more "dynamic."

In general, movie critics did not like *The Candidate*. Several used the
word "superfluous" (e.g., Kauffmann 1972). According to Paul Zimmerman
(1972), "[I]n the end, 'The Candidate' commits the same crime, merchandis-
ing the glamour of politics at the expense of any tough, precise political advocacy." Mimicking the declaration of McQuail (1994) that television is "not
a window on the world . . . but is the world itself" (1994), critic Penelope
Gilliatt (1972), writing in *The New Yorker*, declared, "'The Candidate' is not
about idolatry; it exemplifies it."

Bob Roberts is the story of a self-made investor-cum-right-wing
folksinger who decides to run for the Senate. The campaign is high technology, with a campaign computer center-cum-stock trading floor mounted inside
of a huge black mobile home called "The Pride." Stockbrokers double as
campaign staff, alternating between managing rallies and conversing around
the world in German and Japanese. In addition to the most sophisticated
computers, there are mobile phones and paging systems. Everyone, including
the candidate, wears an earpiece to hear the latest market news. The movie,
framed as a documentary study, follows his general election campaign, including issues of scandal focusing on the campaign manager, Lucas Hunt.
When asked, "What is Lucas Hunt's connection to Bob Roberts's success?",
the immediate response is denial—"No connection!" Everyone on the campaign staff avoids the topic, as if Hunt did not exist.

Apparently, Hunt worked for the CIA, plundered a loan for low-income
housing to establish a foundation called Broken Dove to fly weapons to the
Contras and drugs to the states, and caused the collapse of a savings and
loan. He is accused by Buzz Raplin, a reporter for the fictional *Troubled
Times Journal*, of being "a spook, Langley crowd new guard." Raplin claims
Hunt was involved in the CIA Phoenix program in Vietnam, played a part in
the overthrow of Salvador Allende in Chile, and was a central figure in fly-
ing arms to Nicaragua. The film portrays the original Senate hearings as
chaired by the incumbent, Senator Brickley Paiste. Both the hearings and an
investigation concurrent with the campaign find no wrongdoing. Paiste's underlying theme is concern with secret government, represented by Roberts's
business wealth, generated through stock speculation, and Hunt's Contra and
drug involvement.

Raplin, a crippled African American reporter for an alternative newspaper, hounds the campaign, breaks the Hunt story, and loudly proclaims to
Roberts, "I'm gonna get you." Roberts, exiting from a performance on a nationally televised comedy show à la *Saturday Night Live*, is shot in an appar-

ent assassination attempt. The reporter is accused and arrested, but later exonerated, only to be killed by vengeful Roberts supporters.

Incumbent Senator Paiste is victimized by aggressive negative advertising. The opposition, using selectively edited photographs, accuses the Senator of having sex with a minor, who turns out to be a friend of the Senator's granddaughter. In an indictment of the media, the film shows television reporters and anchors making repeated reference to the allegation, even after it has been disproven. In a slick television advertisement against Paiste, a camera pans across a mockup of the Senator's desk. The message waiting and incoming call lights on the telephone are flashing. The voiceover announces, "Paiste, as he sleeps, we live nightmares." Next to the telephone, scratched on a post-it note, is a handwritten "I love teenage girls." The Senator ignores the tidal wave, asserting, "This is America. Virtue always prevails." Yet Roberts wins.

Bob Roberts is explicitly political. The lyrics of Roberts's songs capture his position. The songs include "This Land Was Made for Me" and "Wall Street Rap." The latter music video features Roberts holding cue cards warning us to "don't get caught" and act "by any means." When asked what the song is about, Roberts responds, "Congress, liberals, Iraq." His three albums are entitled "The Free Wheelin' Bob Roberts" (reached number 23 on the *Billboard* list); "Times Are Changin' Back" (reached number 3); and "Bob on Bob" (immediately went to number 2). The hit single and video entered the *Billboard* chart at number one. The single, a prescient "I Want To Live," is released on election day. Roberts's campaign publicist acknowledges the number one song, "It's as if he knew what was going to happen to him." *Spin* magazine is quoted as calling Roberts a "crypto-fascist clown." The closing song of the movie, "Godless Men," includes the lyrics "This world turns; it's back on God; we must fight to protect him."

As if an intentional mirror to *The Candidate*, Roberts aggressively repudiates the 1960s. He asserts, "The Sixties are a dark stain on our history," in reference to the civil disobedience of the civil rights and anti-war movements. A reporter in the film comments on Roberts's attack on the 1960s, stating, "Bob Roberts is Nixon, only shrewder. . . . The rebel conservative."

Race is a strong undercurrent in *Bob Roberts*, though nonexistent in *The Candidate*. Roberts's nemesis is not Senator Paiste, but the African American reporter from *Troubled Times Journal* who exposes Hunt and allegedly shoots Roberts. Early in the movie, Lynn Thigpen, playing the host of *Good Morning, Philadelphia*, challenges Roberts. The candidate beats the reporter to the punch, accusing her of being a Communist and of betraying her journalist's obligations of fairness, balance, and objectivity. Off the set, the frustrated Thigpen accuses Roberts's one African American aide of "leaving his skin at the door." Later, during a campaign stop, Roberts admonishes everyone, "Don't do crack, it's a ghetto drug."

My focus on Oliver North is about the real-life story of a former Marine lieutenant colonel who, while working for the National Security Council, engineered a complex scheme to rescue American hostages in the Middle East by selling weapons to Iran (in violation of policy) and using the funds to buy and ship weapons to the Contras in Nicaragua (in violation of the law). Called before a nationally televised Senate hearing, he admitted to violating the law, shredding documents, and lying to Congress. Subsequent federal felony convictions were overturned because the evidence used in the convictions came from North's immunized testimony. A darling of the conservative and religious right, North decided to challenge the very institution that attacked him by running for the U.S. Senate. In one of the most expensive Senate campaigns ever conducted, North challenged incumbent Senator Charles Robb. Race and religion, as well as North's potential involvement with drug smuggling, were issues in the campaign (Baker and O'Harrow 1994). While campaigning with Dan Quayle and Jerry Falwell, North translated his campaign speech into a Bible lesson. He declared that he believed the Bible to be literally true and that prayer had healed a back injury (Baker and Jenkins 1994). Paralleling Roberts's attack on the 1960s, North decried what he believed to be the moral decline that began during the Great Society: "With members of the audience yelling 'Preaching it!' and 'Help take our country back,' North said, 'Since this country abandoned faith in our creator and looked to government for every solution, the country has gone straight down the tubes" (Edds 1994a,b,c).

The citizens of Virginia were generally nauseated by the choices, and two other challengers jumped into the race—former Democratic Governor Douglas Wilder, an African American, and former state Attorney General Marshall Coleman. Both men had challenged Robb: Coleman lost to Robb in an earlier gubernatorial race; Wilder was a personal and political enemy, even though of the same party. Wilder withdrew, perhaps not wanting to be the man to split the Democratic vote and be remembered for elevating Oliver North to the Senate. Senior Virginia Republican and senior U.S. Senator John Warner repudiated North. Coleman, running as an independent, hoped to capture moderate Republicans and disenchanted Democrats. The Republican Party was split, with Nancy Reagan, representing her husband, condemning North. Other Republicans, such as James Baker and a reluctant Bob Dole, endorsed North. After a bitter and nasty campaign, North lost.

A brief mention of the first successful U.S. Senate campaign of Rick Santorum in 1994 is relevant to the present chapter. Young, conservative, and outspoken, Republican Santorum defeated older, liberal, incumbent Harris Wofford, who was elected to fill the vacancy left by the death of Republican Senator John Heinz. Wofford is remembered as the man who made health care reform a dynamic and powerful campaign issue in his come-from-behind defeat of former Governor and U.S. Attorney General Dick Thornburgh. Except for some tenure in office, Wofford could be the fictional Brickley Paiste. The race, à la Bob Roberts, took place in Pennsylvania.

Viewing the Films

Two of the three tales in the present chapter may be evidence of the existence of some process of social construction of reality. Viewers, both college undergraduates and college-educated adults, whom I debriefed after viewing these two movies, share similar reactions to the political process as portrayed in the films. They accepted the films as confirmation of the corruption of the political process.

The Candidate and *Bob Roberts* have simple narrative structures and are parallel in general plot. They follow the Senatorial campaigns of young, ambitious challengers—Bill McKay in California and Bob Roberts in Pennsylvania—against entrenched incumbents, from the earliest stages to victory. *The Candidate* begins with the recruiting of candidate McKay, while *Bob Roberts* begins sometime after the primary, which is never mentioned.

As a side note, it is curious that the English documentary filmmaker depicted in *Bob Roberts* never discusses Roberts's rise to political power and candidacy, including the important stage of a primary. Perhaps even more curious, there is no direct reference to political parties of either the challenger or the incumbent. We infer their political preferences based on their policy positions and assertions. Likewise, parties appear to play no role whatsoever in the Pennsylvania election. On the other hand, political parties are central in the California election. Perhaps this is recognition, within the screenwriters, of the decline of the party-centered candidate and the rise of the candidate-centered campaign.

Equally curious is the failure to mention Vietnam in *The Candidate*. There is only passing reference to Vietnam in *Bob Roberts*. Since Roberts was born in 1955, he would have missed the draft. His mother was a "peacenik," and Roberts was raised on a rural Pennsylvania commune. After running away from family and school, Roberts enrolled himself, paying with a forged check, in the fictional Westmoreland Military Academy. (William Westmoreland was the military commander most associated with America's involvement in Vietnam.)

There are stylistic differences between the two films, reflecting their respective eras of production. *The Candidate*, as a result of hair and dress styles, is a film of the late 1960s/early 1970s. Appropriately for the 1960s, *The Candidate* casts a young, liberal, socially committed Democratic outsider challenging an entrenched, conservative, grandfatherly, status quo-oriented, flag-waving incumbent Republican. Film critic Stanley Kauffmann (1972), writing in *The New Republic*, summed up Redford's character:

> The character is modeled, not on individuals [the Kennedy brothers, John Lindsay, and John Tunney were mentioned by Kauffmann], I would say, but on the new political persona of the '60s: slim, sexy, smartly dressed, intelligently humorous, socially concerned and philosophically bland, young in feel if not in fact.

Particularly after his years of stardom, it is difficult to suspend disbelief and accept Robert Redford as a Senatorial candidate. However, California has produced actor candidates Sonny Bono, Clint Eastwood, George Murphy, Ronald Reagan, and Arnold Schwartzenegger. The film utilizes an "eye of God" point of view that follows the campaign from the inside. In effect, with the ability of God, the audience watches the campaign, without any disruption to the action, from the inside. The audience is a "fly on the wall," or better, a "flea on the lapel." We do not forget that this is a movie, though we are captivated (particularly if we viewed it during the era it was made) by its realism. Unless specifically presented as a documentary of that era, the film can clearly be recognized as fiction.

Bob Roberts is a product of the late 1980s/early 1990s, with the technological and media sophistication of that era. Appropriate for Generation X, Bob Roberts is cast as a young, conservative, self-made, Me-Generation, flag-waving outsider (presumably a Republican) challenging an entrenched, grandfatherly, status quo-oriented New Deal liberal incumbent (presumably a Democrat). The movie presents itself as a documentary, and the narrator is conscious of and frequently addresses the camera (as do many of the characters, including Roberts and Hunt). Everyone is aware of the camera, as in most documentary filmmaking, and frequently the camera is part of the story. Several times the lens is blocked by a hand. At least once, the camera is pushed or shoved. At one point, looking directly into the camera, Roberts asks the camera operator for his opinion. On several occasions, the narrator gives instructions to the camera operator. The presence of the camera or its assumed absence, as when the characters believe that the camera is off, visibly affect how the participants behave, or so we are led to believe. We easily accept that we are participating in a documentary project, commenting at how the characters "let their hair down" when they think the camera is off.

We may forget that the characters are actors responding to the directions of a director and creating a fiction.

Both films are powerful because of their use of a number of devices, particularly the abundance of cues in the form of metaphorical symbols and allusions. The movies use real, known, and confirmable locations. They were shot on many of the locations asserted, necessitating extensive travel by the filmmakers around the respective states of California and Pennsylvania.

Both films, particularly *The Candidate*, employ the political commonplace in keeping with the media campaigns of the 1990s. Campaign staffers refer to a newspaper column by Evans & Novak, and Ritchie has a television editorial done by Howard K. Smith. Throughout, there are references to the Field polls, then the leading polling organization in California. There are references to *Spin* and *Billboard* magazines, as well as candidate appearances on prime time television talk and variety shows.

Often, the techniques simulate a live style of filming. Ritchie often has the camera catch the glare of lights and capture apparently natural moments in the campaign. There is a textural feel, heightened by the contrast of course-grained television clips. One reviewer asserted that Ritchie borrowed from the work of director John Frankenheimer: "fast, edgy editing and countless compositions involving television monitors come straight out of *The Manchurian Candidate* . . . , [the staging] giving the viewer the impression that he is looking at unused footage from a television documentary" (Cocks 1972).

Robbins's film presents itself as a documentary by an English documentary filmmaker, who serves as the first person narrator. There are all the angles one would expect from "live" filming—pans, off-centered shots, tracking through crowds after the candidate. The film interweaves testimonials, stills of black and white photographs and newspaper clippings, shots of the interviewer, and captions. The camera catches private moments, as when the Roberts band is in prayer before a performance, and embarrassing moments, as when the Roberts campaign seems to melt down just before a local beauty pageant begins. Both films assert a heightened level of realism.

The films use a lot of unknown actors and "real people." In filming *The Candidate*, Ritchie enlisted the assistance of local California political campaign consultants. One of their tasks was to gather extras to serve as campaign crowds and to orchestra realistic rallies. Unknown professional actors were able to provide the necessary polish for a profitable feature film, while avoiding the appearance of filmmaking. Alternatively, *Bob Roberts* used generally unknown, yet somehow familiar actors in the key roles of newscasters and reporters, personalities of whom we are vaguely aware—Lynn

Thigpen, Pamela Reed, Susan Sarandon (Robbins's significant other), Fred Ward, James Spader, and Helen Hunt, all of whom, when costumed as journalists were familiar yet not recognizable.

Casting of the leading roles can be tricky. A profitable movie usually requires bankable stars, such as Redford. On the other hand, stars can overpower the story, because, instead of the characters, the stars are seen by viewers as themselves or as some previous famous role. (For a time, Richard Thomas and John-Boy Walton were synonymous. For a certain generation, Ed Asner is Lou Grant, and Alan Alda is Hawkeye.) Ritchie cast solid actors for several key roles—Peter Boyle as the campaign manager and Melvyn Douglas as McKay's father and former governor of California. The rest of the major roles were filled by vaguely familiar character actors (e.g., Don Porter as incumbent Senator Crocker Jarman and Allen Garfield as the campaign's media expert) or unknowns. Robbins, the closest person to a star in *Bob Roberts*, cast himself in the lead. Like Ritchie, he cast solid actors for several key roles, particularly the appropriately villainous Alan Rickman as the campaign manager, Lucas Hunt, and the gushing Ray Wise (of the early 1990s television series *Twin Peaks*) as the public relations media rep. Novelist Gore Vidal played the bewildered incumbent, U.S. Senator Brickley Paiste. Vidal, few viewers might remember, scripted the political film *The Best Man* (1964). The rest of the major roles were filled by vaguely familiar actors (e.g., as Giancarlo Espositio, David Straithern, and Bob Balaban) or unknowns.

Both films interweave reality with the fiction. In *The Candidate*, the real Natalie Wood goes backstage to greet the character Bill McKay. Before McKay's first major speech to the party faithful, Ritchie edits in clips of Hubert Humphrey and George McGovern entering through the crowds. Ritchie also uses real journalists, playing themselves, including Van Amberg of ABC News, and California newscasters Roland Post, Ken Jones, and Morey Green. Robbins, tying his movie to a very specific era, intersperses television clips of the looming Persian Gulf conflict of 1990–1991, complete with Saddam Hussein and George H. W. Bush. Candidate Roberts, as expected, takes a stand on the decision to go to war.

The films use "doubles," as when dignitaries rely on look-alikes or actors depend on stunt doubles. The films utilize artifacts that are similar, but different. Robbins has Roberts appear as the musical guest on a fictional live satiric comedy television show, *Cutting Edge Live*. The show is hosted by a celebrity guest star and supported by an ensemble crew who perform recurring skits and characters, including a lobster family. *Cutting Edge Live* is the double for *Saturday Night Live* (1975–), which has all the features of its fictional clone. A less direct double, though one looming over the entire movie, is the parallel between Bill McKay, the son, and John "J. J." McKay, the father, with former governor of California, and Pat (the father) and Jerry (the son) Brown, both former governors of California. Both sons are liberal Democrats who appear to challenge the system, while both fathers were pragmatic Democratic politicians. Another comparison might be with Senators Gene (the father) and John Tunney (the son).

Both films use artifacts that are "almost real," though not doubles for specific real events, things or people, including realistic televised debates, news interview shows, campaign rallies, and negative advertisements. The public has come to accept these as elements of any major political campaign. Ritchie hired experienced political operatives to stage these events. They rented the Paramount Theater in Oakland and packed it with 2,000 "loyal supporters" for one of the rallies. The final ticker-tape parade was staged in the middle of the San Francisco financial district's traditional year-end shower of shredded calendars. One reviewer remarked that "whatever other flaws the film may have, the script's campaign strategy and tactics hit unnervingly close to reality. . . . The film, in fact, is a handbook for today's image-conscious politics" (Fayard 1972). The publicity for *The Candidate* was such that *Life* magazine, in addition to a splashy photo-spread, asked a professional political consultant to evaluate McKay's chances against Sen. Jarman (ibid.).

The Candidate is a fairly straightforward picture of a political campaign, with few allusions. McKay's acceptance of his political corruption comes with a one-hour affair with a young campaign worker. When the son finally approaches the father to get his public support, J. J. McKay asks "What does it feel like to run a campaign in this state these days?" Bill responds, "I don't known, I don't know." Although the polls show a dramatic rise in McKay's popularity, he acknowledges, "I'm not talking to anyone, and I'm not saying anything." Howard K. Smith, decrying the disappearance of the original and honest-spoken McKay, accuses him of "selling himself like an underarm deodorant." Two former legal services workers appear at different times to symbolize the distance McKay has put between his original position and his new persona. In the final "big speech," McKay pulls out all the clichés: "together," "test of courage," "faith in ourselves, faith in our country," and "give it all I've got." Backstage, in momentary passing, a legal services colleague acknowledges, "I know what this is costing you." McKay turns away.

Bob Roberts, on the other hand, is filled with allusions verging on allegory. Roberts leads his campaign caravan, including the massive black motor home, around Pennsylvania dressed head to toe in white, riding a black motorcycle. He is a white knight on a black steed, less in the mold of old Westerns and more in the mold of Clint Eastwood's *Pale Rider* (1985). Eastwood's unnamed gunslinger-cum-preacher is benevolent as a means to a malevolent end. We are warned of Roberts when he mounts his steed to lead the motorcade, only to slide and fall on the gravel. Campaign aides pull out pistols, and Roberts curses at everyone. Roberts is a fallen man. At each campaign stop, Roberts fences with one of his staff. For Roberts, the campaign is just a grand game, and the goal is winning, not some ideal or principle.

The financial sponsor of the Roberts campaign is the foundation headed by Hunt called Broken Dove. Its major purpose is to fund anti-drug campaigns and support rehabilitation clinics for children. The irony of Broken Dove is that Hunt presumably made his money smuggling drugs into the United States by airplanes bought with loans intended for low-income housing. The irony is compounded when a clinic sponsored by Broken Dove and employing Roberts's personal physician awards the candidate its "Patriot of the Year" award.

There are allusions to religion throughout *Bob Roberts*. After singing with a church choir, Roberts is extolled by the minister as the man who will clean up "the devil's mess in Washington." Roberts's followers are fanatical, following the motorcade from city to city. One of the young men tattoos the word "Bob" on his forehead. Another dresses in the uniform of George Washington's Continental Army, taken from one of Roberts's music videos. A supporter, when asked why he supports Roberts, proclaims, "Because he's righteous." When Roberts is shot, followers put up candle altars decked with crosses, American flags, and photographs of the candidate. They march around, sing praises, shout prayers, thumb prayer beads, and swear vengeance on the assassin. They claim visions, and one young woman proclaims her guilt for the shooting. Bob Roberts is their messiah, who rises from the dead.

From docudramas, we have come to expect art to imitate reality. However, *Bob Roberts* predated Oliver North's candidacy. The film was made in 1991/1992 and released in 1992. North battled through the Virginia primary and general elections in 1994. The movie implicates his role with the Contras and Nicaragua, as well as the savings and loan scandal (in which company executives from the 1970s defrauded and bankrupted half of the thrift savings banks) as central motivations of the conservative, populist right to seek power. Although North was not yet a senatorial candidate, *Bob Roberts* makes numerous references to the ex-Marine. In a telling interview, the fictional African American reporter enthusiastically explains the nature of the Hunt conspiracy to the narrator. In the background hangs a large poster of North.

Conservative North, bouncing back from the Iran-Contra hearings and trial, sought to appeal to populist sentiments, particularly in marginalized and disenchanted rural Virginia voters. Roberts toured Pennsylvania in his computerized mobile home, "The Pride." The name appealed to the patriotic renewal of fundamental American values, as espoused in Roberts's conservative folk songs. North was never a few hours from any corner of Virginia in his computerized mobile home, "Rolling Thunder." The name drew visions of God, appealing to the religious right, and the air war over North Vietnam, reminding voters of patriotism. North pushed technology to its limits at the time, using computerized fax-generated mailing lists to respond instantaneously to any campaign crisis or issue. He combined the mastery of direct mail with the technology of instant communication. Both candidates employed an aggressive, in-your-face style, keeping the incumbents on the defensive throughout the campaign. Both employed questionable campaign advertisements, with North having to withdraw one from circulation under pressure.

One piece of evidence indicating the existence of a process of social construction of reality is the belief of many viewers that the actor in a movie or on television has the traits and beliefs of the character she or he portrays. Robbins, unlike Roberts, is a committed, socially active liberal (cf. Associated Press 1994). Fearful of the misuse of the lyrics of Roberts's folk songs, many of which Robbins created, Robbins prohibited the release of a sound track.

Conclusion: The Joke on the Audience

Each story is a morality play and a black comedy about the American political system. Both films end with a punchline.

Bill McKay narrowly defeats the incumbent, surprising himself as well as the audience. The movie closes with McKay alone, staring, asking aloud, "What do I do now?" The joke is on us, for he has become a hollow image, in spite of his struggle to prevent this very occurrence. As the victory celebration leaves the candidate's suite for the main ballroom, the camera lingers on the empty, hollow room. The joke, as well, is on the candidate, for he has become what he so despised. J. J. McKay congratulates his son, "You're a politician." McKay had to become what he despised in order to defeat that which he despised. The 1960s and 1970s were a simpler time, and *The Candidate* is a simpler movie, even with its joke. McKay simply sold his soul.

Bob Roberts narrowly defeats the incumbent, as both he so confidently expected, and the audience so feared. The victory edge was provided by a life-threatening and permanently paralyzing gunshot wound suffered by

Roberts. Of course, the assigned assassin is exculpated. We may never know who fired the election-determining shot. We suspect, with great trepidation, that someone on Roberts's staff fired the shot to guarantee the election victory. But, we reassure ourselves, no one, not even the value-less Roberts would stoop so low. So, we follow our documentarian to the victory ball, where paralyzed Roberts is lifted in his wheelchair chariot onto the stage to perform one of his songs. The camera floats through the happy throng, scanning the stage. Roberts strums his guitar, singing his lyrics, tapping his toe. He smiles directly at us. The joke is on us, and Roberts is the jokester.

The 1980s and 1990s were a more complex time, with Generation X, the religious right, Bill Clinton, and Newt Gingrich. We realize that Roberts was never shot. He manipulated the election and the audience. A protester at a Roberts's campaign stop warned us, "Bob Roberts is not for the people, he is for himself." Film critic Raplin was incorrect in his assertion that "there is no Mr. Smith in Washington; Mr. Smith has been bought." Bob Roberts could not sell his soul, for he had no soul to sell.

Oliver North narrowly lost to Chuck Robb. Virginia continued with a self-destroyed, impotent senator, but a known quantity. A victory for either would be a joke on Virginia. The ultimate joke may be that Oliver North continued to soar, politically and economically, in spite of the crimes he committed and the disrepute that he brought to the Marine uniform. And, for all the liberals and moderates who feared North, they got Newt Gingrich.

The production values improve from story to story, with the North campaign one of the most sophisticated and expensive yet mounted. In various ways, the creators of the three stories utilized the techniques suggested by the typology of Medhurst and DeSousa (1981)—the political commonplace, allusions, caricature, and contemporaneous events, personalities and issues. Perhaps the most striking phenomenon is how audiences respond at the moment of the punchline: Until that moment, film audience—and voters in the film—have accepted one vision of reality. At the punchline, social reality is deconstructed and replaced with a sobering new reality. In a moment, reality is stood on its head.

Epilog

The paradigm presented by *The Candidate* and *Bob Roberts* about elections, validated by the actual campaigns by Oliver North and Rick Santorum, was a social construction of how elections were run when television was the dominant mode of communication. The themes were electoral politics as sport (a "race") rather than a contest of ideas, mindless projection of imagery rather than substance, a public willing to believe anything provided that certain buttons (prejudices) are pressed by candidates, and campaign professionals and interest groups pulling the strings behind the scene. Either film could have been made in any of the years up to 2000.

In the twenty-first century, the same themes have been present in films about elections. *The Manchurian Candidate* (2004) provided an opportunity to update the technology of "brainwashing" during an election campaign. *Silver City* (2004) implied that George W. Bush was bought by special interests in his successful gubernatorial campaign in Texas. *Man of the Year* (2006) showed how voters distrust the two parties so much that they instead would vote for an amusing television personality running as a third-party candidate. *Swing Vote* (2008) played up the refrain that ordinary citizens are ill-informed and, thanks to the media, are subjected to cynical appeals by opposing candidates.

Some observers may feel that the ground shifted in 2007, since Barack Obama utilized social media in his campaign for election in 2008 and re-election in 2012, while FoxNews and MSNBC have addressed different elements of the electorate, demonizing and polarizing their audiences. The Home Box Office film *Game Change* (2012), based on the nonfiction book of the same title by two sympathetic journalists (Heilemann and Halperin 2010), provided a docudrama of the 2008 election without the cynicism of *The Candidate* and *Bob Roberts* and ignoring the insights of Obama's critics (e.g., Suskind 2011; D'Souza 2012). Dinesh D'Souza, sketching out a counterscenario in his documentary *2016: Obama's America* (2012) based on his book, focused on the president's background and ideology, not the way American elections are conducted in the age of social media. Nonetheless, the positive spin of *Game Change* and negative critique of *2016* represent the voices of a deeply divided American political class, which encourages citizens to screen their filmviewing by ideology while also maintaining continuity with the paradigm developed by *The Candidate* and *Bob Roberts* of deeply flawed electoral politics.

5

Escape from the Bowling Alley: Traditional Associations as the Antagonist in Popular Film

Hans Noel

Well, we're safe for now. Thank goodness we're in a bowling alley.—Mayor "Big Bob" (J. T. Nelson), reacting to the sudden introduction of 1990s chaos into the order of his 1950s television town in the 1998 film *Pleasantville*.

The title political scientist Robert Putnam has given to his argument about traditional associations could not be more apt. Not only does "Bowling Alone" (Putnam 1995, 2000) clearly summarize the basic phenomena that he seeks to explain, but it also evokes just the right social setting. Political scientists meeting weekly to watch the Sunday news shows would qualify as building social capital but such a group would not quite capture the spirit of ordinary, hardworking Americans gathering in a public place to do public things in an organized manner. This milieu is something Putnam (1993) and many of the other advocates of small, local community cooperation (from Amitai Etzioni to William Kristol) really admire.

But in this way, "Bowling Alone" also captures many weaknesses of the argument, for this social order is not admired by everyone. A very old counterculture tradition, especially active in the last half-century, sees the bowling alley domain as something to overcome. And they seek their social interaction—and build their social capital—in other, less ordered places. Here, "Bowling Alone" is illustrative in its inaccuracy. The many Americans who are bowling but not bowling in leagues are not, in fact, bowling "alone," They are bowling with friends. And while those friends are hard to record as a "group" that one might join, they still constitute social interaction.

Challenges to the social capital argument are not new. While a number of theorists advance some variant of the social capital thesis, I will herein focus on Putnam's formulation, which has been hard to prove, and hard to articulate. Here, I attempt to outline some of the implications of my critique by using several popular films. In these vernacular films, traditional associations play the role of the antagonists, and the obstacles presented tend to undermine the ability of the protagonist to build social connections and accumulate social capital. The protagonists are forced to find ways to *circumvent* the very traditional associations that are supposed to *help* to build social capital.

The Social Capital Thesis

Of the claims that the associations argument makes, three are of particular interest: (1) Participation in community associations has declined since the 1960s. (2) This decline is alarming, because community associations are essential for democratic life. (3) The causes of this decline are generally structural, and include especially the introduction of television and the replacement of the older "civic generation" by its less civic-minded members of the Baby Boom and Generations X and Y. All three claims are contentious:

(1) The notion of decline is among the more demonstrable of the argument's claims. Among the more specific declines (Putnam 2000): Membership in parent-teacher associations (PTAs) for families with children 18 or under fell from more than 45 percent in 1960 to less than 20 percent in 2000 (ibid., p. 57). Church attendance fell from more than 45 percent of adults to just more than 35 percent in the same period (ibid., p. 71). And famously, bowling league participation fell from 8 percent of all men 20 years old or older to just 2 percent in that time (ibid., p. 112). Nevertheless, the notion of decline has been challenged by scholars who claim that modern Americans have merely shifted their participation to other, less countable places (Bennett 1998).

Although social interaction might have shifted to an informal setting, measurements of many of these also show a decline: Having friends over for dinner, sending greeting cards and informal participatory sports have all declined (ibid., pp. 93–115). Meanwhile, attendance at spectator sports is up, leading some to argue that "watching culture" is replacing "doing culture." But this may be an area where measurement is problematic, since we cannot get a general index of all social-capital-building activities and then control for shifts in behavior. Tailgating before a football game surely counts for something. Even watching a basketball game in a bar is not the same as watching it at home. Nevertheless, it may be valid to presume that informal activity is a poor substitute for formal associations.

Still, most critics are willing to acknowledge that something has happened to Americans since Alexis de Tocqueville (1835) saw a nation dedicated to associations. A great number of today's groups are detached "membership" groups that use membership as a fund-raising tool, such as the American Association of Retired Persons.

(2) The normative claim that we should worry about the decline is supported by both theory and evidence. The theory is that social engagement

breeds the kind of networks needed in a liberal democracy. Lions Clubs, PTAs, and yes, even bowling leagues, serve as a location for democracy as much as does the ballot box. And these groups also provide something like a school for democracy, teaching people how to govern themselves and how to think about solving problems in a community. This theory is supported by evidence showing that where social capital is high, so are markers for democracy, social inequality, good schools, and a host of other desirable community traits (Putnam 1995, 2000).

But there is a darker side to social engagement. Putnam (2000:ch 22) himself noticed the jab from *Pleasantville*. And it's not a new jab. Sinclair Lewis's *Babbitt* (1922) is a deliberate satire on the traditionally "engaged." Others note that the Ku Klux Klan is among the associations that grew in the civic heyday of the early part of the twentieth century. Many of the national and local associations lauded by community advocates did not accept blacks, women or gays and lesbians until recently. It may be no accident that advances in tolerance and individual liberty have come at the same time as the decline in civic associations, as I demonstrate below. Michael Schudson (1998) argues that these gains might be worth the price of declining bowling league membership.

(3) Finally, the claim that the decline is due to television or a lack of civic spirit among the younger generation is perhaps the least supported. However, if there has been a decline—or even a shift—in social engagement, it should have some cause. This puzzle has motivated much of social capital research. Putnam (2000:Section 3) lays out a cluster of explanations, largely structural. First, changes in work habits and urban sprawl have reduced the opportunities for social activity. More importantly, face-to-screen television has replaced face-to-face social interaction as a dominant pastime. People who are watching television are not out building social capital. The use of television is especially prevalent among the younger generations, who in general are less likely to engage in civic activity: The generational difference may play an even larger role. Baby Boomers and members of Generations X and Y, born and raised after World War II, were not exposed to the national sense of purpose that the war encouraged. Thus, they were not as acclimatized to civic involvement.

Most of these explanations are largely circumstantial. While they may account for some of the decline, Putnam himself acknowledges that there may be more culprits. And his two main causes—television and generational changes—both have logical flaws. Television may have adverse effects, but in Putnam's study of social capital in Italy, television ownership is greater in the more civically engaged north. And the war effort might have encouraged civic activity, but Putnam's "civic generation" suffered no decline in the lag period between World War I and World War II. Something more may be at play.

The Discussion in the Movie Theory

Insight into the issues raised by the social capital thesis is found in an unlikely place. Inside the darkened movie theatre, several films, made mostly for commercial purposes, explore the same issues. Social capital issues can be found especially in six films: *Animal House* (1978), *Caddyshack* (1980), *Revenge of the Nerds* (1984), *Footloose* (1984), *Dazed and Confused* (1993) and *Pleasantville* (1998). These films have more than just social capital in common. The first three are clear cases of the nerd or romp movie (Gaslin and Porter 1998; Wieland n.d.), and the latter three have elements of that genre. Many themes discussed below are common in that genre. All six films depict groups of young people responding to and rebelling against the older generation. Commercially successful, each film qualifies as high-profile, either through its significant box office gross or through its recorded audience popularity (Table 6.1).

Looking at measurable social data can tell us many things that looking at a small selection of popular films cannot. But looking at popular culture can prompt a perspective that the data alone might not suggest. The six films suggest several things to us. In all six, the antagonist role is played by a traditional civic organization or its representatives. Thus, the challenges faced by the protagonist come directly from the organizations and structures that are meant to engender social capital. What's more, the goal of the protagonists in these films is to build social capital and civic engagement. The heroes are not trying to be left alone to watch television. They want the same things that traditional associations are meant to provide. But in these narratives, traditional associations serve the opposite purpose. The films illustrate several strategies for overcoming the traditional associations, and these strategies have resonance in real life.

The way these narratives play out speaks directly to the three claims that I highlighted above. First, the protagonists engage in civic community in ways that may be hard to measure and detect, lending credence to the thesis that much of the decline could be a shift to something new. Second, the protagonists come to consciously oppose traditional associations, supporting a normative perspective that is more critical of traditional associations, and they might even welcome their decline. Third, conscious and deliberate disengagement suggests a different explanation for the decline—choice.

Table 5.1. Comparing Six Films

Film	*Animal House*	*Caddyshack*	*Footloose*	*Revenge of the Nerds*	*Dazed and Confused*	*Pleasantville*
Writer	Douglas Kenney Harold Ramis Chris Miller	Brian Doyle-Murray Harold Ramis Douglas Kenney	Dean Pitchford	Jeff Buhai Tim Metcalfe Miguel Tejada Flores Steve Zacharías	Richard Linklater	Gary Ross
Director	John Landis	Harold Ramis	Herbert Rosa	Jeff Kanew	Richard Linklater	Gary Ross
Producer	Ivan Reitman Matty Simmons	Mark Canton Douglas Kenney Jon Peters	Lewis J. Rachmill Craig Zadan	Tim Field Peter Samuelson	James Jacks Sean Daniel Richard Linklater	Jon Kilik Gary Ross Steven Soder-bergh
Principal Cast	Tom Hulce Stephen Furst Mark Metcalf Kevin Bacon Karen Allen Tim Matheson Peter Riegert Donald Sutherland John Vernon	Chevy Chase Rodney Danger-field Ted Knight Michael O'Keefe Bill Murray	Kevin Bacon Lori Singer John Lithgow Dianne Wiest Chris Penn Sara Jessica Parker	Robert Carradine Anthony Edwards Timothy Busfield Curtis Armstrong Ted McGinely John Goodman	Jason London Joey Lauren Adams Mila Jovovich Adam Goldberg Parker Posey Matthew McConnaughey Ben Affleck	Tobey Mac-Guire Jeff Daniels Joan Allen William H. Macy J. T. Walsh Reese With-erspoon
Distributor	Universal Pictures	Orion Pictures	Paramount Pictures	20th Century Fox	Gramercy Pictures	New Line Cinema
Release	6/1/78	7/25/80	2/17/84	11/1/85	9/1/93	10/24/98
Gross*	$141,600,000	$39,800,000	$80,000,000	$40,900,000	$7,993,000	$40,468,000
IMDB Rate	7.4	6.9	5.8	5.9	7.1	7.4
Time of Plot		1980	1984	1984	1976	mostly 1950s

*As of March 2001

Before engaging the films, it is appropriate to question why I treat these "popular" films politically. Scholars have a range of theories about what makes a "political film." On one extreme, some see political material in nearly every film. All films have some message, even if unintentionally. And auteur theory (e.g. Hillier 1985) would hold that the director often is intentionally grafting a message. At the other extreme, we find those who find very few political films. With the exception of conscious propaganda, film is commerce first, art second. And politics gets in the way of commerce. Most film theorists try to find a middle ground. Michael Genovese (1986), for instance, offers three criteria for a political film: (1) It serves as a vehicle for social change. (2) Its major intention is to foment social change. (3) Or it is designed to support the status quo. Under this framework, the six films discussed here do not quite qualify as "political films." Their *major* intention is not to bring about social change, but to entertain and make money. But this does not mean that the films' creators are unconscious of their place in the political world.

The six films might also be seen to fall short of criteria offered by Ernest Giglio (Chapter 3 herein), who prefers considering both the film's *intent* and its *effect*. Certainly the primary intent of these six films is not political. And there is little independent evidence that these directors were deeply motivated by a desire to make a political statement. Meanwhile, I do not claim that these films *caused* any decline in social engagement, so they did not have that kind of effect.

Peter Haas's typology, as noted by Giglio in Chapter 3, has similar criteria. He asks to what degree a film has *political content* and *political intent*. The two questions help to decide how to think about the film politically. In this framework, the films considered here could be judged as having little (or only secondary) political intent, and no explicit political content. These are films Haas calls "socially reflective," because they give insight into the social setting of their time.

Without attempting to develop fully an alternative framework for defining political film, I offer the following perspective: Most films have some sort of artistic message, which is the collective work of the many creative talents involved. The artistic message is usually subordinate to the demands of commerce, but that only tempers it. And an artistic message can be explicitly political, as with *Bulworth* (1998) and *Traffic* (2000), or only incidentally political, as with *Planet of the Apes* (1968) and *Dirty Harry* (1971). And that political content is worth exploring.

This discussion is important, because it is an easy mistake to assert politics—or any other meaning—where there is none. We need to believe that the filmmaker is trying to make a statement. On the other hand, if film is expression, then the best place to look for that statement is in the film itself. The crucial criterion is that the film must support the weight of the politics asserted. And if the film as a whole is political, then evidence needs to be sought not only in the script, but in the other elements of the film as well, such as mise-en-scène, editing techniques, or framing decisions.

So, can the six films support the weight of politics? While the films are rarely considered "art," that may be because comedy is not well respected by auteur theorists. Even so, they are not hack products.

Directors John Landis and Harold Ramis, who wrote *Animal House* (1978) and wrote and directed *Caddyshack* (1980), are both comedy legends, mostly for creating loud, slapstick-oriented fare, including *The Kentucky Fried Movie* (1977). Among Landis's other credits as director are *The Blues Brothers* (1980), *Trading Places* (1983), *Coming to America* (1988), *Beverly Hills Cop III* (1994), *The Stupids* (1996), *Blues Brothers 2000* (1998), and *Burke and Hare* (2010). Ramis later directed *Vacation* (1983), *Club Paradise* (1986), *Groundhog Day* (1993), *Multiplicity* (1996), *Bedazzled* (2000), *Analyze That* (2002), *The Ice Harvest* (2005), and *Year One* (2009).

Dazed writer/director Richard Linklater was among the early darlings of the 1990s explosion of independent films. He later directed *SubUrbia* (1996), *The Newton Boys* (1998), *Waking Life* (2001), *The School of Rock* (2003), *Fast Food Nation* (2006), *Me and Orson Welles* (2008), and *Bernie* (2011).

Pleasantville earned Gary Ross the Golden Satellite Award for best original screenplay and the Producers Guild of America Golden Laurel's Nova Award for "Most Promising Producer in Theatrical Motion Pictures." Primarily a writer, he is also known for directing *Seabiscuit* (2003) and the 2012 version of *The Hunger Games*.

Herbert Ross *of Footloose* later directed *The Goodbye Girl* (1977) and *Steel Magnolias* (1989), *My Blue Heaven* (1990), *True Colors* (1991), *Undercover Blues* (1993), and *Boys on the Side* (1995).

Of the six, *Revenge of the Nerds* has the worst pedigree, but the film is perhaps the most perfect example of the nerd movie genre. All in all, while they may be fun and popular comedies, they are *good* fun and popular comedies.

Looking Around

Footloose, *Revenge of the Nerds*, and *Caddyshack* all take place in the "present day" of their release from 1978–1984. *Animal House* is set back to 1962, and therefore depicts a period right at the beginning of the decline in traditional associations. The film is based on the college experiences of co-writer Chris Miller, who was at Dartmouth from 1960 to 1964, though much of the sensibility seems to come from the 1970s.

If the phenomenon under study began in the 1960s and had made a major impact by the 1990s, then these are films that were made during and are about the time period in question. A film, of course, can take more than a year to produce; the initial inspiration for the story probably comes from a few years before its release data. Since the decline in attendance at traditional associations began before the films were released, we can not argue here that the messages spread by the films changed people's attitudes and led to any decline (although film can be influential in that way). Rather, these films are efforts by their creators to reflect the world around them. The fact that they were successful suggests that their themes spoke to the issues that matter in the lives of their audiences.

Barred at the Gates in *Caddyshack*. Harold Ramis's 1980 film *Caddyshack* is a true comedy romp. The story roams over varied territory, making it more a collection of gags than an organized narrative. Still, each of the subplots contributes to the same themes about the country club where they take place. The original script of *Caddyshack* was meant to focus more on the caddies and their relationship to the golfers. However, big names like Chevy Chase and Bill Murray were brought in to play adult roles, so the focus of the comedy shifted to them. The central story concerns Danny Noonan (played by Michael O'Keefe), who takes a summer job as a caddy to earn money—and a shot at a scholarship. He knows that success comes from the social connections that he can develop through the country club, and he cultivates one with Judge Smails (Ted Knight), who can help deliver the scholarship. Unfortunately, Danny inadvertently offends Smails, and the deal is off.

Meanwhile, newly wealthy Al Czervik (Rodney Dangerfield) also wants access to the social-capital-building resources of the country club. However, Czervik is crass and obnoxious, and this, too, offends Smails and the other powers-that-be in the country club. The club is exclusive ("I hear this place is restricted, Wang," Czervik tells his Asian golf partner, "So don't tell 'em you're Jewish, okay?"). Czervik does not fit, even though he can buy acceptance. Importantly, the attack on Czervik is not through specific exclusionary rules but through social pressure and the exercise of discretionary power on the part of the club leadership.

To the rescue is Ty Webb (Chevy Chase), who mentors Danny and allies with Czervik when Smails and the others try to drive him out. Webb exercises a typical strategy that insiders can use when they do not approve of the restricted, uptight nature of the traditional organization. He ignores it. He loves golf (religiously), but he does not keep score or play in the club's tournaments. (He golfs alone!) Webb can get away with this strategy because his father was a founding member, and because he is wealthy. However, he eschews many of the social capital networks of the association to which he belongs, because they come at the price of socializing with Smails. However, when Smails tries to ally with Webb—and implies that Webb's father agreed that "some people simply do not belong." Webb chooses sides against the association.

The narrative themes are echoed in the mise-en-scène and iconography. Bushwood Country Club *is* the site of important social networks, and membership is important to building social capital. It also provides access to the golf greens, a more physical (and cinematic) resource. The shots on the country club grounds establish it as a privileged and pleasant place, with expanses of green that are defended from gophers by wacky groundskeeper Carl Spackler (Bill Murray). Contrast this with the images of Danny Noonan's crowded house and the dirty caddyshack where Noonan and the other caddies fight over access to a soft drink. The country club becomes a metaphor for class distinction, and the Horatio Alger story of social mobility is shown to be false, as both Noonan and Czervik are barred from entry. Since this is a comedic fantasy, they prove victorious in the end, but only because insider Webb takes their side in the climactic showdown on the links. Outside the country club, both Noonan and Czervik have more access to social capital. Noonan also faces challenges in the caddyshack, but since it is less formal, it is easier for him to overcome them. And Czervik's obnoxiousness gets less in the way of his money when he is not on the links.

The protagonists do not fit the civic disengagement story. They want to join, but are nearly forced out. And we see evidence that their civic spirit would remain were Smails successful in excluding them, although it might have to be expressed in less formal ways. The normative take on the country club is far more critical. And the reason for their possible exclusion is related to normative issues rather than any structural changes. Real life echoes these patterns. Even after many exclusive country clubs opened their doors to minorities, the social powers-that-be can still exercise a great deal of control against unwanted members.

An End Run Around the Rules in *Footloose*. Midway through the musical drama *Footloose* (1984), John Lithgow gives an eloquent and carefully crafted defense of the small-town life he is shepherding as the town's spiritual leader, Rev. Shaw Moore:

> You know I was down in Denver, last year, for about a week, at a Bible convention there. And the whole time I was there, people would come up to me, and ask me, "Reverend how can you live, in such a small town, so far away from the hustle and bustle of the 20th century?" I'd say to them, "You'd never ask me that, if you could just once, just for one minute, experience the feeling of family that comes from knowing that all of our lives are tied up with each others. That we feel all the same joys, the same sorrows, and that we care, each and every one of us cares for the other." I told them, "I just feel close to my Lord out there, and I feel closer and safer with my people. And I think they feel closer to me. The Lord smiles on us out there. And that's where I'm staying."

The speech is given to several audiences, which provide a litany of social capital-building groups in small-town America. The scene opens as Lithgow speaks to a group gathered on the porch of a country house. As Lithgow's Moore continues talking, it shifts to a crowd of teenagers, possibly a Bible study group, in a school library. And it ends at a table where a group of women is joining the reverend for dessert. The reverend's words articulate much of the value of social capital. Caring for one another and feeling close to each other is exactly what civic engagement is all about. The message continues in the film's mise-en-scène: Moore moves comfortably from one social setting to another. He knows all the children's names in the town, and those children are happy and cared-for in the community that his church helps to protect. In a typical scene, Moore and another town father walk through a daycare center. While their conversation is elsewhere, Moore picks up children and hugs them as he moves through their world.

But Moore is not the hero of *Footloose*. He is more than a villain. In fact, Moore may be the most dynamic character in the film, since he does begin to have a change of heart. He represents the church in the role of antagonist, to Kevin Bacon's Ren MacCormack, the protagonist. MacCormack comes from Chicago to the small town of Beaumont, where he finds a law against public dancing. First, he goes through proper channels, hoping to change the law so the senior class at his high school can have a prom. But the town council and the social networks of the church are tightly related. The laws against dancing, drinking, and other social evils were passed by Moore and others in the first place, in response to a tragic accident. And they will not listen to MacCormack now, even when he cites the Bible in defense of dancing. So as a last recourse, MacCormack and his high school allies decide to hold their prom in a warehouse just outside the town limits.

Here, the civic networks of the church not only provide an obstacle to building social capital; they reach out and prevent other social interactions that are not sanctioned by the church. A powerful establishing scene introduces us to the young people in Beaumont. The frame explores a crowd of teenagers listening to a tape of the forbidden song (written for the film) "Dancing in the Sheets" by Shalamar. We see the music creating a public sphere in which we might imagine social capital could grow. But the rock song is unapproved: Moore arrives to stop the music, and the public sphere collapses. Indeed, a school dance is a perfect example of the kind of public space that Putnam and others advocate. Indeed, Putnam specifically mentions dances as the kind of activity he would like to see cultivated as a remedy for declining social capital. But since the social network of the church is so pervasive, it can stop other networks it does not like.

The strategy that MacCormack and the other teenagers take is illustrative. Unable to form their organization within the town, they go outside. But a shadow prom, held outside the law, probably would not show up in an attempt to count voluntary associations. To the extent that this strategy is tried in the real world, it would be hard to measure. So again, we have evidence of unconventional association, a different normative perspective on traditional association, and a possible withdrawal from traditional associations based on that normative perspective.

Form Your Own in *Animal House* and *Revenge of the Nerds*. There is no more "fraternal" organization than a fraternity. But fraternities do not fare well in the world of movies. *Both Animal House* (1978) and *Revenge of the Nerds* (1985) tell similar stories about fraternity life. In both films, new freshmen arrive on campus and attempt to join a popular fraternity. But they are turned away because they are too geeky. So they join or form an alternative fraternity whose status is tenuous. The popular fraternity, in league with the powers of the school, directly attacks the outsider fraternity, with some success.

In *Animal House*, Delta Tau Chi already exists. It provides a sort of shadow social network of mentors and resources for the ostracized. But Delta Tau Chi is already at war with the college and with Omega Theta Pi, the popular fraternity. And it is clearly the anti-fraternity, with none of the respectable practices of the traditional association. The disheveled set of the Delta House stands in contrast to the posh Omega House.

Ultimately, the Omegas conspire to get the college to oust Delta House. Why? Because the values of the Deltas (partying, of course) are different from those of the Omegas, or of Faber College. The outsiders attempt to create their own voluntary association but fail because the other associations will not tolerate it. Robbed of their formal organization, the Deltas stick together for one last, outrageous prank.

In *Revenge of the Nerds,* an alternative fraternity must be created. The outcasts apply to form a local chapter of Lambda Lambda Lambda, a black fraternity, which cements the analogy between nerds and other outcast groups. Indeed, the nerds are a laundry list of social outsiders—a gay, a child prodigy, computer geeks, a musician, and a smelly kid. But empowered by their voluntary association, they are able to challenge the popular fraternity (the "Alpha Betas," lest the social hierarchy be unclear to the audience). Their challenge succeeds, but the Alphas attack their fraternity house anyway. *Nerds* has a happier ending—the black alumni of their fraternity arrive in the nick of time, and an impassioned speech brings out the "inner nerds" in the crowd, who join the heroes in solidarity. The threat is overcome, but it is the same threat that succeeds in *Animal House*: The established associations are not as accepting of other associations because of what they see as corrupt values.

Both films portray something that may not find a literal parallel in real life. If one bowling league rejects you, you form another league. It is unlikely that the first league will destroy the new association. But the threat is metaphorical. Traditional associations do not simply exist to promote social capital; they have specific values that they endorse. This is very much a part of the value of these social institutions. But as with the church in *Footloose,* these institutions can go too far in enforcing those values. Misfits who do not endorse (or are even condemned by) those values can attempt to form alternative associations. But the new associations can find it difficult to thrive in a society that is so heavily permeated by traditional values. Homophobia is pervasive enough that you can imagine representatives of the traditional public sphere being very hostile to the formation of a gay or lesbian support group, especially in a small town. You can even imagine the violence against them, as suffered by the Deltas and the Tri-Lambdas.

Looking Back

Pleasantville (1998) and *Dazed and Confused* (1993), the two most artistically respected of the six films, differ from the first four films in that they do not depict contemporary life. They both look back at the world during the time of the biggest decline in traditional associations and reflect on that period from the vantage point of 1990s. They are responding not just to the world around them, but to memory as well. While directors Gary Roth and Richard Linklater may have been cognizant of the social capital literature, they are aware of the admiration of and the struggle over the traditional associations that they place in their films.

Anti-Nostalgia in *Pleasantville*. Explicitly about the social capital thesis, the film begins with a simple (and recycled) premise. Suppose two siblings from the 1990s were transported into the sanitized world of a 1950s family sitcom, like *Father Knows Best* (1954–1960) or *Leave It to Beaver* (1957–1963). In this case, David (Tobey MacGuire) and Jennifer (Reese Witherspoon) begin to tamper with the old-fashioned rules of the black-and-white 1950s. They import from the 1990s not crime or hip slang, but liberation. And not liberation from the 1950s per se, but from the black-and-white world that never existed but that may be our idealized conception of the period. As their liberation spreads, the black-and-white image gains color, to capture the metaphor.

A nice scene, which suggests that Roth may well be familiar with *Bowling Alone*, takes place in a bowling alley. The embattled town elders who want to protect the old way take shelter in the still black-and-white bowling alley, and the mayor (J. T. Walsh), even notes that they are probably safe there.

It is important that the past in *Pleasantville* is not the real 1950s, but a 1990s image of the past. The film expresses the inaccuracy of the image by poking fun at the absurdity of living in the ideal, where the temperature is always 72°, and firefighters only rescue kittens because tragedies like house fires never occur. Before the 1990s, when the two emissaries arrive in Pleasantville, the books in the libraries had no words or pictures because the themes in literature would have upset the perfect balance. Those who defend that perfect balance, then, sound less like voices from the past than voices from the present longing for the image. As a response to the difference, the mayor and town council lay out a set of rules *after* the town's liberation begins. Consider these words of Mayor Big Bob:

> If you love a place, you can't just sit back and watch this kind of thing happen, now can you?
> Up until now everything around here has always been, well, pleasant. Recently certain things have become unpleasant. Now, it seems to me that the first thing to be done is to separate out the things that are pleasant from the things that are unpleasant.
> There must be a code of conduct that we can all agree to live by.

And as satire, audiences are not merely expected to hear the voice of modern culture warriors in the mayor. Instead, the voice of this defense of the modern culture warriors speaks against gays and drugs and modern culture. Roth wants you to believe that, even today, it takes effort to live in color.

Anti-Nostalgia in *Dazed and Confused*. Whereas *Pleasantville* is an over-the-top satire, *Dazed and Confused* is a much subtler criticism of social traditions. The film follows high school students on the last day of school in 1976. With the final bell, juniors become seniors, and those finishing middle school become freshmen in high school. Tradition requires the seniors to haze the freshmen. Boys are chased and paddled, and girls are taunted and made to perform humiliating tasks. Assuming, of course, that you are chosen.

In one scene, girls are piling into a pick-up truck to be taken to the school parking lot for their hazing. A senior has one more space to fill, so she walks over to a crowd of near misfit freshmen and selects the most pretty to join her. The others are excluded. Mike Newhouse (Adam Goldberg) comments on the whole exercise:

> Now, see, what's fascinating is the way that not only the school, but the entire community, seems to be supporting this, you know, or at least turn their heads. I mean, they apparently have permission to use the parking lot. No parents seem to mind. They're selling concessions.

The ensemble cast weaves around and through the public sphere, visiting Little League games and middle school dances, talking with town elders and football coaches. The high school's star quarterback (Jason London), who is thinking about giving up football, casually talks with an older man, who is more interested in the team's prospects than in the quarterback himself.

The quarterback, Randall "Pink" Floyd, has friends who are football players and who are stoners. His social world *is* larger than that of most athletes, and his coaches do not approve. He is running with a "bad" crowd.

Students in Linklater's community are not in open conflict with the social order, as in the other films examined here. (The biggest rebellion in the film is that Pink refuses to sign a pledge not to do drugs—the equivalent of promising to give up the informal social networks that he knows in favor of the traditional ones.) Many characters participate in the perpetuation of tradition. But they are becoming aware of the injustice and pain caused by the tradition, which brings people together; but so does the informal party in the woods that the teens arrange on the fly during the night. And the informal groupings may be superior. Pink points out to his teammates that they could get all the social benefits of playing football if they were in a band instead. The students recognize that these days are not so halcyon. The film, then, like *Pleasantville,* is challenging our memory of a more ideal past. As Pink puts it: "All I'm saying is that if I ever start talking about these like they were the best years of my life, remind me to shoot myself."

Discussion

The debate over traditional associations is not especially new. And it should not come as a surprise that some films take positions against the establishment. But we should take something more from these films than that.

Essays about social capital tend to view the observed decline as a surprising and perhaps hidden development. Thus, the academic explanation for the decline is structural. Something happened in the world, which led to a change that we were unaware of. But the significance of traditional associations has long been known by the people who take part in them. It may be possible that the way people relate to these associations is deliberate. Scholars can advance normative positions about whether traditional associations are good for Americans. But Americans, too, can have normative positions, and they can *act* on them. They can leave the easy-to-recognize associations and interact in very informal ways in an attempt to reach the same social capital ends by different means.

This is not to say that these Americans are right. It may be that their alternatives are inferior to the more formal traditional associations. The Internet and self-help groups may be poor at building social capital and teaching liberal democracy. But it is not enough to demonstrate that traditional associations are necessary. And it may not be enough to assert that they need not be threatening. Putnam and his allies would not defend the behavior of traditional associations depicted in these films. They might even argue that this behavior is not always an accurate picture of most traditional associations. The perception, however, is real.

The fears of many Americans ought to be taken seriously. Taking them seriously may imply a different solution to civic disengagement. If structural change is merely robbing us of the opportunity to participate in traditional associations, Americans can fight those structures. But if the associations themselves are prone to abuse, something else might be needed.

In the end, the six films identify a paradox in liberalism. Classical liberals like John Stuart Mill (1859) argue that people should not persecute differences. But they also argue that truly deviant behavior can be discouraged through subtle social pressures and leading by example. This is a significant difficulty in liberal theory, and one that affects everything from hate speech to violence on television. It is a fine line between persecution and subtle pressure. But the example set by these films suggests that persecution is, indeed, a danger worth worrying about.

6
The Politics of Disaster Films
Elizabeth Haas

Since the beginning of the 21st century, disasters, both disparate and interrelated have brought about what Matthew Gross and Mel Gilles (2012) refer to as a cultural "turn toward the apocalyptic," occasioning a distinct renewal of the disaster genre at the box office. Although rare, the two strands have even shared multiplexes. In sober and at times angry and angst-filled fashion, these documentaries carefully construct narratives to account for what hours and hours of repetitive television news cycles never can and ordinary feature films gloss—cogent explanations of horrifying events that seem as inexplicable and fickle as the tornado that wipes out one side of the street and leaves the other intact. In the present chapter, I identify how filmmakers have dealt with disasters, past and present, and examine the political dimension which their representations imply, especially as those films figure the bodies of individuals as suggestive of a relationship to political agency.

Although an under-studied genre of political films, disaster films frequently feature high levels of both political intent and content. Typologically, they border overtly political films in their shared invocation of government action and ideologically driven plot points. To sketch a context for the resurgence of disaster documentary and fictional films, I begin with a panorama of the disaster-filled twenty-first century.

Disasters and Rumors of Disaster

The beginning of the twenty-first century was marked by disasters of nature as well as of economics and politics, including the unprecedented 9/11 terrorist attacks. Among the natural disasters count the Deep Horizon oil spill in the Gulf of México; the apparent efforts of global climate change, including massive snowstorms and tornados across the midwest; uncontrolled wildfires and flash floods across the southwest and west; and the landmark devastation of Hurricane Katrina in the south followed by Hurricane Sandy in the northeast. Recent landslides and sinkholes, which have struck with lightning speed, have pulled the very earth from under the unlucky.

The collapse of the world economy in 2008 hit more than individual markets, as oil prices topped $100.00 a barrel for the first time, Lehman Brothers declared bankruptcy, and housing prices fell off a cliff. The financial debacle at the end of George W. Bush's White House only gathered speed and competed for top billing with the inauguration of the United States' first African American president, Barack Obama. Financial industry collapse and uncertain rescue, skyrocketing unemployment, and loss of wealth across all classes cascaded into the worst economic conditions since the Great Depression of the 1930s.

American political disasters include the disputed presidential election of 2000, finally settled in an unprecedented intervention by the Supreme Court but later disavowed by Justice Sandra Day O'Connor, who supported it at the time. The presidential election of 2004 had claims of voter fraud connected to computer balloting in the crucial swing state of Ohio. And legislative grid-lock followed the 2010 and 2012 elections. Meanwhile, Democrats and even a few disillusioned Republicans worried that the republic could not withstand President Bush's unprecedented assertion of presidential powers, including statements issued when he signed legislation into law which said he would not enforce the parts of the law that he considered in violation of constitu-tional provisions directing the president to supervise the "unitary executive branch." The Patriot Act and other provisions for secret surveillance of Americans were followed by justifications of torture and other human rights violations issued by Justice Department lawyers.

President Obama's policies riled opposition groups like the Tea Party, Libertarians, and conservative Republicans who bemoaned Obama's "social-ism" and "the end of liberty" at his hands. Supporters of campaign finance reform would also list the Supreme Court's *Citizens United* ruling as a politi-cal disaster while all but a few diehard Bush officials consider the Iraq War and, increasingly, the Afghan War, unmitigated disasters, exacting an unjus-tifiably high price in the nation's "blood and treasure." Other social catastro-phes include a failing public education system, an over-priced and ineffective public health care system, and a plague of gun violence that kills some 30,000 Americans a year (Cane 2012), including massacres in a movie thea-ter in Colorado, at a Sikh temple in Wisconsin, and in an elementary school in Connecticut.

Beginning with the turn of the century and proceeding to 2012, chrono-logical markers bookended these disastrous times. Y2K anxiety led ordinary people to stock bunkers in the wilderness, drain their bank accounts, and stuff cash under mattresses in preparation for an end of the familiar and the start of something wild and uncharted. Commercial and government institu-tions joined in the preparation, leading to the most expensive mass response to the forecast of a secular catastrophe ever recorded, with the U.S. alone spending over $100 billion (Slate 2000).

Twelve years later obsession with the Mayan calendar's apparent prediction of global cataclysm on December 21, 2012, again had some people storing distilled water jugs and beef jerky in their basements, gripped anew by fear of a future cataclysm. In between, religious groups and self-proclaimed prophets declared other revelations of "end of times." After the physical, emotional, psychological and economic devastation of the 9/11 attacks—gleaming birds setting fire to a clear blue sky—doomsday scenarios resonated with secular and non-secular citizens alike.

Armageddon anxiety even broke through the stage-managed protocol and mainstream reporting of a George W. Bush press conference when the president was asked if he believed the "war on terror" and Iraq invasion heralded the apocalypse. Although the president shrugged it off by declaring himself a "practical man," all these dates came and went without incident but did not vanquish the feeling of dread about the future and vague fear of the terror-tinged present. Dubbing the start of the new century the "apocalyptic decade," two cultural critics (Gross and Gilles 2012) summed up the phenomenon: "Americans of all beliefs and backgrounds are turning increasingly to apocalyptic scenarios to explain and understand a world and nation that look radically different from just a decade ago."

From Disasters to the Renewal of Disaster Films

Current fictional disaster films flirt with the possibility of human extinction or irreversible degradation of the human habitat, earth, or conversion of the mortal body into a technologically prosthetic hybrid (an early twentieth century futurist's dream body), and sometimes all at once. Post-apocalyptic films circle the ethical and political dilemmas that survivors face as they struggle to prevail in their brave new world. But that world and the creatures it shelters exist in a blurred condition between corporeal, natural fragility and time-defiant, presumably incorruptible technology. The 1950s science fiction disaster monsters were radiated mutants like *The Beast from 20,000 Fathoms* (1953) and *Godzilla* (1954), creatures roused from the depths of time by nuclear experimentation, but twenty-first century disaster movie mutants are complicated by their relationship to humans—they are not always the source of fear. In *Pacific Rim* (2013), the giant robotic fighters made to combat the Godzilla-like monsters unleashed by the effects of pollution on Pacific coast nations resemble their enemy. In films like the *Iron Man* (2008–2014) series and *Elysium* (2013), technological prosthetics are implanted into and arrayed atop the hero's body so that he is a sign of machinery and mutation, the blurred lines between monster and human, enemy and friend. In this context, the vulnerable bodies of the non-heroes register politically as sheep in need of a shepherd. Their political will counts for little when their bodies and minds are so permeable and easily manipulated. Such a gap between the technologically prosthetic, heroic body rendered capable of taking momentous action with politically significant consequences suggests a corollary that says the voting public can hardly be counted on to make the right decision. A strong man properly altered, however, can always save the day, perhaps motivated by the dispossessed but ultimately in service of restoring some former order.

Politically, disaster films of all stripes reflect, perhaps even verify and perpetuate, widespread suspicion that what was as recently as the 1990s proclaimed to be "the end of history" has instead turned out to be the end of the "American experiment," an ideological victory of liberal democracy and capitalism over fascism and socialism so hollow it tastes like defeat. In these disaster-filled times the former order's battle over political ideologies appear beside the point as increasingly prosthetic-dependent heroes (*Iron Man* series, 2008–2014; *Transformers*, 2009–2014; *Pacific Rim*, 2013; *Elysium*, 2013; *Edge of Tomorrow*, 2014) in computer-generated imagery-driven, dystopian fiction films come calling with their dark distracting fantasy and mythological underpinnings. Their cultural influence, as demonstrated at the box office, suggests that the end of the human body as we have known it, and the earth that has cocooned it, seems improbable enough or existentially unfathomable enough to offer escape from the very real troubles that have helped to spur a golden age in the feature-length documentary.

At the same time, enhanced heroes like *Elysium's* Max (played by Matt Damon) recall the trope of patriarchal authority figures triumphing against all odds in 1970s disaster films like *Towering Inferno* (1974) and *Earthquake* (1974) and the apocalyptic films *Omega Man* (1971) and *Soylent Green* (1973). For, despite aspects of a post-human appearance, the heroes of films like *Elysium* and *Edge of Tomorrow* always manage to register their masculinity in familiar displays of bodily heroics. (Max's nemesis in *Elysium* is Secretary Rhodes, a determined woman.) In *Oblivion* (2013), the time-traveler Jack (Tom Cruise) experiences nostalgia for events that he is not even certain he ever experienced. Superbowl football games, New York Yankees baseball caps, the Brooklyn Bridge, and the Empire State Building haunt his perfect yet barren post-apocalyptic present. He has a partner willing to do anything for him sexually and romantically, but still he longs for a vision of a woman he does not know he knows. His nostalgia ultimately translates to support for patriarchy and traditional masculinity when the woman haunting his dreams eventually materializes and despite the fact that she, too, is a government astronaut like Jack, she is also Jack's wife. She arrives weak and dependent on Jack to defeat the alien force that Jack has been duped into thinking they had already vanquished. The movie ends on a vision of the two of them ensconced in a handcrafted shelter in an Edenic spot of unspoiled earth. They will begin the world again. Whereas techno-bodied cyborgs may represent the promise of transcending gender in films like *Pacific Rim*, where men and women occupy identical robot bodies irrespective of gender, the apocalyptic body with all its mechanical appendages and gadgetry most often re-engenders the vulnerable body to restore traditional masculinity in line with the restored political order. The re-humanized body is re-masculinized along with or accompanied by the promised of a restored body politic.

Documentary versus Fictional Disaster Films: An Overview

In general, contemporary fiction films that exploit disaster to entertain and documentaries that report facts about disasters to inform serve different political purposes. Documentaries frequently support activism by educating viewers on a particular, often politically charged topic. They may even urge a specific form of action to take. In this, they are optimistic about human agency and democratic government: If we want something enough and try hard enough, they tell us, we can change our world. On the other hand, disaster fiction films layer escapist fantasy with postmodern anxiety and aim to thrill and disturb in a visceral yet ultimately transitory way. As Susan Sontag (1965:42) wrote of the 1950s–1960s cycle, "Part of the pleasure, indeed, comes from the sense in which these movies are in complicity with the abhorrent." In other words, "they inculcate a strange apathy concerning the process of radiation, contamination and destruction which I, for one, find haunting and depressing." Worse even than illustrating cartoonish politics, disaster films to Sontag were complicit with the dangers they depicted, inuring people to the very issues they most needed to rebel against.

Present-day films, too, are unlikely to foment civic action, though the twenty-first century is no less dangerous an environment than the Cold War. Less concerned with nationalism or specific international tensions than their Cold War forerunners, their depiction of political circumstance and social struggle increasingly serves twenty-first century interconnectedness as achieved through social media and concern for the global fate of humanity. The globetrotting heroes, different languages spoken, and prominent role of the United Nations in the zombie apocalypse film *World War Z* (2013); the generic "earth" settings of *The Matrix* (1999–2005) series, *After Earth* (2013), and *Oblivion*; the multinational cast and Hong Kong setting of *Pacific Rim*; the multilingual, multinational cast of *Elysium*; and the mobilization of official multinational groups like the World Health Organization (WHO) in *Contagion* (2011) demonstrate this shift of disaster mise-en-scène onto the world stage. As in the 1950s nuclear disaster cycle, the doomsday premise, so popular that a 2013 movie news headline announced, "These Days the End is Always Near" (Wallace 2013), distinguishes the apocalyptic subgenre in its confidence that the end is coming and the only real questions are how it will occur and who, if anyone, will survive.

Documentaries often "speak truth to power" as their mode of address, how they acknowledge their audience. Frequently, they rely on "talking heads," medium- and close-up shots of experts, witnesses, or people with firsthand experiences to relate as a cinematic verification: This event or disastrous situation really occurred or continues to plague us, believe you me. Documentaries tend to rely on the analog value to viewers of featured speakers. Their unembellished embodiment is part of what allows us to relate to these "talking heads" as people, not physically stunning movie stars or technology-enhanced cyborgs. As one critic explains the recent surge in documentary production and popularity, people are "more alert about, and suspicious of, the mainstream media and eager for a form that talks to them about real events in a real way" (O'Hagan 2010). The "real" body of the documentary suggests an authenticity despite the fact that documentaries are typically shot using digital cameras and thus are also "virtual."

Our perception that their "real" bodies are at stake in the center of documentary form provide a signifying power to disaster documentaries that their fictional counterparts increasingly bypass, instead literally and metaphorically consigning the actor's body to the same heap of useless nostalgia as celluloid and a devastated earth. Digitally produced films more typically rely on computer-generated-imagery, both independent of and appended to actor bodies to convince audiences of their scope and potential veracity or to enthrall with the stuff of nightmares.

Of course, documentary style and purpose varies. As film critic Eric Hynes (2010) reminds us, documentaries can be as entertaining and cinematic as narrative films and formally more daring: "The truth is that docs can and should be as varied and unruly as the world they capture. No matter how well-reported or well-meaning, there's an element of dishonesty to wrapping up a complex story in a simple package."

Reviewer A. O. Scott (2010) puts it more bluntly, "Documentary is, at present, heterogeneous almost to the point of anarchy." Politically, disaster documentaries frequently assume an investigative posture to expose a political truth that has been suppressed by those with vested interests in keeping the public in the dark or one that has been hiding in plain sight and requires a documentary to bring its significance to light. As Scott puts it, "The dominant approach to documentary filmmaking nowadays is more argumentative, even prosecutorial" (ibid.). Documentaries like 2010's *Inside Job, Waiting for "Superman,"* and *Gasland* (and the 2013 sequel, *Gasland Part II*) address "complex, highly politicized and enormously consequential issues in a way that combines explanation with advocacy" (ibid.).

In contrast, twenty-first century Hollywood disaster films more pessimistically suggest that government is either responsible for impending catastrophe or incapable of stopping it, serving up singular heroes to fight on two fronts—a blockheaded bureaucracy and whatever external disaster government malfeasance, ineptitude, or venality enables and abets. And there is nothing for us to do but wait for "Superman" to arrive. Almost without exception, heroes succeed without political authority, even if acting in the interests of that authority. In *White House Down* (2013), the bodyguard hero saves the day despite having just been turned down for a job with the Secret Service to protect the president, while *World War Z*'s hero is a former United Nations agent reluctant to take back his old job just because a few million zombies are on the attack. Only when his family's safety is on the line does he relent.

Two Case Studies: *The Invisible War* and *Contagion*

Exemplifying several features standard to current documentary form, including a prosecutorial, advocacy-based approach, *The Invisible War* (2012) takes on an unusual form of disaster—the epidemic of sexual assaults within the American military, the corrupt and biased institutional response to these crimes, and the military chain of command that allows the epidemic to continue unabated and under-reported. Says director Kirby Dick, "There are hundreds of thousands of survivors in this country. They were completely voiceless. I've never come to a story where fewer people knew the story than this story" (Rosenberg 2013). His attempt to give them a voice and shine a righteous light in the shadowed corners of the military justice system includes scenes of rape victims speaking to the delegates of democratic power—Congressional representatives—the truth of their abuse first by their assailants, many of whom were in positions of authority over them, and then by the command structure that favors perpetrators over prey. The film reports that since World War II over 500,000 military men and women have experienced sexual assault. Out of more than 3,000 reported cases of sexual assault in one year, fewer than 200 ended with a perpetrator facing punishment (cf. Matthews 2013). Abandoned by the armed forces, the victims describe lives frayed almost beyond repair, while their rapists are reported to have escaped serious punishment, some even going on to thriving military careers. "They gave him the military professional of the year award during the rape investigation," explains one victim about her rapist. Accounts of psychological pain punctuate the film: "I have never seen trauma like I've seen from veterans who have suffered military sexual trauma," says one psychologist—lasting physical damage sustained during sexual assaults, and blatant injustice— "You'd see a guy get five years for drugs and two weeks for rape," says one investigator. In the words of Dave Robson (2012), this documentary was "made . . . to change the world" and the movie's website provides a number of ways for viewers to take action, including signing a petition and donating money to the Artemis Rising Recovery Fund founded by the filmmakers.

Nominated for a 2012 Academy Award for best documentary, *The Invisible War* has had one of the biggest political impacts of any recent documentary. It directly advocates that the prosecution of military rapes be taken out of the chain of command. Two days after seeing it, United States Defense Secretary Leon Panetta announced that prosecutorial decisions would no longer be left in the hands of victims' and perpetrators' immediate supervisors. A few months later, Republican Senator Susan Collins and Democratic Senator Claire McCaskill, in a determined show of bipartisanship, offered a bill to limit a military commander's ability to dismiss a court-martial conviction for sexual assault and to mandate dismissals or dishonorable discharges for anyone convicted of rape or sexual assault in the military. As Chris Willman (2013) puts it, "That's the documentary equivalent of a box office blockbuster." Although Congress' bipartisan response falls short of what the filmmakers and the film's subjects want most—to take prosecution of these crimes out of the military altogether—the film's producer calls Panetta's decision "a good first step. We're not thrilled with it, but it's not bad. At least it's something."

That "something" is more than most documentaries can claim, a concrete effect on politics and the military institution. As such, it fulfills its director's goal to effect political change: "Absolutely it's a political film, made to have an impact on policy" (Gavin 2013). Whether this policy change will translate to stopping the epidemic remains to be seen but unlike Michael Moore's *Bowling for Columbine* (2002), a study in the culture of gun violence, *Invisible War*'s goal is much more precise: Its spotlight shines not on the military ethos underlying criminal sexual behavior or the epidemic's relationship to continued integration of women into combat positions but turns solely on exposing the fact of the epidemic and the insufficient, indeed immoral, remedy available to sufferers. *The Invisible War* counts a male victim among its featured subjects and makes a point to include men in its statistics and general discourse. The film's mission is not to diagnose the military but to point out the problem and force changes to a corrupted, failing system.

The Invisible War's epidemic is social, criminal, yet also an integral part of the national defense and stands in contrast to the epidemic of infectious disease in the fictional disaster film, *Contagion* (2011). Both concern the widespread occurrence of the standard definition of disaster as a "particular undesirable phenomenon." Yet on the face of it, *The Invisible War* would not seem like a disaster genre documentary especially in comparison to works like *When the Levees Broke: A Requiem in Four Acts* (2006) and various others about Hurricane Katrina and its aftermath. Both use the trope of infection and the invisible means by which it spreads to get at the social dimension of experiencing and responding to disaster. And both position government—as it exists in practice and as idealized in theory—at the core of any human answer to the hazards that spread destruction if untreated.

Directed by Steven Soderbergh, famous for *Traffic* (2000) and *Side Effects* (2012), *Contagion* typifies the disaster fiction film and its apocalyptic subgenre by engaging viewers as armchair political philosophers—how are scarce resources best allocated among people battling with each other and against extraordinary conditions to survive? Is martial law inevitable? Is life worth living if individual freedom is so restricted and a single touch from another person can mean painful death? Once the virus has reached the United States, Lawrence Fishburne's character, Dr. Ellis Cheever of the Centers for Disease Control (CDC), gives his wife special treatment by letting her know before everyone else that Chicago is about to be quarantined so that she can flee before it takes effect. Suspecting that Cheever is privileging his loved ones over ordinary citizens, a maintenance worker chides him, "I got people, too, Dr. Cheever. We all do." Already uneasy over the ethics of his actions, this exchange disturbs Cheever and with hope finally in sight determines the generous decision that he makes at the end of the film. When he insists on inoculating his maintenance worker and son before himself, this act of selflessness signals the film's dénouement as much as the discovery of the treatment itself. And when the disease is running its merciless course, mutating like a 1950s science fiction monster to adapt to any potential treatment, a few people like Matt Damon's character, Mitch Emhoff, show signs of immunity even as his wife, also played by a name-above-the-title star, dies near the film's start, the epidemic's first casualty. Barricaded in his home with his children and a rifle, Emhoff turns from doting father to self-appointed sheriff, policing his children to keep them inside and warding off anyone who might infect his safe haven, including a teenage boy in a budding romance with his daughter. Emhoff wears his newfound militarism clumsily but with an emotional certitude suggesting that he can imagine no other option. His attitude echoes in scenes throughout the film of countless

Army troops enforcing civilian compliance with quarantines and other emergency laws.

Like *Traffic*'s take on the drug war, multiple yet sharply focused slices of life in *Contagion* illustrate a range of sociopolitical responses that such an outbreak might provoke in individuals, institutions, and groups of people acting as one. Each character responds differently to the ensuing panic and widespread civic breakdown. Jennifer Ehle's Dr. Ally Hextall tests the virus in animals but then, ever more desperate for a cure, turns to experimenting on her own body. Another scientist, played by Kate Winslet, exposes herself to the infection to assist others and track the disease's rapid spread. When she begins to exhibit symptoms, her first reaction is to warn anyone who has been in contact with her, including the service workers in her hotel, and then to report her condition to Dr. Cheever, who vainly promises her rescue. Not everyone is so professionally rigorous or altruistic.

In a murky subplot, Jude Law plays a fringe blogger hyping a conspiracy theory to exploit the epidemic for money. *Contagion*'s production values do not translate into the dazzling display that characterizes many disaster genre films—*Titanic* (1997), *The Day After Tomorrow* (2004), *The Core* (2003), and the more recent *Oblivion* and *Elysium*. Instead, scenes set in contemporary hospitals, suburban neighborhoods, and city streets, and references to actual government agencies like the Federal Emergency Management Agency (FEMA) and the World Health Organization create a realistic and therefore all the more frightening account of an airborne viral epidemic that kills with efficiency and indifference. The human body and its susceptibility to disease are vital to the film's premise, and the man who appends a self-designed prosthesis in the form of a plastic face shield to his head looks more foolishly selfish than heroic. Eventually he is revealed to be just that, a charlatan seeking only to profit from the pandemonium that the government has helped to cause in its ineffective response to the disease.

Soderbergh's pathogen from a future frighteningly like the present resists disaster movie protocols that demand a film to save its biggest names and prettiest faces for last-minute triumph. (A convention captured in the title of Nick Roddick's study "Only the Stars Survive: Disaster Movies in the Seventies" from his 1980 book *Aspects of Popular Entertainment in Theatre, Film and Television, 1800–1976.* With one marquee star already dead on a hospital stretcher, midway through *Contagion*, another's body tumbles unceremoniously into a mass grave. In a tactic reminiscent of the color-coding that distinguishes different storylines in *Traffic*, the post-disease world looks washed out and increasingly antiseptic as people face a bleak, trust-no-one future, especially in contrast to the deeply saturated colors dominated by glossy reds, oranges and yellows of pre-transmission scenes when life still had its pleasures like gambling and drinking in foreign casinos; when illicit physical contact was the old-fashioned, adulterous kind.

As with other films in the genre, effects of realism result in part from *Contagion*'s nod to remediation or the embedding of other media like television into the film's mise-en-scène and story structure. When real-life CNN chief medical correspondent Dr. Sanjay Gupta interviews Fishburne's Dr. Cheever in a news segment presented as part of the film's story, reality and fiction blur. Gupta appears in the film doing what he actually does on American television and so *Contagion* presents Gupta not as an actor playing a fictional part but as the expert many viewers already know him as. Reminding us of Gupta's real profession as a medical commentator creates a sense of transparent immediacy and the quality that most distinguishes television from film, "liveness," the perception that what unfolds before the viewer's gaze is happening now. It also lends the film a quality of truthfulness, the very value typically associated with documentary.

At the same time, however, remediation also creates the distancing effect of hypermediation, a term that refers to audience awareness of *Contagion* as merely another media presentation. Hypermediation occurs when the film showcases Gupta not as his private or "unproduced" self but as his televisual personality of TV doctor and when it features other screens within its frame (cf. Bolter and Grusin 1999). Audiences are reminded of their own activity— watching a movie—when they observe characters participate in the production of television news, in the case of doctors Gupta and Cheever, and in the consumption of it in the case of various characters shown throughout the film turning to various monitors for information. By using other media to provide narrative exposition—in this case, television news, and elsewhere in the film, laptop, and cell phone screens—*Contagion* reminds us that we are watching a movie. It reminds us that we are not experiencing reality but consuming media just as we do when we watch television and Gupta comes on to report on medical issues—or when we check our tablets for the latest weather report or use cellphones to take pictures to send to others. This immediacy-hypermediation paradox balances effects of "liveness," transparency, and realism with self-references that tug in the other direction, situating viewers in the mediated and therefore filtered, edited, fictional present. This paradoxical effect compounds the signifying role the unadorned or analogic body plays in depicting contemporary disaster. In a mediated world, the body as a site of epistemological work is easily overlooked, indeed actively suppressed in films that rely on Common Gateway Interface (CGI) depictions of the body as a site of embedding or bearing media: The body does not stand apart and "know"; the body becomes the site of transmission. Instead, the body in *Con-*

tagion carries and infects or contaminates others with a virus. Going "viral" in other films refers to bodies as part of the "going viral," as it refers specifically to media: the body transmits the way of knowing that media always/already signifies. . . . wtf?

The political process is inextricable from twenty-first century 24-hour news cycles, and the quality of disaster response depends on how effectively and quickly information spreads. This means that remediation, a hallmark of current moviemaking, is especially prevalent in political and disaster films. From the barebones newspaper staff at the center of *The Day the Earth Caught Fire* (1961) to the desperate lone shouting of the whistleblower detective in *Soylent Green* (1971), to the television newscasters first reporting on and then being trapped by zombies in *The Dawn of the Dead* (1978) and the conspiracy theory blog "Truth Serum" in *Contagion*, gathering and disseminating information inevitably repeats as a disaster film feature, a thread thickened in the contemporary disaster trend by nearly omnipresent screening technology and multiple news platforms. Social media, for example, compounds the intensity of the news culture, as one incident posted to *YouTube.com* or Tweeted by someone with many followers will spread and regenerate like spores in the wind across multiple platforms, user to user. These infectious and saturating qualities of social media and contemporary screening technology mean that their depiction in a contemporary disaster movie will not appear solely as part of the film's mise-en-scène but will feature as an important plot mechanism. The term "goes viral" further pins the remediation at the core of *Contagion*'s plot and mise-en-scène to its ostensible subject, a killer highly contagious and thus "viral" disease.

Not for nothing do we refer to Internet videos going "viral." Noting the increasingly affordable availability of high-end digital cameras and laptop technology, one critic even compares the rise in documentary filmmaking to "malaria," calling it a "virus that's spreading fast and far and wide" (O'Hagan 2010). The feeding frenzy that characterizes contemporary news generally and impending disaster reports specifically resembles a spreading contamination at the center of an epidemic, whether criminal or social or microbial, and unleashes instinctive human responses played on by *Contagion*'s promotional taglines: "Nothing spreads like fear," and "Don't talk to anyone. Don't touch anyone." Managing information about a particular epidemic— dismissing, quashing, or undermining it in the case of sexual assault reports in *The Invisible War* and, alternatively, using it in unorthodox ways for scientific testing or to free information from the global media conglomerates in the form of independent blogging in *Contagion*—is a topic both kinds of contemporary disaster films must address. Political control of facts lies at the heart of many disaster films.

The Invisible War provoked actual political change and went "viral" among military personnel. So did *Contagion*, which stopped Tea Party Republicans from gutting the CDC budget.

Changes in disaster films more often result culturally and incrementally, as political awareness and public opinion must absorb real-world disasters and their aftermaths and also catch up to disaster fiction films' imaginary circumstances and fictive predictions. *Contagion's* haunting images of empty airports, desolate streets overrun with garbage and outbursts of frantic mass looting reverberate from their appearance in other disaster epidemic films like *The Invasion* (2007) about a space shuttle exploding and releasing an alien virus that recodes human DNA. The 2009 world outbreak of the H_1N_1 virus clearly inspired *Contagion*'s fictional MEV-1 virus. And the more recent interspecies viral transmission reported in China eerily resembles the origin of transmission depicted in *Contagion*'s closing frames. As reported in spring 2013, "Chinese scientists say the virus has been transmitted to humans from chickens, though the World Health Organization says 40 percent of people infected with H_7N_9 had no contact with poultry . . . The U.S. Centers for Disease Control and Prevention has said the current strain of bird flu cannot start a pandemic but notes there is no guarantee it will not mutate and cause a serious pandemic" (Koh 2013).

Similar to their predecessors, current fictional disaster films often begin with historical precedent—atomic bombs, earthquakes, astronomical events, space travel, flu outbreak, and dwindling natural resources—and then ask, "What if?" Note the historical progression: What if atomic testing caused common ants to mutate into giant man-eating monsters, as presented in *Them* (1954)? What if detonated atomic bombs knocked the earth out of its orbit and sent it careening into the sun, as dramatized in *The Day the Earth Caught Fire* (1961)? What if the sight of a meteor shower was radiantly beautiful but also blinding and created an outbreak of flesh-eating plants as found in *The Day of the Triffids* (1962)? What if, for no discernable reason, common birds began to attack and kill people with uncommon viciousness, as in Alfred Hitchcock's *The Birds* (1963)? What if your emotionally unavailable boyfriend had really been replaced by an alien duplicate—*Invasion of the Body Snatchers* (1956, 1978)? What if a world dependent on fossil fuels ran out of gasoline—*Mad Max: The Road Warrior* (1981)? What if the 2003 Space Shuttle *Columbia*'s explosion spread an alien virus—*The Invasion* (2006)? What if declining birthrates turned into the sterility of the entire world—*Children of Men* (2006)? What if the H_1N_1 virus transmitted from animal to human and from human to human and instead of a debilitating flu caused quick but painful death (*Contagion*)? What if the wealth gap between the one percent and the rest of the United States turned into the wealthy living in a luxurious, trouble-free space station while everyone else was stuck on a crumbling earth (*Elysium*)? The invariably ugly answer paints a bleak picture of humans stripped bare of creature comforts and civilizing social cues, driven by fear and need.

The disaster film's crystal ball effect substitutes for the documentary's actual political influence. The strongest political message of such films? Government fails us or even authors our destruction and cannot or, when either the self-interest of bureaucrats or their soulless calculus of social costs and benefits trumps any other consideration, will not save us. Only brave individuals can perhaps save themselves; and, if the public is lucky, one of them, by bucking government safeguards that look more like senseless obstacles, will single-handedly find the cure and save the public despite its having foolishly trusted "the system." Hollywood genres writ large privilege individual effort over communal or government action (with the possible exception of war or sports team films that depend on scenes of group-orchestrated action to provide context for individual acts of courage or talent and the like). Disaster films emphasize that same ideology of individualism in genre conventions that include depictions of inept government response and such mass misbehavior as large-scale looting.

A contrary view might press the fact that the disaster film genre as realized in *Contagion*, while not validating any particular political response beyond martial law, at least partially endorses existing government institutions and safeguards, as well as the current conglomerate-controlled mass media that can seem if not in cahoots with government at least willing to toe its official line until something better comes along. *Contagion*'s disaster subsides only when a selfless, driven scientist working for the Centers for Disease Control discovers the vaccine. When he cannot get the film's fictive mainstream paper, *The Chronicle*, to publish his work, Jude Law's lone wolf reporter goes rogue with his "Truth Serum" blog, only to be revealed as a charlatan. Even so, *Contagion* subverts trust in a variety of governmental institutions by depicting them for much of the film as incompetent, self-centered, or worse, as other CDC and WHO staff, public health and safety officers, public employee unions and others fail to stop the spread of the killer virus and the social mayhem thereby unleashed. In the end, audiences learn to feel lucky and perhaps even trust that such a virtuous and nearly super-powered individual as Dr. Hextall exists to transcend our political and administrative systems.

Similar to all generic distinctions, the lines dividing disaster documentaries from their fictional counterparts can be elusive. As with 1952's *Invasion, U.S.A.*'s use of documentary footage from the London Blitz to depict a fictional vaguely Eastern Bloc nation invasion of the United States, such films as *Contagion, Children of Men,* and *The Road* (2009) feature settings and imagery that are not the computer-generated disasters of a *Pitch Black* (2000), *The Island* (2005), *I, Robot* (2009), *Oblivion* (2013), or *Elysium* (2013), but were derived from photojournalism and shot on-location in the very places where documentaries fix their critical eye. Their plots play out on all too vulnerable human beings, not technologically advanced hybrids. In fact, *World War Z* ironically renders the mortal body of non-zombies even frailer in order to repel zombie attacks. Only through self-inflicted weakness and disease do the survivors overcome the zombie apocalypse.

Contagion depicts stadiums converted to FEMA camps that are familiar from 2005's Hurricane Katrina. On the other end, Al Gore's Academy Award–winning documentary *An Inconvenient Truth* (2006) used computer-generated images of Manhattan under water and a polar bear struggling to stay alive atop ever-shrinking ice floes to dramatize with breathtaking effect an earth sure to be decimated by climate change unless humans reverse course. While no one would ever confuse the generic categories of the documentary *An Inconvenient Truth* and the feature film *The Day After Tomorrow* (2004), their overlapping imagery of cracking Arctic ice shelves and scientific diagrams suggests similarities between the nonfiction and fictional genres, as each borrows strategies from the other to maintain viewer interest—to induce suspension of disbelief in the case of fictive disaster films and to break through denial in the case of documentaries.

Concluding Thoughts

The Invisible War and *Contagion,* as representatives of their respective film genres and the political values associated with each, are unexpectedly alike in their departure from the gender politics of today's disaster films. The computer generated imaging technology that both allows and encourages the mise-en-scène typical of such members of the genre as *Dredd* (2012), *Oblivion* (2013), *Pacific Rim* (2013), and the *Transformers* franchise (including the redundantly named latest installment, *Transformers: Extinction,* 2014) remains largely absent from these two films. Instead, the prosecutorial style of *The Invisible War* and the politically philosophically engaged *Contagion* depend upon, even demand, a far more familiar conception of the physical body and of the characters those bodies represent. Matt Damon's Max undergoes technological enhancement and implantation to enable him to cross the definitive divide between rich and poor in *Elysium,* something he must do to counteract the impact of radiation poisoning on his working-class body. In *Contagion,* the same actor's upper-middle-class Mitch is inherently immune to the viral disease that kills his adulterous wife, an echo of the retributive nature of death in the 1970s disaster cycle. The most vividly presented deaths and scenes of scientific experimentation center on women's bodies. In this way *Contagion* is like *The Invisible War* and its victims of the war, who also are predominantly women and mainly suffer as a result of their physical availability and gender positioning. The psychological trauma of rape is certainly on display in the film, too, but the violence happens first to their bodies. In *Contagion* central women characters die horrible deaths or withstand experimentation like Dr. Hempstall, who penetrates her own body with the experimental serum, while the key male characters survive unscathed with fully intact bodies. With earnestness, *Contagion* teaches reliance on the body and what it stands for in its equation of gendered bodies with penetrability, vulnerability, and mortality.

What both films impress upon viewers is the hopelessness of relying on current government agencies and institutions. *The Invisible War* presses for and, in some respects, is on its way to achieving change, whereas *Contagion* blames political ineptitude and its self-serving agendas for failing the public.

On the other end of the digital filmmaking divide, we find that the blockbuster digital fantasies of *Oblivion*, *Pacific Rim*, and *Elysium* set the stage for the restoration of the sort of nostalgia-seeped, old-order institutions that implicitly failed the world as it was prior to the apocalyptic annihilation that these types of films take for granted at film's start. While hardly an endorsement for government institutions and the political system that viewers participate in outside the theater, they ironically prepare audiences for their seemingly inevitable demise and necessary rehabilitation. In either instance, the politics of disaster at the movies is a no-way-out pessimism with present and future political agency and government action each equally incapable to prevent imminent doom or to restore civilization when doom has struck.

7
The Blending of a Kaleidoscopic Culture: Films on Asian Americans
Andrew L. Aoki

The present chapter examines questions of inclusion and community in the United States, questions as old—or older—than the United States, and they have loomed large in American politics for just as long. Superficially, the issues may appear to be social rather than political, but, questions about difference—especially racial difference—have animated a good deal of American politics from the earliest years. My concern here is with the context for inclusion and community in American politics—focusing specifically on the context relevant to Asian Americans.[1]

Historically, these issues have often led to questions about assimilation and pluralism (e.g., Higham 1955, 1984; Barth 1969; Sollors 1986; Alba 1990; Waters 1990; Barkan 1995; Conzen et al. 1992; Gleason 1992; Nagel 1994). To what extent do immigrants maintain the cultural patterns that they bring to a new country? To what extent are they changed? Should maintenance of cultural patterns in the next generations be encouraged and celebrated, or should it be discouraged and feared? Are newcomers unwilling to change?

I look at how these questions have been addressed by Asian American filmmakers who have produced work about Asian Americans. Therefore, I do not look at films such as Clint Eastwood's *Gran Torino* (2008), since, while it meets the second criterion, it obviously fails the first. Nor do I look at films of Asian filmmakers who have made movies featuring Asians in America—such as works by Mira Nair as *Mississippi Masala* (1991) and *The Namesake* (2006). I also do not examine the work of Asian American filmmakers who have made films about Asians. For instance, although Ang Lee's *Crouching Tiger, Hidden Dragon* (2000) was tremendously influential, and his *Eat Drink Man Woman* (1994) is a thoughtful look at tensions between tradition and modernity, neither look at Asian Americans. Finally, I focus on fiction, not documentaries, thereby excluding some excellent work, such as those by Renee Tajima Peña. Her *Who Killed Vincent Chin?* (1987) or *My America . . . or Honk If You Love Buddha* (1997) are well worth viewing, but they seem in much less need of interpretation. I do not attempt an exhaustive review of Asian American film, but rather a selective examination of those that offer insightful visions of the American struggle with issues of inclusion and community.

Inclusion and Community in Asian American Films

Questions of inclusion and community are not unique to Asian American films. These issues are found in many books and movies about the immigrants in America—e.g., Richard Rodriguez's *Hunger of Memory* (2004), or Barry Levinson's semi-autobiographical movie *Avalon* (1990). This is a recurring story, the struggle to preserve traditions and community in the face of the continual erosion caused by exposure to a new society. For some groups, however, this struggle is complicated by the simultaneous challenge of winning acceptance in a society which seems determined to brand the group as alien and unassimilable. The first effort—to preserve the immigrant traditions—is ultimately a losing battle. The second challenge is, for some groups, an unfinished task, felt more acutely by the second and third generations, as their immigrant heritage fades to little more than a symbolic memory.

The old order changeth. Wayne Wang's *Chan Is Missing* (1982) is a low-budget film of epic vision. Even thirty years after its release, it continues to provide the dominant frame for an exploration of the questions of inclusion and community for Americans of Asian descent. Virtually all subsequent similar movies on Asian Americans build on the paths that Wang blazed in this groundbreaking work.

The title itself is a clever pun, spoofing Charlie Chan movies while seeking to erase their images. *Chan Is Missing* is a Chinese American detective story, but there is no Charlie Chan. Instead, we have Jo and Steve—authentic Chinese Americans, not the ersatz version found in Charlie Chan films—who are hunting for another Chan—Chan Hung, an immigrant who has struggled to acculturate. Jo and Steve had given Chan Hung the money for a cab license, but Chan has disappeared. They search Chinatown for signs of him, but, as with the reporters who tried to find the identity of Charles Foster Kane's "Rosebud," they find only strikingly different descriptions of the missing Chan.

Jo and Steve are both native-born Americans, but Jo is considerably older, and has deeper ties to immigrants, such as Chan Hung. Jo is perplexed at Chan's disappearance, but Steve is irritated. Jo seeks understanding, and attempts to "think Chinese," trying to see into the layers of Chan's mind, but

Steve thinks only as Americans do, and presses for more direct action—calling the police.

What they learn about Chan suggests a man deeply embedded in the world of his birth and never able to be comfortable in his immigrant home. Chan's estranged wife, also an immigrant, declares that he is "too Chinese," and complains that he did not even want to become a citizen. Chan's daughter is more sympathetic. But she, too, notes that her father struggled to adapt to America, unlike her mother. Old world problems also plague Chan, in the form of conflicts between supporters of mainland China and supporters of Taiwan, conflicts which have erupted into violence that may somehow involve him.

In a hilarious scene, Wang shows that language can create differences in many ways. Jo and Steve meet an Asian American sociologist, who explains that she is "doing a paper on cross-cultural misunderstanding." Rather than aim for the cheap laughs typically generated by having academics spew nonsense, we get an authentic discussion of intercultural communication problems, in language that one might hear at a scholarly conference—completely dumbfounding Jo and Steve. They react with confusion, irritation, and even pity for this communications expert who cannot speak a language they understand. This scene, like so many throughout the film, shows us that "Chinese Americans" are a diverse group of people, like any other subpopulation of that size.

In the end, the money is returned. Chan is only missing, not transformed. Chan Hung would never abscond with a friend's money, but he might find America so overwhelming that he fades from sight. His story reminds one of the haunting words of Tennyson's King Arthur: "The old order changeth, yielding place to new."

"Too late to go back." Steven Okazaki's *Living on Tokyo Time* (1987) offers a poignant portrait of the realization that we cannot return to an earlier time. In its opening scene, the film perfectly captures part of the worldview of older Japanese Americans, and seems to suggest a continuing gulf between them and the larger society. The movie opens with a white waitress—a *hakujin*—taking an order from what appears to be a *Nisei* (second generation) Japanese American couple in their late fifties or early sixties. As the waitress leaves, the man says to the woman, "Why do they have a *hakujin* waitress? . . . I wonder if the food's any good." In that brief scene, Okazaki perfectly depicts the sentiments of many *Issei* (first generation) and *Nisei*: Japanese cultural practices remain beyond the reach of those who are not *nihonjin* (of Japanese ancestry).

But a very different perspective enters the film when the central character appears—Ken, a *Sansei* (third generation) drifting through life with only the most tenuous connections to things Japanese. At a local cafe, the Japanese American proprietor suggests that Ken should like *manju* (an extremely sweet bean paste pastry); one bite quickly convinces Ken that *manju* requires a taste that he has no desire to acquire. Ken's images of Japan and Japanese seem only slightly less realistic than that of non-Japanese Americans, and his great musical passion is not for jazz—that American export which has won such a devoted following in Japan—but for heavy metal rock, the antithesis of Japanese artistic sensibilities.

When Ken's casual attitude toward life leads his Japanese American girlfriend (whom his mother felt was hardly Japanese) to leave him, a friend convinces Ken to enter into a marriage of convenience to Kyoko, a Japanese national who wants to stay in the country, but whose visa has expired. Just as he casually watched his old girlfriend leave, Ken casually decides that this marriage might be the key to his happiness.

But the marriage only highlights Ken's distance from Japan, and symbolizes the distance between Japanese Americans and Japanese. Ken knows he is not Japanese, but he does not know what it *is* to be Japanese. His ignorance of the gulf separating him from Kyoko allows him to imagine that their marriage of convenience can turn into an enduring relationship, not realizing that their enormous cultural differences will create an unbridgeable chasm between them.

Ken's sister has a better understanding of this distance. Without telling her of his marriage, Ken reflects on their parental preference that their intimate associates have strong roots in Japanese culture, and he asks his sister if she thinks he "should . . . marry a Japanese girl." His sister replies, "I think that this is not Japan, *bochan* [little boy]." That his sister is herself married to a *hakujin* serves to emphasize that fact.

Okazaki repeats his theme with perfectly formed slices of Japanese American life. A Japanese American co-worker tries to warn Kyoko of the folly of marrying Ken, but her efforts are frustrated by her reliance on a patois in which American terms are freely interjected when the speaker is at a loss for the Japanese translation—a type of Japanese widely used by the diminishing number of Japanese Americans who speak any Japanese at all. Kyoko's inability to comprehend the woman's warning serves not only as a touching reminder of Kyoko's failure to understand her differences with Ken, but also suggests that the gap is created by culture, not gender. Kyoko can understand Japanese American women no more than she can understand Japanese American men.

As the film progresses, however, Kyoko begins to observe her distance from Ken. When Ken tells her that he does not like Japanese food, a surprised Kyoko replies, "But you are Japanese," to which Ken responds, 'No I'm not. Not like you." Gradually, Kyoko comes to see just how different they are: Writing to her friend, she concludes "He [Ken] does not understand me, but it is not his fault." Kyoko lives on Tokyo time, a mode Ken does not even recognize.

Ultimately, Kyoko decides to return to Japan. To preserve her pride, she tells those in Japan that Ken has died, and that she is too overcome with grief to stay. Leaving Ken an apologetic note, she departs, only to return when she can experience America within a truly Japanese context—a package tour of Yosemite National Park.

Ken, stunned to find her gone, finds sympathy from his friend Lambert, whose own experience serves as a symbol for Ken's failed brief relationship. Lambert, a Chinese American who emigrated from Taiwan, notes that his hopes have also gone astray. Rather than finding fortune and fulfillment, Lambert has found a job that pays little better than minimum wage, and he has only frustration in his search for female companionship. Ken asks Lambert why he does not return, to which Lambert replies, "Too late to go back. When you stay too long, you have to stay. Too hard to go back now."

Lambert expresses what Ken failed to realize: Japanese Americans have also stayed too long. They are no longer Japanese in America, but Americans whose families happen to have originated in Japan. Ken's hope of finding happiness through Japan is doomed, because Japanese and Japanese Americans have become culturally distinct groups. For those who dream of a return to the culture of their ancestors, it is too late to go back.

Japanese Americans may be the most assimilated of Asian Americans. Extremely high rates of *Sansei* and *Yonsei* (third and fourth generation) intermarriage, combined with highly integrated housing patterns, raise the possibility that a distinctive Japanese American ethnic group will largely fade away in a few generations. It is worth noting that eighty years ago, concerned scholars worried about the "second-generation Japanese problem"—the challenge that *Nisei* would face when trying to enter a society often unwilling to accept them (Strong 1934).

We're all alone. Tony Chan's *Combination Platter* (1993) is a touching complement to Okazaki's exploration of third-generation Asian Americans and the gulf between them and their co-ethnics in Asia. Chan, however, explores this from the other side of the cultural divide, focusing on a Chinese immigrant, Robert, who works at the Chinese restaurant "The Szechuan Inn," and is trying to figure out how he can get a Green Card. His roommate, Andy (an Asian American who does not face this problem), urges him to look for a sham marriage, and he introduces Robert to Claire, a lonely white woman who does not know the reason behind Andy's matchmaking. What unfolds is a penetrating and sad depiction of cultural divides and language barriers.

As we watch life swirl in the restaurant, we see many different cultural gaps. Robert is very dubious that things can work between him and Claire, even for only a sham marriage. Over time, though, he comes to appreciate that Claire is a very nice person, and says to Andy, "If she weren't an American . . . "

For many of the Asian immigrants, including Robert and Andy, "American" is equated with "white." Earlier, Andy had tried to facilitate a sham marriage between Robert and another American woman (Michelle), but Michelle was of Asian ancestry, and Robert showed none of the reluctance that he had with Claire. The cultural divide is just as great, though. Michelle had backed out of the agreement, telling the two that Robert should get "a Chinese wife," to which Robert exclaims "*You* are Chinese," but Michelle sees the distinction. "I mean a real Chinese—you know, *Chinese* Chinese," she says, "someone who can speak his language."

This cinematic equation of "American" and "white" seems to reflect the perspective of actual immigrant families. Jennifer Lee and Frank Bean found that many immigrants and their children equated marrying a white partner with marrying an "American" (Lee and Bean 2010).

Others see the distinction between Asian and Asian American, however, and Asian Americans are well aware of it, sometimes painfully. Sam, one of the Chinese-speaking waiters, notes that the owner's niece Jennie is an "ABC" (American-born Chinese) who cannot understand the wait staff as they converse in Cantonese. Later, Jennie and the white busboy, Benny, talk about their discomfort when the other staff speaks Chinese. Jennie says her situation is worse than Benny's: "The Chinese treat me like an American, and then the Americans treat me like I'm Chinese." For many Asian Americans born in the United States, the homeland of their parents and grandparents is a foreign place, and American society is all they know. But, even those in the third or fourth generation find that many white Americans continue to see them as foreign.

We see this acted out by some of the white characters in the film, including an extraordinarily obnoxious customer who wants his money back after eating most of his food. The owner explains that he cannot give a refund when most of the food has been eaten, but the obnoxious customer continues to demand his money back, declaring "This is *America*. In *America*, we give refunds when the food sucks!" The obvious implication is that the owner and his American-born niece are not Americans, a message that Asian Americans have received for decades (e.g., U.S.-born Asian Americans being asked how they learned to speak English so well).

The film skillfully explores other cultural divides as well. One day, Robert arrives before the Szechuan Inn has unlocked its doors, so he strikes up a conversation with the Chinese immigrant dishwasher, who is also waiting for the doors to be unlocked. As their conversation progresses, they struggle to understand each other, because they speak different dialects. We see this same gulf in the kitchen, where the waiter Sam cannot understand the Mandarin-speaking chefs, as Sam speaks Cantonese. One chef tells of tensions over his son's fiancée, because the young woman speaks only Cantonese, not Mandarin.

Yet another difference is played out in the repeated visits that James and Noriko make to Szechuan Inn. James is white, and Noriko is Asian American, likely U.S.-born. She and James argue over things, and, when Robert first observes them, he seems to see it as a cautionary tale of the gulf between him and Claire. We see, however, that the dispute is a different type of communication tension—one found every day in America: "James, you just don't *listen* to me," Noriko complains. Later, Robert seems to realize also that Noriko is an Asian *American*. As Robert and another waiter, Stanley, observe the couple, Stanley asks Robert why "such a nice Asian girl" would go out "with an American." Stanley has been in the United States for five years, but he too equates "American" and "white." Robert is beginning to see things differently, though. Stanley, looking at Noriko, asks Robert, "You think she's Korean, Japanese, or what . . . ?" Robert replies, deadpan, "What?" Robert may still not be sure what an Asian American is, but he is starting to see that it is part of this large, complicated thing called *America*.

In the end, the communication differences create a painful rupture. Robert feels increasingly bad about misleading Claire. He tries to explain, but his halting command of English does not allow him to describe the complicated chain of events and his growing remorse. Claire misunderstands him and thinks that he is still trying to get her to enter into a sham marriage, but Robert wants only to apologize for the deception. Sadly, he does not have the English skills to explain, and Claire angrily walks away. The cultural gap is too great, even for two decent people to understand each other's good intentions.

The film closes by returning to James and Noriko. Although they had tense moments, the two of them work from shared American cultural understandings, and they become engaged. The great wall between American and Chinese (explored by Peter Wang—see below) was too much for Robert and

Claire, but James and Noriko share the same cultural context—even if many around them fail to understand that.

Another brick in the Great Wall. Before *Combination Platter* (1993), Peter Wang's *A Great Wall* (1986)[2] examined similar cultural differences, but centered the story around Chinese Americans. Wang takes America to China, giving an Asian perspective of the great barrier separating Chinese from Chinese Americans.

When Leo Fang learns that an expected promotion has gone to someone else, he decides to take his family on an often-postponed trip to China to visit family whom he has not seen in the four decades since he emigrated to the United States. One of Leo's first discoveries upon their arrival in China is that the walls of Beijing—which Leo remembered from childhood—have been torn down. In a metaphor for the post-Cultural Revolution China, these walls—which originally kept outsiders out and insiders in—have been taken down to make room for modernization.

But when the Fangs arrive at Leo's sister's house in Beijing, cultural barriers are more durable than physical ones. Three neighbors are mystified by these Chinese Americans, aliens so foreign that they cannot even be identified:

> Who are these strange people? Japanese?
> No, Filipinos, maybe.
> I don't think so.

Even Leo's brother-in-law is puzzled by this strange American amalgamation: "Two of your brother's family can't speak Chinese," he muses to his wife, "but they all can use chopsticks."

Like other American filmmakers of Chinese or Japanese ancestry, Peter Wang portrays Asian Americans who have undergone substantial assimilation and have become bicultural—both Chinese and American. When an American friend assumes—incorrectly—that Leo's wife speaks Chinese, his wife responds, "Can't you tell? I'm an American!" Unlike some immigrants, Mrs. Fang understands the substantial distance between herself Chinese Americans and Chinese.

A lengthier and more striking example of this bicultural amalgamation unfolds in a conversation between Leo and Paul (Leo's son), concerning Paul's white girlfriend, Linda. Leo, mentioning that he thought Paul had stopped seeing Linda, then asks "Whatever happened to that nice Chinese girl, Margaret Wei?" "She's goin' out with some white guy," Paul retorts. Pursuing the advantage, Paul challenges Leo: "Why don't you like Linda as my friend? You know, the only reason you don't like her is because she's not Chinese."

Paul has challenged Leo with an American offense—judging by group identity, rather than individual qualities. Leo's response is instructive: "Come on," he protests. There is no impassioned defense of maintaining cultural purity in the family, only embarrassed reaction. Whatever Leo may think (and it seems that he *would* prefer that Paul marry a Chinese American woman), he will not admit to violating the norm of treating people as freely choosing individuals, independent of their group affiliations. Indeed, only a short time ago, after being denied a promotion, he had hurled the same charge at his boss—"You don't believe that a Chinaman is good enough to be the director!"

The very context of the conversation establishes that Leo and Paul are tied together with American bonds. Although the walls of the Fang home are decorated with Chinese art, the attention of father and son is focused on the television—watching pro football. As they share a beer and root for the same team, we see that any cultural gap between Paul and Leo is minuscule compared to the gulf that they will find between themselves and their overseas relatives.

When the Fangs return to the United States, they come back only marginally changed. Paul notes the irony of being seen as the outsider in both places—"In America people think I'm too Chinese and in China they think I'm too American"—somewhat similar to the predicament of Jennie in *Combination Platter*. But it is clear: The Fangs may have somewhat more affinity for China than Americans not of Chinese descent, but their trip has reinforced, not reduced, the differences. We can see more than ever that the Fangs stand on the western side of the wall that separates Americans from Chinese.

Not that the Fangs have been incorporated into white society, losing any of their own distinct identity. There is no "identificational assimilation," a stage, marked by a "development of peoplehood based exclusively on [the] host society" (Gordon 1964). Part of the Fangs's identity is still based on their Chinese ancestry, and that identity is reinforced by the perceptions of the whites around them.

But structural assimilation—large-scale entrance into cliques, clubs, and institutions of the host society, on the primary group level (ibid.)—seems to have arrived at the Fang household or, at least, is knocking on the door. Although Leo had dumped coffee on his boss and quit his job before the Fangs left for China, the supervisor comes calling after they return, presumably to make amends and to try to lure Leo back to a lucrative position. And, given

Paul's continuing relationship with Linda (his white girlfriend), it would seem that marital assimilation might be soon to come. For the Fangs, the larger American community seems the only option, as the gulf between them and their ancestral heritage grows larger with each generation.

Mother and child reunion. Amy Tan's *The Joy Luck Club* (1983)[3] also looks at the cultural gulf between Asians and America, but offers a glimmer of hope for those fearing cultural estrangement. Weaving together the stories of four mothers and daughters, they are connected in a tapestry that spans two continents and five decades. Each daughter struggles against barriers similar to those that their mothers overcame in their youth—barriers which now push mother and daughter apart. As each story draws to a close, the common threads in their lives once again pull them together, and the viewer understands that America has transformed but not obliterated their Chinese inheritance.

An-mei Hsu sees her daughter Rose gradually lose her sense of self in her marriage. She does so decades after An-mei's own mother made the supreme sacrifice so that An-mei's life would not be lost to the whims of others: An-mei's mother had been disgraced when her family refused to believe that she (An-mei's mother) had been raped by the wealthy Wu Tsing. To survive, she had lived as Wu Tsing's concubine, given the lowly status of fourth wife; and, when she had given birth to Wu Tsing's only son, she had been forced to surrender the boy to Wu Tsing's second wife. Using the only resort she had to prevent her daughter from inheriting her disgrace, An-mei's mother had committed suicide, thereby freeing her spirit and allowing it to pass to An-mei, who, armed with the power of her mother's ghost, then forced Wu Tsing to give An-mei and her brother the high status of children of a first wife.

Now, as Rose moves aimlessly toward a divorce, An-mei tells her story to Rose in order to pass on the spirit of An-mei's dead mother. Revived by this ancestral inheritance, Rose rallies to confront her soon-to-be ex-husband and is once again able to consider and express her own wishes. She demands that she be allowed to keep the house, drawing on the power of a Chinese ghost to fortify her in that increasingly common American contest—a marital property dispute.

For Waverly Jong, however, the challenge is to wrest control *from* her mother, Lindo. Waverly, a child chess prodigy, came to resent how her mother seemed to present her like a trophy on display. When she rebelled, she was surprised that her mother responded not with fury but ostracism. But although that penalty had stunned Waverly as a child, such a socially based sanction could never be as powerful in America as it was in China.

In Asia, Lindo's future husband had been selected when she was a small child. Her own mother could only regretfully prepare Lindo for a marriage and life that would be controlled by others. After her marriage, Lindo's in-laws had complete control over her life, and she was able to gain her freedom only through an elaborate ruse.

In contrast, Waverly is able to chart her own path, although she feels that her mother has an inescapable power over her. Waverly can and does select her own mate, and her choice of a white man underscores how much her mother's culture has lost its hold in America.

The search to find the ties that bind is most movingly portrayed in the tale that provides the bookends for the other stories—the saga of Jing-mei ("June"), her mother Suyuan, and the babies that Suyuan had "lost" while fleeing wartime China. After Suyuan's death, June learns from her mother's closest friends (An-mei, Lindo, and the third mother, Ying-ying) that the long-lost daughters have been found.

Suyuan had been part of a wave of desperate refugees fleeing the Japanese invasion during World War II. Near death from dysentery but unable to convince anyone to help her and her children, Suyuan had guessed that the sight of healthy abandoned babies would be too compelling to pass by, so she had made the wrenching choice to leave them, while she staggered off to die alone. What her mother had never imagined was that she would be saved, condemning her to a lifetime of pondering the fate of her daughters.

June is charged with traveling to China and telling them about the mother they had long wanted to see, but June worries that she will not know what to say. Her mother's friends are dismayed to hear this, and June realizes that she has given voice to their greatest fears—that their own daughters, in whom they have placed so many hopes, might have taken very little of what they have tried to give.

The opening monologue expresses that fear poignantly:

The old woman remembered a swan she had bought many years ago in Shanghai for a foolish sum. This bird, boasted the market vendor, was once a duck that stretched its neck in hopes of becoming a goose, and now look!—it is too beautiful to eat. Then the woman and the swan sailed across an ocean . . . stretching their necks toward America. On her journey she cooed . . . "In America I will have a daughter just like me. But over there nobody will say her worth is measured by the loudness of her husband's belch. Over there, nobody will look down on her, because I will make her speak only perfect American English. . . . She will know my meaning, because I will give her this swan—a creature that became more than what was hoped for."

But when she arrives in the new country, the immigration officials pulls the swan away from her, leaving the woman with only one swan feather for a memory.

For a long time now the woman had wanted to give her daughter the single swan feather and tell her, "This feather may look worthless, but it comes from afar and carries with it all my good intentions."

June's tearful unification with her half-sisters symbolizes all the stories. In America, too, mother and daughter have been lost to each other, and the older generation ponders how such a sad result could come from such good intentions. In the end, though, the mothers find that America has not destroyed their hopes but transformed them. Although they have grown into a world culturally distant from the one of their parents' youth, the daughters also come to cherish what the mothers have brought from China: In America, mother and child can be reunited around an old culture in a new world.

A little help from my friends. While Chinese and Japanese Americans often explore the complexities of life in white America, other Asian American filmmakers address experiences within an ethnic community. Chris Chan Lee's *Yellow* (1997) does this through the eyes of Korean American youth. The key plot device makes no sense, but there are a host of interesting characters and some hilarious scenes as Lee explores how youth navigate between the life they have made and the ones their parents have tried to create for them.

Sin Lee's family owns a small grocery store. Sin is ordered to close it on his own when his parents make their weekly Friday night trip to his grandmother. Sin, however, has planned to go with his friends to a graduation party. As he angrily cleans up, three African American youth enter, and Sin yells at them that he is closing. They look at Sin, smile at each other, and the camera fades to black.

The next scene shows us Sin visiting his girlfriend, Teri. Without a word, he reaches out to her for comfort. We then jump to a gathering of all the friends, and they ask Sin how much the robbers got. Sin tells them $1,500, and says he will be working at the store forever to pay for the loss. They ask if he called the police, but agree it would do no good ("Might as well call Domino's," Gracie says drolly, "at least they'll come out"). Sin's friend Alex declares that they will not let that happen, and demands that everyone pitch in whatever they have to cover the $1,500. Interspersed with their ill-fated quest for cash is a series of scenes of teen life, cruising the streets, stopping at parties, dealing with their parents and others of the older generation.

One blurb advertised the film as a "*Korean American Graffiti*," but the comparison is flawed. The joyful and sometimes hilarious depiction of teenage life does indeed merit some comparison to George Lucas's pre-*Star Wars* masterpiece, but there's little distinctly Korean about *Yellow* other than the fact that the central characters all happen to be of Korean ancestry. Director Lee seems to be showing us what such scholars as Mia Tuan or Nazli Kibria have found when talking to second- and third-generation Asian Americans: From their own perspective, their lives have much in common with many other second- and third-generation Americans of any ancestry (Tuan 1998; Kibria 2002).

Korean American youth sometimes have clashes with their parents—especially Sin, whose father is almost a caricature, but so have millions of other youth. Like other children and grandchildren of immigrants, these kids are used to interacting with foreign-born adults, but their cultural preferences are drifting ever-farther away. When Sin's mother comes looking for him, she finds only some of his friends, and takes them to the apartment of a Korean American acquaintance, who offers them ethnic food which makes them cringe. With just a few changes, this could be the Norwegian *lutefisk* dinners that Garrison Keillor gently parodies.

In the grand tradition of *Chan Is Missing*, *Yellow* leaves us with an open-ended conclusion. We learn that Sin has in fact taken the money himself, and the movie closes as he heads to confess to his parents and to an uncertain fate. What seems somewhat clearer is that this slice of Korean American life looks very much like slices of life in many other parts of America.

There's no place like home. In Gene Cajayo's *The Debut* (2000), we get another look at ethnic teen life, but this film shows us much more interaction between the Asian American and white worlds. However, central character Ben Mercado is trying not so much to manage these two cultural worlds as to segregate them. In the opening scene, we see that Ben moves easily and happily outside the Filipino American community that defines his family. But when his non-Asian friends Rick and Doug need to stop at his house to use the bathroom, he quickly hustles them out the door before his mother can get them food to eat, even racing to the kitchen to try to air it out, because, he says, "It stinks in here."

In clumsy fashion, this scene sets up a morality play not unlike *The Wizard of Oz*. By the end, Ben will learn that no matter how far away he wanders, if he ever wants to find his true heart's desire, he need look no farther than his own figurative backyard.

The entire Mercado family, as well as countless friends and relations, are cheering Ben on a path which runs through the University of California at

Los Angeles and then, apparently, on to med school. But Ben wants to study drawing at CalArts, which his father ridicules as "drawing cartoons."

The movie gets its name from the eighteenth birthday party to be held for Ben's sister Rose. Roland's postal worker pay has not given him the means to pay for a full-blown debutante party, but this will serve as her debut into Filipino American society. As we see, though, it will be a transition for Ben as well.

At the party, we see how culturally estranged Ben has become. While his sister has worked to develop a rudimentary knowledge of Tagalog, Ben knows not a word, and does not even know how to give a proper Filipino blessing to his grandfather, who has come to America for the event.

We also begin to see the complex way that race plays out in this community. A family friend, Alice, arrives with her non-Filipino husband, drawing dubious looks from two Filipina American women, who declare "She thinks she's so great. Just because she hooked a white guy." Later, Ben wants to leave the party, and is confronted by his sister Rose, who tells him

> You actually think you're better than all of us, huh? Just 'cause you hang out with white boys and want to study art in college, you think you're the shit. . . . Wake up little brother. 'Cause, you know what, you're just as brown as the rest of us.

Ben's friends Doug and Rick come to take Ben to another party, but they want to stay awhile when they see Rose begin a special dance for the guests. Ben reluctantly agrees. But, after a while, he too is impressed by the skill and artistry of the dancers, and he begins to gain some appreciation for Filipino culture.

Eventually Ben, Rick, and Doug make their way to the other party, a virtually all-white affair. The three find themselves playing "Never Have I Ever," a drinking game in which participants admit intimate facts about themselves by taking a drink when a statement doesn't apply ("I never masturbate"). One girl, Susie, has been goading them on, and Rick counters with one targeted at Susie ("I never swallow"), which prompts the three of them to make several jokes at her expense.

Susie gets mad, and says to Ben, "All right, then, I've got one for you: I never . . . ate a dog!" Ben's smile disappears and his expression drops, while Doug and Rick look shocked, and Susie's friend is visibly uncomfortable. Susie feigns regret: "Oh, I'm sorry," then continues, "I never . . . ate a cat!" and breaks out laughing. When Rick tells her "that's not cool," Susie retorts "All those Orientals do it." Everyone other than Susie wants to change the subject, but then Ben accidentally spills a drink on Susie, who explodes:

"Look at me! I'm soaked, you fucking Chink!" Ben is stunned, and can only mutter "I'm not Chinese," before fleeing the party.

Ben, Doug, and Rick head back to Rose's party, where things go considerably better for a while. There's a dance battle pitting boys against girls, with a little breakdancing, suggesting a younger generation comfortably acculturating without completely losing grasp of the traditions of their immigrant parents. Ben is surprised to see his dad singing, learns about his father's singing career in the Philippines, and begins to realize this his own dreams of success as an artist were preceded by his father's hopes of a music career.

Ben hits it off with a new girl, Annabelle. But, as they talk, Ben is confronted by Gusto, Annabelle's former boyfriend. Gusto, a gangbanger wannabe, taunts Ben, calling him a "sellout" and a "white boy," noting that Ben only hangs out with white friends. After Gusto shoves him and calls him a "fucking coconut,"[4] Ben hits him and a fight ensues. Later, though, Ben says to Annabelle that maybe he *is* a coconut, a sellout. Annabelle assures him that Gusto is hardly a model of ethnic pride, having once tried to braid his hair into cornrows.

Through these scenes, we see Filipino American youth struggling to navigate multiple worlds. Gusto tries to embrace black gang culture but still yearns for the approval of his mother, and, by extension, the heritage she represents. Ben has moved easily in the subculture of white youth, but he has had a rude awakening, learning that some whites view him as a racial alien. His close friends, Doug and Rick, accept him and are impressed by Filipino culture, but the night's tumultuous events seem to imply that Ben will not find happiness by drifting too far away from his family and his heritage.

All ends well the next morning. Ben admits to his dad that he has taken out all his savings, sold his comic book collection, and used the money to pay his first semester's tuition at CalArts. He shows his dad his portfolio of drawings, which were the basis for his admission. Roland looks at the artwork for a long time, stunned by his son's talent, then quietly says to Ben, "I'll talk to your mother about this Cal-Arts thing," implying his acceptance.

We are left with a reconciliation not unlike that in *The Joy Luck Club*, although this time it is father and son who have created common ground out of the old and the new. A new life does not require rejection of the old, and may even have greater potential when built on the foundation of the immigrant heritage.

A place for us. Asian America hits the fast lane in Justin Lin's *Better Luck Tomorrow* (2003), ending up not sure where it's going. This hyperkinetic story is a bit like Asian America's *Godfather* (1972) or *Once Upon a Time in America* (1984), with a group of (mostly) good kids descending into crime and violence. Like the Italian or Jewish characters in those epic films, the Asian American youth here are probably only a generation away from their immigrant roots, and they too are uncertain of how much acceptance they can find in America. Unlike the Italian or Jewish youth of those other films, however, the life of crime itself brings social acceptance, rather than being just a way-station on the path to inclusion.

In some ways, the film is a clear departure from the landmark Asian American movies of the late twentieth century. One difference is the way the characters largely blend into a pan-ethnic—a pan-Asian—identity. While there are some references to possible Chinese ancestry, there is no mention of ethnic difference. Three of the central characters may be of Chinese ancestry, but at least two other seem to be of Filipino descent. Whatever the ethnic differences, they seem insignificant here.

Another difference is the type of challenge thrown at the "model minority" image of Asian Americans. At first, it seems as if all are stereotypical "model minorities." The central character, Ben Manibag, is the epitome of over-achievement: A repeated employee-of-the-month at his fast food job, he strives to improve his already-high SAT results, seeking a perfect verbal score by memorizing a new word each day. His friend Virgil Hu is Ben's academic equal, and the two of them seem to spend every spare minute on community service and extracurricular activities. They, in turn, look up to Daric Loo, "an academic All-American," who is editor of the school newspaper and seemingly leads every school club of any consequence.

The movie seeks to expose and subvert these images, though. Daric sports a letter jacket, but Ben matter-of-factly notes "don't let that fool you— it's for tennis"—not a sport that will command respect in their school's social hierarchy. Indeed, at a party, a white athlete treats them all dismissively, yelling "The Bible study's next door!" and mocks Daric's letter. We repeatedly see how the extraordinary achievements of Daric, Ben, and Virgil fail to win them social acceptance. Even when their life of crime has brought them riches, a prostitute they hired cannot comprehend them in anything other than a stereotypically Asian American frame. After a party featuring liquor, drugs, and sex, she asks, "So what are you guys, anyway?" to which Virgil replies, "We're a club." "Like a math club?" she responds.

We see that Ben and his three friends were never a model. "Our straight A's were our alibis, our passports to freedom," says Ben, as we see them covering a house with toilet paper. Over time, they move easily into more serious crime, such as theft and drug dealing.

Notably, there is Han, Virgil's cousin, who seems the wild one. Unlike Virgil or Ben, Han seems to find sex easily, fences stolen goods, and gets his booze by bribing liquor store clerks. Han seems to be the anti-model minority, but, when the group begins to fall deeper into violence and crime, Han seems most troubled by what they are doing.

The "model minority" is empty, Lin is suggesting. All their academic accomplishments win them no respect from their white peers, and the primary direct benefit seems to be their ability to sell "cheat sheets" to less talented classmates. Ben, Virgil, and Daric often cynically note that the reason for their community service and extracurricular activity is to gain yet another line on their college applications. At no time do we see them gain any intrinsic benefit from their academic achievements or volunteer work.

But, as the group's criminal activity gains notoriety for their exploits, they gain popularity and esteem. They have gained acceptance, it would seem, by moving ever farther away from the stereotypical image of Asian American students.

The film does not suggest an embrace of the thug life, however. The final episode in the downward spiral of the four is the murder of Steve Choe, who had sought their help in robbing his own house. Steve's life seems to exemplify the pinnacle of Asian American achievement. He attends a private school, is assured of admission to an Ivy League school, wants for nothing—and yet despises his life. His rejection of his parents' achievements does not sit well with Ben's friends, however, and they decide to doublecross Steve and teach *him* a lesson. Things go terribly wrong, though, and they end up murdering Steve and burying his body. For Daric, the ends seem to justify any means, so when Steve's death seems the best way to extricate them from a scam gone wrong, Daric does not hesitate to kill him. But Ben, Virgil, and Han are shocked and distraught.

The Asian American youth of *Better Luck Tomorrow* are not caught between two cultures so much as they are pursued by both. They have continued their lives of intense work and high achievement even as their criminal activity and wild night life grew, suggesting that pursuit of academic excellence is something which they cannot easily abandon. Their lifestyle, presumably reflective of the lives of their parents, brings them no respect from most of their non-Asian peers, however. On the other hand, the deviant lifestyle may win them acceptance in the larger youth society, but they come to realize that it is a dead end. *A Great Wall* had suggested hopefully that Asian American youth could exist in two worlds, living biculturally, but *Better Luck Tomorrow* portrays a choice between two nightmares.

The movie closes as Ben finally wins over Stephanie, the girl of his dreams. Stephanie, an adoptee from China, is another high-achiever, but has not followed the path of Ben and his friends, and she is unaware of what has happened to Steve. As the movie closes, she and Ben drive off, but we do not know where they are headed, as we hear Ben's voice tell us "For the first time in my life, I don't know what my future will hold. . . . All I know is that there's no turning back."

Like Ken and Lambert in *Living on Tokyo Time*, Ben must continue searching to find where he belongs in America. A life of high achievement has not gained him acceptance, and a wild life of crime is not viable. He and Stephanie drive away with high hopes, but uncertain whether they can escape the ghosts of the past.

Living in a Kaleidoscopic Culture

The collective vision of the films described above depict what Lawrence Fuchs (1990) has called a kaleidoscopic culture. Americans of Asian ancestry have not melted into some indistinguishable mass, nor have they preserved ancestral traditions as if they are living in some dusty museum display. Within the same ethnic group, there is both continuity and change, but the change sometimes threatens to overwhelm the continuity. *The Joy Luck Club* gives the most touching depiction of this, when the immigrant mothers fear that little of them has survived in their American-born daughters, but the theme of generational tension over cultural difference runs through many of these films.

Observers have long warned that America is being overrun by immigrants who are changing the country for the worse. Those prophecies of doom (e.g., Nelson 1994; Brimelow 1995), dating to the early years of the republic, are as persistent as they are unfounded.

The films reviewed here offer a very different view. The worlds depicted do indeed teem with immigrants, but immigrants adapting to as well as shaping the society around them. In *Chan Is Missing*, Jo and Steve are not confined to an isolated ethnic enclave. Rather, they can move within both the immigrant and the larger society, and the few immigrants who cannot do so are fading from the scene. In *A Great Wall,* the Fang family seems literally removed from any ethnic enclave; and, when we look past the couch (often occupied by Peter Fang and his white girlfriend), we see an expansive view suggesting that the Fang house is perched in what realtors call a highly desirable location. The Korean American teenage world depicted in *Yellow* is little different from the world of other American teenagers in the late twentieth and early twenty-first century.

We see more immigrant stories—not surprising, since over half of Asians in America are immigrants[5]—but the stories seem old and familiar, only somewhat altered versions of the challenges that faced immigrants of previous generations. Parents struggle to understand children, and the younger generation pushes back against what they see as the restrictive or old-fashioned ways of the immigrant generation. As with waves of youth before them, though, the younger Asian American generation typically ends up building bridges between the world of their parents and their own, although not without tension and anger, as many of these movies suggest.

Data on immigrant incorporation suggest that the silver screen is offering a realistic appraisal. For example, immigrants today seem to be learning English even faster than earlier newcomers, and immigrant interest in learning English seems very high (Martin and Midgley 1994:37–39). Second-generation youth often manage to draw on the strengths of the immigrant culture that their parents brought with them as well as on the American cultural traits that can help them to overcome the constraints of ancestral traditions (Kasinitz et al. 2008).

The challenge is not immigrant adaptation but immigrant acceptance—i.e., Asian immigrants and their children have acculturated to American society, but they often still find themselves viewed as alien. In *Better Luck Tomorrow*, we see extremely high-achieving Asian Americans still not able to win acceptance from the dominant cliques in their high school—at least until they descend into an ever-widening life of crime.

What is striking is how many of the movies end in uncertainty. In *Chan Is Missing*, Jo observes that he has trouble seeing Chan Hung in the one picture which he has of him, and the film closes with images of San Francisco bay, both in constant motion and never changing. Both *Better Luck Tomorrow* and *Yellow* end with the central character reflecting on his uncertain future. And in *Combination Platter*, we are left uncertain whether Robert will figure out a way to get a Green Card before he is swept up in the immigration raids that are targeting the area restaurants. For a century and a half, Asians have been in America, seeking to make their way just as countless others have done, but for just as long they have faced an uncertain acceptance.

At the same time, each film suggests hope in the communities that have emerged, each thriving in its own way. As Lambert tells Ken in *Living on Tokyo Time*, it is too late to go back. So Ken presses forward, buoyed by the support of his friends—Chinese Americans, Japanese Americans, European Americans—his community of choice, in a kaleidoscopic culture.

Notes

1. Japanese Americans in Hawai'i represent a sufficiently different case as to fall outside the scope of this analysis. Far from the United States mainland, Japanese there were never threatened by pressures to assimilate to American culture, although they faced other pressures from Americans of European ancestry. It is important to note also that my concern here is with Americans of Chinese, Filipino, Japanese and Korean descent, not with Chinese, Filipinos, Japanese and Koreans.

2. This film was subsequently re-released in 1986 with the less elegant title, *The Great Wall Is a Great Wall*, an unintentional example of forcing mainstream American practices (in this case, removing any trace of subtlety and replacing it with a painfully self-evident title that even the most obtuse could understand) onto an effort to blend Asian and American elements.

3. The film *The Joy Luck Club* states that it is "based upon a novel by Amy Tan." Oliver Stone and Janet Yang were the executive producers, Wayne Wang the director. Amy Tan and Ronald Bass co-wrote the screenplay, and Wang, Tan, Bass, and Patrick Markey are given credit as producers. This is not to suggest, however, that the film is as much the product of Tan as was the book. Nevertheless, the film seems to be an accurate representation of Amy Tan's book, and so I refer to the film as the work of Amy Tan.

4. "Coconut" is just one of a list of insults used by ethnic Americans to imply that they are "white on the inside," regardless of the color they appear to be on the outside: e.g., for African Americans, "Oreo" (black on the outside); for American Indians, "apple" (red on the outside); for East Asian Americans, "banana" (yellow on the outside). "Coconut," of course, implies brown on the outside.

5. According to the latest *American Community Survey* (U.S. Department of Commerce 2013), approximately two-thirds (66 percent) of Asians in America in 2010–2012 were foreign born, though Japanese Americans are an exception: Most are native born.

8
Films about Thailand and Vietnam
Michael Haas

How, based on portrayals in films, does the world perceive various countries around the world? How do films inside countries differ from portrayals of the same countries abroad? In the present chapter, I focus on two countries where foreign stereotypy is common—Thailand and Vietnam. The two questions are important not only for their tourist industries but also for the foreign relations of the United States and other countries toward the two countries. American filmmakers can complicate American foreign policy as well as confuse American tourists into misbehaving in Thailand or Vietnam or even toward Thais and Vietnamese living in the United States. In addition, nearly half of the profits from American films are derived abroad, so culturally inappropriate films can hurt Hollywood at the box office (Eller and Muñoz 2002:A26). Whereas previous chapters have focused on films from Hollywood, the narrative below compares films made by Thai and Vietnamese companies with American films and films of other countries that focus on Thailand and Vietnam.

Thailand

First, the reality of Thailand, a country of some 67 million persons (34 percent urban) that has had dramatic changes in socioeconomic indicators in the last decade, with per capita national income rising to $6,572, an infant mortality rate cut in half to 11 per 1,000, and 35 percent of college-age young adults are enrolled in higher education, a 50 percent increase. Within Southeast Asia, only urbanized Malaysia and Singapore have better profiles. A burgeoning Thai Town in Los Angeles has been a mecca for immigrants; massage parlors and restaurants, the most visible signs of expatriate Thais, have been spreading across the United States.

Thailand has the freest press in Southeast Asia and a democracy with competing political parties and free elections. Although there is a long tradition of corruption and nepotism as well as military coups, democratic practices took root in he 1990s. Thailand's monarch is the longest reigning king in the world; not a mere figurehead, he has disciplined errant prime ministers and promoted charities to such an extent that he is widely revered, presiding as a special person who does what is best for the country.

Thai Buddhists practice compassion for others in order to assure a good place for themselves in their next reincarnation, and parents raise children very affectionately. Thais believe that "smiles are free," so everywhere people smile and enjoy telling delightful jokes to one another.

Tourists come to see jeweled palaces and temples, Thai dancing, kickboxing, tasty food, silk clothing, floating markets, and magnificent art and stoneware—that is, those who are not on sex tours for their own self-indulgence. Bangkok has many tall buildings, an elevated rail system, a subway, swanky hotels, and gleaming shopping malls with bargain prices for quality merchandise. The countryside, with 66 percent of the population, consists of less educated farmers and their children, who are not enjoying much trickle-down from booming Bangkok. Accordingly, many younger Thais migrate to Bangkok with marketable skills important for the tourist industry—sweet, charming personalities.

Unlike other countries in Southeast Asia, Thailand has never really angered Americans, even though a little-known fact is that Siam declared war on the United States during World War II. Japan, which militarily occupied the country, was pleased with the declaration of war and largely left the country alone. Siam's half-hearted alliance was reversed afterward, when Bangkok served as the headquarters of the now-defunct South-East-Asia Treaty Organization.

In short, most Americans and Europeans probably see Thailand as an exotic place to visit and to play. If they learn vicariously about the country, they do so through film.

Films produced in Thailand. Using the International Movie Database (IMDB), I have found nearly 1,200 films in which Thailand was the subject of a film or a filming location. American studios made the first films featuring Thailand. During the twenty-first century, the output of the Thai movie industry has increased greatly, with the result that some film studios abroad now have joint productions with Thai film companies. Productions exclusively made by Thai film companies number 568, mostly since the year 2000.

Including joint productions, there have been 97 American films. Hong Kong productions come next—9 while a British colony and 11 since the reversion to China in 1997. Britain accounts for 9 films involving Thailand, and France's 6 is next. Australia accounts for 5, Korea 4. Canada and Italy tie at 3. Bulgaria, Germany, Iceland, India, Japan, Malaysia, and Norway have 2. The remaining countries (Cambodia, Ireland, Israel, the Netherlands, Poland, Singapore, Taiwan, Turkey, Sweden) have only one film made about

Thailand. In recent years, actors and directors from other countries have gone to Thailand to make films.

However, six films about Thailand were shot outside the country because the script did not obtain the approval of the Thai government. In four cases, the films are different versions of the fabricated biography of Anna Owens. The fifth case is *Brokedown Palace* (1999), which has a plot similar to *Bangkok Hilton* (1989), an Australian film depicting abominable prison conditions in Thailand that was approved by Thai authorities. In all five cases, the depiction of the king was said to violate the law of lèse majesté by showing the king violating court protocol, even behaving in what would be considered a vulgar manner. Quite simply, a Thai king would not talk on an equal basis with a commoner, let alone strip to the waist in public. That a well-educated king would rely on advice from a mere tutor, as in *Anna and the King of Siam* (1946), even when remade as *Anna and the King* (1999), presents a preposterous fiction.

Why have American filmmakers deliberately broken Thai law? The story of Anna Owens, with three re-takes and counting, is just too much of a box office success to be modified to satisfy Thai authorities. In 2000, some writers of letters to the editor to Thai newspapers complained that the censorship contradicts the guarantee of freedom of press in the Thai constitution.

Regarding *Brokedown Palace*, Hollywood had a gratuitous scene in which the two American girls are among several persons in a queue seeking clemency from the king. Although such a scene might make sense in a film about King Solomon, no such practice exists in Thailand. The reason given by the Thai government for refusing to allow Twentieth Century Fox to film *Brokedown Palace* in Thailand was that the "entire enterprise is based on falsehood and fiction." Nevertheless, according to the film's director, Jonathan Kaplan (2002), the original story of Adam Fields was based on interviews in Thailand with "dozens of imprisoned English, French, German, Australian, Swedish, Kenyan, Jamaican, Irish and Scottish young women," including one American girl. The location was switched to the Philippines instead.

In 2012, a sixth film was banned. The Thai government did not allow a version of *Macbeth* (*Shakespeare Must Die*) to play in Bangkok cinemas, presumably because some Thais might find parallels with contemporary politics in the country. However, the same year *Fatherland* was perhaps the most explicit Thai "problem film" ever made, focusing on the insurgency within the Muslim provinces in the southernmost provinces. In that film, an officer is sent to quell the uprising but instead finds agreement with the rebels and converts to Islam.

Hypotheses. To determine whether American films stereotype Thailand, I have undertaken a pair comparison, counting the types of principal characters in American films, Thai films, and films of other countries. My hypotheses are as follows: (1) Thai films feature a much larger range of characters, reflecting a less stereotypical image of the country, than films about Thailand made by studios elsewhere. (2) Thai films feature more positive characters than films about Thais produced elsewhere, which have more negative characters. (3) American films are more stereotypical of Thailand than other films made outside Thailand.

Method. The quantitative method is a content analysis. The sample consists of all characters identified in film synopses and lists of characters portrayed, which means that some films do not enter the sample because information is missing. After identifying characters, they were classified as positive, negative, or ambiguous based on their role in the film story. Percentages are calculated in each column to facilitate comparison (Table 8.1).

Table 8.1. A Statistical Comparison between Portrayals of Thai Characters in Films Made in Thailand, the United States, and Other Countries

Characters	USA Films	Thai Films	Other Films	Total Roles
positive roles	37 (43.5%)	862 (32.4%)	22 (31.0%)	921 (32.8%)
ambiguous roles	34 (40.0%)	1101 (41.4%)	29 (40.8%)	1164 (41.3%)
negative roles	14 (16.5%)	696 (26.2%)	20 (28.2%)	730 (25.9%)
Total roles	85 (100%)	2659 (100%)	71 (100.0%)	2815 (100.0%)

Range of characters. Based on a category scheme that is perhaps a bit crude, American films featured 85 characters, Thai films had 2,959 characters, and films made elsewhere depicted 71 characters. Hypothesis 1 is confirmed, as Thai films portray a larger range of characters; films made elsewhere focus on more stereotypical understandings of the diverse Thai culture. Looking at specific characters, the data show that Thai films are much more likely to portray families and people in love than other films about Thailand. Until the Tony Jaa films, Thai kickboxers were of more interest to filmmakers outside Thailand than inside. In recent years, gay and lesbian themes have become more common; "ladyboys," that is, men acting and dressed as women, have almost routinely been cast in comedy films.

Positive characters. According to Table 8.1, American films have a higher percentage of positive Thai characters than Thai films and other films made outside Thailand. Regarding negative portrayals, American films have the lowest percentage, other films made outside Thailand have the highest, and Thai films are in the middle. There is no difference between the three categories regarding ambiguous characters. Hypothesis 2 is not confirmed: American filmmakers view Thailand through rose-colored glasses, while Thai filmmakers present a wider range of positives and negatives, and other filmmakers outside Thailand (largely Hong Kong) exploit negative stereotypes.

Expatriate stereotypy. The count of portrayals for Hypothesis 1 has already revealed that American films are less stereotypic than films made by film producers from countries outside Thailand. A final test, however, is to subtract portrayals in all three subcategories, using Thai percentages as the norm. American films differ from Thai films by 22.2 percentage points, whereas other non-Thai films differ by 4.0 percentage points. Hypothesis 3 is confirmed: American films stereotype Thailand more than other non-Thai films.

Conclusion. Films tend to be made about cardboard characters, seeking profits from entertainment. Accordingly, many movies are made in and about Thailand, one of the most fascinating countries in the world. Headlines emerge when the Thai government turns down a request from Hollywood to make a film, eclipsing other cinematic ventures. The phony story about a British tutor teaching the King of Siam a thing or two has both made money and the enmity of the Thai government because of an undignified treatment of a revered king. Although Americans may not understand why the Thais are so sensitive, they would react quite negatively to a Thai film falsely portraying Abraham Lincoln as a sadomasochistic sex maniac, but such a film might not be banned due to the actions of censors in a horrified Washington. Nevertheless, many Soviet bloc films were not imported into the United States for political reasons during the Cold War.

Rather than focusing on one film that has been remade so many times, the paper reports a content analysis of all films made about Thailand on the International Movie Data Base to test three hypotheses. The data show that Thai films portray a broad range of characters, while films about Thailand made in other countries feature a narrower range of roles. Despite the narrow range, American films present Thai people in a more positive light than do Thai films. The range of stories in Thai films is broader, containing some legends about demons and ghosts, while American film audiences pay to see happy endings. Finally, although American films about Thailand are stereotypic, films made in other countries are even moreso. American filmmakers evidently are more captivated by the beauty and charm of the Thai people.

Nevertheless, Americans are unlikely to have a realistic view of the country by viewing films made in Hollywood. To improve the perception of Thais, more movies made in Thailand would have to be imported. One Thai film released in Los Angeles in 2001 is an excellent example. *The Iron Ladies*, a film about the gay volleyball team that won the national championship in 1996, is particularly profound in articulating Buddhist principles that not only sustained the solidarity of the team in the face of much prejudice but also served to break down those very barriers. A comedy with many serious moments, *The Iron Ladies* depicted cultural and generational conflicts in Thai society, ultimately making the point that "To triumph over oneself is the greatest triumph of all." Those who saw the film gained new respect for Thailand and its people. However, *Iron Ladies 2*, released in 2003, did not have the same impact abroad.

Few Thai films are exported to Western countries, partly because ghosts and reincarnation are popular themes for Thais in Thailand, providing both elements of morality and suspense that Westerners may find difficult to appreciate. Thai films, however, are more often screened within Asian countries, where such themes have more resonance.

Vietnam

At war almost continuously from World War II to 1989, Vietnam does not have the same portrait as Thailand. The population is 90 million (larger than Thailand), with 30 million living in urban areas. Per capita income is $3,547, infant mortality is 18 per 1,000 births, and only 10 percent of the college-age population is enrolled in higher education. Although the country has a tourist industry, neither Hanoi nor Ho Chi Minh City (Saigon) are popular destinations for world travelers. Heavy industry has not developed as in Thailand, so cities are improbable magnets for young Vietnamese to move for a better life. However, the millions of expatriate Vietnamese professionals and small business owners who live in Australia, France, and the United States provide funds for their relatives until they can immigrate.

The Communist Party controls the constitutional government, press and speech are tightly controlled, and democratic reforms are not planned. There is civilian control of the military and few outbreaks of dissent. Vietnam is allied with neither China nor Russia, is a member of the Association of South-East Asian Nations, and has established cordial ties with the United States in recent years. Vietnamese are hardy, industrious, and friendly, and expatriates have done well in France, the United States, and elsewhere.

Besides Vietnamese restaurants, cosmetic nail shops have arisen with Vietnamese ownership in the United States and other countries, while Vietnamese are famous for fishing in the Gulf of Louisiana and for rice farming in southern France. Many expatriates are professionals, including Dustin Nguyen, who starred in the American weekly television series *21 Jump Street* (1987–1991) with Johnny Depp. However, Nguyen and his brother have returned to make films in Vietnam for Vietnamese. Hollywood's quest for authenticity in films has long meant that talented Asian actors are almost never considered in Western-oriented films.

Hypotheses. Vietnam has been plagued by war. Accordingly, the major hypothesis is that foreign filmmakers will tend to make war films, while Vietnamese producers will want to get beyond war to entertain Vietnamese.

Method. The sample of films selected for analysis is again derived from IMDB, which lists 218 films with Vietnam as the country of origin (Table 8.2). Currently, about a dozen films are produced each year in Vietnam, sometimes in co-productions with other countries. Excluded from the list are films about Vietnamese Americans and films about Vietnam veterans that have no scenes about Vietnam. I include *Air America* (1990), a film about the famous drug traffic from Laos that went through Vietnam.

Table 8.2. Classification of Films about Vietnam by Theme and by Decade

Language	War	Other	Before 1970	1970s	1980s	1990s	2000+	All Years
Chinese	3	2	0	0	2	3	0	5
English	54	14	10	6	22	20	11	69
French	6	18	1	1	1	5	15	23
German	1	4	0	0	0	0	5	5
Italian	2	0	0	0	2	0	0	2
Japanese	1	3	0	0	0	2	2	4
Korean	0	1	0	0	0	0	1	1
Pilipino	1	0	1	0	0	0	0	1
Russian	3	0	0	0	3	0	0	3
Spanish	1	0	0	0	1	0	0	1
Vietnamese	19	117	7	16	32	32	82	169
Total	89	169	19	23	63	62	115	282

Most of the earliest films were in English, primarily American. Vietnam, which has developed a vibrant movie industry, is now is the most numerous source of films about the country. Aside from English-language films, the 22 French films (most recently by French Swiss) edge out those in other languages. German and Japanese films are quite recent. Americans are clearly haunted by their involvement in Vietnam's civil war, just as French are nostalgic for the days of the colonial empire.

Most foreign-made films are about war, whereas films of Vietnamese directors are primarily set in peacetime. Most but not all American films have an anti-war theme.

The first film about Vietnam, *Red Dust* (1932), was Victor Flemings's film on a rubber plantation. There were two other films in the 1930s, one only in the 1940s, two in the 1950s, and thereafter the number of films focusing on Vietnam has increased in each succeeding decade. From 1990, the return of peace to Vietnam was associated with a surge in films, though primarily by Vietnamese filmmakers.

The themes of the 1930s and 1940s were primarily about love triangles involving Westerners in an exotic location where natives "knew their place." The only films in the 1950s were the prophetic *The Quiet American* (1958), based on the 1955 novel by Graham Greene, in which Audie Murphy plays the role of a naïve diplomat who is educated about the subtleties of Vietnam while caught up in a murder mystery. A remake of the film appeared in 2002, but with is a love triangle involving Michael Caine and Brendan Fraser as rivals for a Vietnamese beauty. In 1963, *The Ugly American*, based on the 1958 novel by William J. Lederer and Eugene Burdick, had another prophetic message, albeit ignored by President Lyndon Johnson and those holding onto the Cold War mentality. Nearly everyone understands that the country of Sarkan in the film was Vietnam.

Aside from *The Ugly American*, only two other American films focused on Vietnam in the 1960s. *The Green Berets* (1968) presented John Wayne's point of view, focusing entirely on the American role, totally ignoring the situation in Vietnam. That same year, Brian De Palma made his first full-length feature film *Greetings* (1968), which satirized the American role in Vietnam as well as many other shibboleths.

During the first six years of the 1970s the theme of the films was how American soldiers were haunted by their war experiences. But it was not until South Vietnam was overtaken by the North that subtle critiques emerged, especially *The Deer Hunter* (1978) and *Apocalypse Now* (1979). In 2001, Francis Ford Coppola released an uncut version of *Apocalypse Now* to provide more scenes that represented how he really felt about the war.

During the 1980s, after Ronald Reagan's remark about the Vietnam War as a "noble cause," many prominent filmmakers were eager to dispel that notion, though they had to compete with pro-war Rambo-type films. Oliver Stone's *Platoon* (1986) began the avalanche.

According to IMDB, the most popular film about Vietnam is *The Lover* (1992), a French film set in 1929. A French girl falls in love with a Vietnamese man of Chinese ancestry, both knowing that they cannot consummate their relationship in marriage because of prejudices in both communities.

Something happened to change the way in which Vietnam was perceived after Bill Clinton moved into the White House and eventual American normalization of relations with Vietnam was assured. Most films from 1994 have been made in Vietnamese, but the success of *Forrest Gump* in 1994 seems to have signaled a new slant to American films about Vietnam. Gump gets a medal for his role in Vietnam, but the favorable images of Americans involved in Vietnam continue in *Operation Dumbo Drop* (1995), *The Walking Dead* (1995), *Behind Enemy Lines* (1996), *A Soldier's Sweetheart* (1998), and *Rules of Engagement* (2000).

However, the most serious portrayals of postwar Vietnam are found in two films, both made in Vietnam and by Vietnamese film directors, about peacetime conditions in Vietnam. The first was *Cyclo* (1995), directed by Anh Hung Tran, the director who earlier gave us *The Scent of Green Papaya* (1993). The second film was *Three Seasons* (1999), directed by Vietnamese American Tony Bui, who earlier directed *White Lotus* (1995). Both films focus on the human cost of the long war and how Vietnamese are coping with conditions that are less than favorable. Both give prominent play to the poverty of Vietnam and even to the plight of prostitutes. I would like to analyze both films, which have not entered the consciousness of the American mainstream, but nevertheless represent powerful depictions of postwar Vietnam with a painful trace of the American imprint on the country:

Cyclo, which was re-run on the Independent Film Channel, is one of the saddest films ever made. The theme is similar to the 1998 Chinese film *So Close to Paradise*. Indeed, I suspect that the Vietnamese film inspired the Chinese film, as the presence of a Vietnamese prostitute in *So Close to Paradise* seems to serve as an acknowledgment of the story's origin. The focus is on how Vietnamese are trying to earn a living to survive. At the center of the story is a cyclo boy (played by Le Van Loc) in Ho Chi Minh City, who lives with an elderly grandfather whose war injuries prevent him from working, a sister who cooks at a local restaurant, an older brother who is a pimp, and another older brother who is insane. When the cyclo driver stops to take a leak one afternoon, gang thugs steal his vehicle. Penniless, his brother gets him a job doing dirty work for the same gang; then, when he obtains happy pills one day, he takes an overdose and dies. The pimp, whose grandfather does not approve of his profession, has a favorite prostitute, who is a virgin; but when a client deflowers her, the pimp kills the client and sets fire to the house of prostitution. The insane brother dies from the explosion of a firecracker set by mischievous boys. While chaos reigns in the streets and sadness in the apartments, the camera also shows tourists at a five-star hotel enjoying the good life. Throughout the film, we hear traditional Vietnamese music, especially twice at a school during a class of very young students. *Cyclo*, thus, says that those who lived through the war are cursed, but perhaps the younger generation will have an opportunity for a better life.

Three Seasons was also shot in the environs of Ho Chi Minh City, with more scenes that should be characterized as cinematic postcards of the beauty of nature. Once again, we view people in various lines of work in an economy where personal survival is not assured. In the beginning of the film, we observe Kien An, a female orphan (Ngoc Hiep Nguyen), whose application to be a lotus picker and street seller has just been accepted. In due course, she finds redemption by translating poems of Teacher Dao, her employer (Minh Cuong Tran), who is disabled by leprosy, while her fellow lotus-pickers are content to enjoy singing as they work. Among the cyclo drivers, who await customers outside opulent hotels, Hai (Don Duong) tries to court Lan, a prostitute (Zoe Bui, the director's spouse); lacking families, they are ultimately drawn together by his tenderness. Woody, a five-year-old urchin (Huu Duoc Nguyen), tries to sell junk trinkets to survive, and has to endure rudeness from hotel management staff while pursuing his craft, but he finds joy in a game of soccer with boys his age in the rain. An American war veteran, James Hager (Harvey Keitel, who is also the executive producer of the film), returns to locate his daughter, an Amerasian whose rejection by Vietnamese society means that she can only obtain income as a prostitute for foreigners. The pained expression on his face while he searches, often drinking in the open-air Apocalypse Now bar, speaks volumes of his guilt, a collective sentiment that the director evidently wants to convey in light of the fact that few Amerasians have been claimed by their fathers, even though thousands live in the United States today. Lives of some characters crisscross, but that is not the point of the film, which challenges filmviewers to determine which are the three seasons. One interpretation might be that the three seasons are birth, life, and death, but most of the film focuses on life as survival. We could also assume that the three seasons are the dry season, the hot season, and the wet season. Instead, I feel that the three seasons are psychological—the recognition of the need for redemption, the striving for redemption, and the joy of achieving redemption. Whichever interpretation you choose, *Three Seasons* was the rage of the 1999 Sundance Festival, winning the Grand Jury Prize, the award for Best Cinematography, and the Audience Award. Censors in Vietnam cleared the film in its present form, which appears to tell Americans, in Hager's words, to find "some peace with this place" by returning.

However, *Three Seasons* appears designed to be unsettling to Americans, who are collectively responsible for the tragically fragmented society and could, if motivated by unselfish impulses, claim the children that they fathered, adopt adorable orphans and urchins seeking a better life, and provide humanitarian assistance to a highly cultured and literate country that heroically refused to be "bombed into the Stone Age." Some Americans doubtless exited from commercial screenings of *Three Seasons* unmoved and unimpressed; but at Sundance, *Three Seasons* received a standing ovation at its first screening.

In contrast with *Cyclo* and *Three Seasons*, American directors in the late twentieth century seemed to believe that filmviewers were still haunted by the Vietnam War—or perhaps the directors are the monomaniacs about portraying Americans caught in the quagmire of a lost war. Some films about war, any war, now treat Vietnam as the paradigm case. The first of what I could call the pseudo-Vietnam genre was Jon Avnet's *The War* (1994), in which small children start a conflict that almost results in a death of one child. The actor who plays the role of the father, as if to hint at the analogy, is a Vietnam veteran who calls a halt to the absurd tit-for-tat conflict escalation of the children. His implication, that there is something wrong with American culture, seems to hark back to the time presented in *The Quiet American* and *The Ugly American*.

Similarly, two 1998 films, *Saving Private Ryan* and *The Thin Red Line*, appear by inference to contrast the just war aims of World War II with the unjust aims of the American role in Vietnam's civil war. The ferocity of the combat especially nails down the message that war should be reserved for causes that enjoy wide public support, especially when the aggression is outside their countries.

In 1999, two films made the same point by focusing on regional wars. *One Man's Hero* shows Irish immigrants in the U.S. army, about to be courtmarshaled for celebrating Catholic mass with Mexican Americans, who defect to the Mexican side and end up defending México from the United States in President Zachary Taylor's war. *Three Kings* cleverly attacked George H. W. Bush's Gulf War by showing that the outcome in Iraq was an anarchy that left Saddam Hussein in place. Both films have anti-American sentiments, showing a clear pattern in which the Vietnam War fits.

Thirteen Days (2000) provided a window into the careful deliberations of President John Kennedy that served to avert nuclear catastrophe, an obvious contrast with Lyndon Johnson's sloppy decision about Vietnam. In *Deterrence* (2000), the American president nukes Baghdad, which appears to be a stand-in for Hanoi circa 1965. In *The Patriot* (2000), the Americans are the guerrilla fighters against the superpower of the day, Britain. *Gladiator* (2000) spotlighted a conflict in which adversaries are bombed back to the Stone Age yet the victors are uncelebrated when they return home to Rome.

In the final scene of *Company Man* (2000), the film tried to suggest that the Central Intelligence Agency (CIA) sent jerks to Vietnam. *Pearl Harbor* (2001) returned to the just cause theme; the tagline, "From an end to innocence to a nation's greatest glory," suggests that Americans should be proud of themselves rather than dwell on the failure of Vietnam. In fact, as a condition of allowing filmmakers access to Pearl Harbor, the Navy insisted on toning down Vietnam-type elements of the script, notably conflicts between enlisted men and officers (Perry 2001:8).

Two more American films, *Going Back* (2001) and *We Were Soldiers* (2002), dwelled on a reliving of war experiences in an effort to come to terms with unresolved psychological conflicts. In short, Hollywood's films about war were still treating Vietnam as a paradigm case. But after 9/11, American involvement in films about Vietnam has been limited to co-productions and films on nonwar themes.

Then came *Letters from Son My* (2011), produced by UNESCO Vietnam Cinema and Multimedia Center and directed by Dan Le. Filmed in My Lai and based on a true story, the film focuses on the life of Lt. William Calley from the time of the massacre of at least 350 Vietnamese in 1968 until his first public apology in 2009 and later return to the village to atone for his misconduct. American filmmakers clearly missed an opportunity to make such a poignant film. But Vietnam has all but been forgotten and replaced by concerns over terrorism.

Conclusion

Films about Thailand and Vietnam present a stark contrast—lighthearted versus serious, happy-go-lucky versus guilt-ridden. Americans in particular do not appear interested in knowing the inner thoughts of Thais, but they do feel remorse about the Vietnamese. Films about Thailand under-prepare foreigners for a visit, whereas those about Vietnam over-prepare.

Nevertheless, both countries continue making their own films in their own way for their own people. Judging from films for the residents of both countries, Thai people fear that ghosts will punish them in the present and afterlife for their misdeeds, while Vietnamese want to enjoy simpler matters, such as love and getting on with life in a poor country.

More subtitled films from both countries seen abroad will better serve to understand the people, but they are unlikely to be chosen to make box office profits. When they are distributed, they should be treasured.

Epilog
Using Political Films in the Classroom
Michael A. Genovese

All great art is by its very essence in conflict with the society with which it coexists, it expresses the truth about existence regardless of whether this truth serves or hinders the survival purpose of a given society. All great art is revolutionary because it touches upon the reality of man and questions the reality of the various transitory forms of human society. —Erich Fromm

Those interested in using films in the classroom—either incorporating films into standard political science courses or developing a course in Political Films—face a myriad of decisions. I will focus my attention on those considering a course in Political Films.

One of the first decisions is how to approach the course: A generic/eclectic course, or a Theme course. I have been teaching a course in Political Films for many years. At first, I used the generic/eclectic approach; if there was any discernable theme, it was "Michael Genovese's favorite political films." This was a very good way to get my feet wet, as it allowed me to roam widely instead of explore deeply. The lack of focus did not appear to be a problem for students. I would use 8–10 standard films: *The Candidate* (1972), *Citizen Kane* (1941), two or three Frank Capra films, for example.

Before long I found myself introducing two or three films in a row based on a theme. In the early 1980s "nuclear war" films proved effective and relevant (e.g., *Dr. Strangelove*, 1972; *Fail Safe*, 2000; *On the Beach*, 1959). By the late 1980s, I shifted to films on race (e.g., *Alamo Bay*, 1985; *Malcolm X*, 1992; and, yes, *The Birth of a Nation*, 1915).

As a response to the recognition that a more multicultural approach might be useful, I have often organized my course around the question: What does it mean to be American? This question is broad enough to allow for a great deal of flexibility, but also maintains a thread of focus which runs throughout the course. The course is organized in two parts: In part one, I have used some standardized introductory films to introduce students to viewing films as political documents—*The Candidate* (1972), *Bob Roberts* (1992), *Citizen Kane* (1941), and *The Battle of Algiers* (1966). In this section, I have the students read my own book *Politics and the Cinema: An Introduction to Political Films* (1987), and I then have them compare a leftist-oriented book on film, Michael Parenti's *Make-Believe Media* (1992), and one of two conservative books, either Michael Medved's *Hollywood vs. America* (1992), Richard Grenier's *Capturing Culture* (1991), or Steven Ross's *Movies and American Society* (2002). Next, I moved to a more focused sequence dealing with the following themes—immigration (*Avalon*, 1990), race (*Alamo Bay*, 1985), "un-American activities" (*The Front*, 1976), individualism (*The Searchers*, 1956), rule of law (*The Man Who Shot Liberty Valance*, 1962). As times goes on, issues change, and I adapt accordingly.

Some may wish to develop a theme for the entire semester. I know colleagues who have focused on race, gender, fascism, and a variety of other themes in their political film courses. Whatever approach used, the results will almost certainly be positive—regardless of what some colleagues "may" say.

When Colleagues Complain

> *To be deprived of art and left alone with philosophy is to be close to Hell.*
> —*Igor Stravinsky*

Some colleagues may complain: "This film stuff isn't academic enough," or "You are just pandering to the tastes and short attention span of our pop culture kids," or "This stuff just isn't politics or science." How to answer these colleagues?

Some colleagues will never be converted, but several responses might be useful:

- I use films in class because they work! They serve as useful political documents that explain and enlighten.
- Students respond! They get into the films and respond with interest and enthusiasm.
- I use films not as a replacement for books but to use with and complement books.
- The very best discussions I have had in the classroom came as a result of post-film exchanges.
- In an era of cutbacks and number-counting, Deans like courses that draw, and a good political film course draws students from a wide range of disciplines.

These responses have worked, and students have continued to benefit!

Editor's Note: The Political Film Society offers a *Syllabus Series* for purchase at a nominal cost from its website (*www.polfilms.com*).

Appendix
Films Nominated by the
Political Film Society, 1986-2014

The following films have been nominated by members of the Political Film Society over the years. Winning films are in boldface:

Award Year	Category				
	Democracy	Exposé	Human Rights	Peace	Special Award
1987			*Matewan* Project X	*Gardens of Stone* **Platoon**	**The Killing Fields**
1988	**The Milagro Beanfield War** Stand and Deliver	*A Cry in the Dark* The Milagro Beanfield War Patty Hearst	The Accused **Cry Freedom** A World Apart	**Good Morning, Vietnam** 1969	*Vietnam*
1989	**The Dead Poets Society**	Blaze **Scandal**	A Dry White Season Listen to Me **Mississippi Burning** Talk Radio	**Casualties of War** Do the Right Thing Fat Man and Little Boy	*A City of Sadness*
1990	Born on the Fourth of July	Air America Reversal of Fortune **Roger & Me** Romero	Driving Miss Daisy Glory Longtime Companion Quigley Down Under Romero	**Dances with Wolves** Dreams Come True	*Pele's Appeal*
1991	**City of Hope** JFK	Boyz 'n the Hood **Guilty by Suspicion** JFK Paris Is Burning	Boyz 'n the Hood Come See the Paradise Guilty by Suspicion Jungle Fever The Long Walk Home	**Boyz 'n the Hood** JFK	*City of Hope*
1992	**Bob Roberts** City of Joy Howards End The Power of One	*Hoffa* Malcolm X Thunderheart	Europa, Europa **The Power of One** Sarafina! School Ties Thunderheart	**Grand Canyon** The Last of the Mohicans Mr. Saturday Night	*Midnight Express*
1993	Dave **Indochine** The Piano The Secret Garden	**In the Name of the Father** Rising Sun Schindler's List Short Cuts	Dragon: The Bruce Lee Story Geronimo: An American Legend In the Name of the Father Indochine Orlando Philadelphia **Schindler's List**	**Heaven and Earth** In the Name of the Father	*Farewell, My Concubine*
1994	**Rapa Nui**	*Quiz Show*	Go Fish On Deadly Ground	The War	*Dragon: The Bruce Lee Story*
1995	**Beyond Rangoon**	Beyond Rangoon **Nixon** Panther	Beyond Rangoon **Murder in the First** Picture Bride The Scarlet Letter	**Beyond Rangoon** Murder in the First Picture Bride The Scarlet Letter	*Bombay* **Picture Bride**
1996	Basquiat Dead Man Walking The People vs. Larry Flynt	**Dead Man Walking**	The Crucible Dead Man Walking Get on the Bus **The Ghosts of Mississippi** The People vs. Larry Flynt	Dead Man Walking **Michael Collins**	*Six O'Clock News*

Award Year	Democracy	Exposé	Human Rights	Peace	Special Award
1997	**Red Corner** Rainmaker	Amistad The Peacemaker **Rosewood** Seven Years in Tibet	L.A. Confidential Midnight in the Garden of Good and Evil **Rosewood** Seven Years in Tibet	**Seven Years in Tibet**	*Poverty Outlaw*
1998	Enemy of the State **Four Days in September** Primary Colors The Siege The Truman Show Wag the Dog	Bulworth A Civil Action Four Days in September Regeneration	**A Civil Action** Enemy of the State The Siege Wilde	American History X The Boxer Men with Guns Regeneration Saving Private Ryan **Savior** The Thin Red Line	
1999	East of Hope Street Fight Club **The Insider** Naturally Native Three Kings	Bastards **Boys Don't Cry** Cabaret Balkan East of Hope Street The Insider Naturally Native One Man's Hero Three Kings Three Seasons	Boys Don't Cry The General's Daughter **The Green Mile** Hard Naturally Native One Man's Hero Three Kings Xiu Xiu	Cabaret Balkan Earth Light It Up One Man's Hero **Three Kings** West Beirut	
2000	The Contender Human Resources The Hurricane It All Starts Today Steal This Movie! **Sunshine**	**Before Night Falls** But I'm a Cheerleader Catfish in Blackbean Sauce Erin Brockovich From the Edge of the City The Hurricane It All Starts Today Luminarias Remember the Titans Steal This Movie! Thirteen Days Tigerland Titanic Town Traffic X-Men	Before Night Falls But I'm a Cheerleader The Contender Erin Brockovich The Hurricane It All Starts Today **Remember the Titans** Sunshine X-Men	The Cell Crime and Punishment in Suburbia It All Starts Today It's the Rage Kippur The Terrorist **Thirteen Days** Titanic Town X-Men	
2001	Anti Trust Atlantis: The Lost Empire Bread and Roses **Lumumba** The Majestic	Ali Baby Boy Behind Enemy Lines Born Under Libra Bread and Roses Greenfingers The Hidden Half The Iron Ladies Journey to the Sun Lumumba Our Lady of the Assassins **Uprising**	Atlantis: The Lost Empire Born Under Libra Bread and Roses The Closet **Focus** Greenfingers The Hidden Half The Iron Ladies Journey to the Sun Lumumba	Atlantis: The Lost Empire Divided We Fall Journey to the Sun **Lumumba**	**The Distinguished Gentleman**
2002	Das Experiment John Q Max Secret Ballot The Town Is Quiet 24 Hour Party People **Y Tu Mamá También**	**Antwone Fisher** Ararat Circuit Enigma Evelyn Green Dragon The Grey Zone John Q K-19: The Widowmaker Kandahar Max Rabbit-Proof Fence Skins To End All Wars	**Ararat** Das Experiment Evelyn The Grey Zone John Q Rabbit-Proof Fence To End All Wars Tricky Life	Antwone Fisher Das Experiment K-19: The Widowmaker **The Quiet American** The Sum of All Fears Time of Favor To End All Wars	

Award Year	Democracy	Exposé	Human Rights	Peace	Special Award
2002 (cont.)		Tricky Life Y Tu Mamá También			
2003	Herod's Law Runaway Jury Sandstorm **Shattered Glass** Veronica Guerin	All My Loved Ones Amen Beyond Borders The Dancer Upstairs Dark Blue Dirty Pretty Things Emerald Cowboy Green Card Fever Herod's Law La Casa de Los Babys Lilja 4-Ever The Magdalene Sisters Marooned in Iraq Runaway Jury Sandstorm Shattered Glass The Statement Taking Sides Tycoon: A New Russian **Veronica Guerin**	Amen Beyond Borders Dirty Pretty Things The Life of David Gale Lilja 4-Ever **The Magdalene Sisters** Sandstorm The Statement Twilight X-2: X-Men United	Beyond Borders Cold Mountain The Dancer Upstairs **Sandstorm** X-2: X-Men United	
2004	The Assassination of Richard Nixon Moolaadé The Motorcycle Diaries **Silver City**	Blind Shaft Carandiru The Day After Tomorrow The Gatekeeper Hotel Rwanda Imagining Argentina **Kinsey** The Motorcycle Diaries Osama Rosenstrasse Tae Guk Ki The Yes Men	Carandiru The Gatekeeper **Hotel Rwanda** Imagining Argentina Moolaadé The Motorcycle Diaries Osama The Sea Inside Two Brothers Vera Drake The Yes Men	Carandiru Hotel Rwanda **Tae Guk Ki** A Very Long Engagement	
2005	Downfall **Machuca**	Assisted Living Before the Fall Crash Downfall **Good Night & Good Luck** The Great Water In My Country Innocent Voices Lord of War Machuca Munich The Ninth Day North Country Paradise Now Turtles Can Fly	Caché **The Constant Gardener** God's Sandbox The Great Raid The Great Water In My Country Innocent Voices Machuca The Ninth Day **North Country** The War Within	Before the Fall Downfall In My Country Jarhead **Munich** Private	
2006	Cautiva Death of a President The Listening Man of the Year The Queen **Sophie Scholl: The Final Days**	Cautiva Fast Food Nation Glory Road The Good Shepherd **Kekexili** The Listening The Queen The Road to Guantánamo Sophia Scholl: The Final Days	Babel Blood Diamond Cautiva Glory Road **The Last King of Scotland** The Road to Guantanamo Sophia Scholl: The Final Days	End of the Spear **Joyeux Noël** Letters from Iwo Jima	

Award Year	Democracy	Exposé	Human Rights	Peace	Special Award
2007	*Amazing Grace* *September Dawn* *Shooter*	*American Gangster* *Amu* *Bamako* *Beyond the Gates* *Black Book* *Black Friday* *Breach* *Charlie Wilson's War* *The Great Debaters* *Holly* *The Hunting Party* *A Mighty Heart* *Offside* *Persepolis* *Redacted* *September Dawn* *Strange Culture* *The Situation* *There Will Be Blood* *Trade* *The Wind That Shakes the Barley*	*Amazing Grace* *Bamako* *Beyond the Gates* *Charlie Wilson's War* *Holly* *The Hunting Party* *In the Valley of Elah* *Offside* *Persepolis* *Pierrepoint* *Redacted* *Rendition* *September Dawn* *Southland Tales* *Strange Culture* *Trade*	*Black Friday* *In the Valley of Elah* *O Jerusalem* *Pierrepoint* *Redacted* *September Dawn* *The Situation*	
2008	*Changeling* *Flash of Genius* *Milk* *Nothing but the Truth*	*The Bank Job* *Battle in Seattle* *Changeling* *Che* *The Counterfeiters* *Defiance* *Frost/Nixon* *Milk* *Miracle at St. Anna* *Still Life* *W.* *Walkyrie*	*Battle in Seattle* *The Boy in the Striped Pajamas* *Changeling* *Hunger* *Milk* *Miracle at St. Anna*	*Gran Torino* *Stop-Loss*	
2009	*Invictus*	*12* *American Violet* *The Baader Meinhof Complex* *The Cove* *Fifty Dead Men Walking* *Flame & Citron* *The Hurt Locker* *The Informant!* *Invictus* *The Last Station* *Punctured Hope* *Sin Nombre* *Skin* *State of Play* *The Stoning of Soraya M* *Storm* *The Sun* *A Woman in Berlin* *The Yes Men Fix the World* *The Young Victoria*	*American Violet* *Avatar* *The Cove* *District 9* *Fifty Dead Men Walking* *Invictus* *Punctured Hope* *Skin* *The Stoning of Soraya M* *Storm* *A Woman in Berlin* *The Yes Men Fix the World*	*A Woman in Berlin* *Avatar* *Brothers* *Fifty Dead Men Walking* *Flame & Citron* *The Hurt Locker* *Inglorious Basterds* *A Woman in Berlin*	*Cider House Rules*
2010	*Blood Done Sign My Name* *Formosa Betrayed* *John Rabe* *Princess Ka'iulani*	*Agora* *Casino Jack* *Extraordinary Measures* *Fair Game* *Formosa Betrayed* *John Rabe* *Mao's Last Dancer* *Princess Ka'iulani* *Shake Hands with the Devil* *Vincere*	*Agora* *Blood Done Sign My Name* *Eichmann* *Formosa Betrayed* *The Ghost Writer* *Green Zone* *Howl* *John Rabe* *Made in Dagenham* *My Name is Khan* *Princess Ka'iulani* *Shake Hands with the Devil*	*Formosa Betrayed* *The Ghost Writer* *Green Zone* *John Rabe*	*Princess Ka'iulani*

Award Year	Democracy	Exposé	Human Rights	Peace	Special Award
2011	*Amigo* *Elite Squad 2* **The Lady** *Of Gods and Men*	*5 Days of War* *Amigo* *The Bang Bang Club* *City of Life and Death* *The Conquest* *The Conspirator* *The Devil's Double* *Elite Squad 2* *In Darkness* *The Iron Lady* *J. Edgar* *Kinyarwanda* *Machine Gun Preacher* *Oranges and Sunshine* **Silenced** *The Whistleblower*	*5 Days of War* *Amigo* *City of Life and Death* *The Conspirator* *The Devil's Double* *Elite Squad 2* **The Help** *In Darkness* *The Flowers of War* *In the Land of Blood and Honey* *Kinyarwanda* *The Lady* *Machine Gun Preacher* *Oka!* *Oranges and Sunshine* *Silenced* *The Whistleblower*	**5 Days of War** *Amigo* *City of Life and Death* *Elite Squad 2* *The Flowers of War* *Kinyarwanda* *In the Land of Blood and Honey* *Kinyarwanda* *The Lady* *Machine Gun Preacher* *Of Gods and Men*	
2012	**Lincoln** *Promised Land*	**Argo** *Compliance* *For Greater Glory* *Lula, Son of Brazil* *Mulberry Child*	*For Greater Glory* *Mulberry Child* *Red Tails* *A Royal Affair* **West of Thunder**	*War of the Buttons* **West of Thunder**	
2013	**The Butler** *Capital* *Mandela: Long Walk to Freedom*	*Aftermath* *Dallas Buyers Club* *A Dark Truth* **Emperor** *The Fifth Estate* *The Reluctant Fundamentalist* *Saving Lincoln*	**12 Years a Slave** *42* *A Dark Truth* *All God's Children* *The Butler* *A Dark Truth* *Fruitvale Station* *Mandela: Long Walk to Freedom* *Out in the Dark* *A River Changes Course* *Wajdja*	*Zaytoun*	
2014 (up to May 15)	*Cesar Chavez*	*Bethlehem* *Cesar Chavez* *The Monuments Men* *Omar* *The Railway Man* *Walking with the Enemy*	*Bethlehem* *Cesar Chavez* *Devil's Knot* *The Monuments Men* *Omar* *The Railway Man* *Walking with the Enemy*	*Cesar Chavez* *The Railway Man*	*Philomena*

Life membership in the Political Film Society is available for US$5.00, payable by check or money1 order to Political Film Society, P.O. Box 461267, Los Angeles, CA 90046, or on the website *www.polfilms.com* by PayPal. Members are entitled to vote for the best political films in the various categories and are emailed film reviews of the latest films released in Los Angeles at regular intervals close to the dates of their release.

Combined References

Alba, Richard D. (1990). *Ethnic Identity: The Transformation of White America*. New Haven, CT: Yale University Press.

Anderson, James A., and Timothy P. Meyers (1988). *Mediated Communication: A Social Action Perspective*. Newbury Park, CA: Sage.

anon. (n.d.). *moviegeek.com.http://www.moviegeek.homestead.com/files/featprod1.htm.*

anon. (2012). "Soviet Union: Films Behind the Iron Curtain," *BZ-Film.com*, March 23 (accessed May 15, 2014).

Associated Press (1994). "Activist Movie Actor Makes Art and Politics Mix," *The Telegraph*, March 6, p. B-4.

Austin, Bruce (1989). *Immediate Seating: A Look at Movie Audiences*. Belmont, CA: Wadsworth.

Baker, Donald P., and Kent Jenkins, Jr. (1994). "North Says U.S. Military Unable to Stop Saddam," *Washington Post*, October 10, pp. Dl, D5.

———— and Robert O'Harrow, Jr. (1994). "North Calls Post Report on Drug Tips 'Hogwash'," *Washington Post*, October 23, p. B3.

Barkan, Elliott R. (1995). "Race, Religion, and Nationality in American Society: A Model of Ethnicity—From Contact to Assimilation," *Journal of American Ethnic History*, 14 (1): 38–101.

Barth, Fredrik (1969). "Introduction." In *Ethnic Groups and Boundaries: The Social Organization of Cultural Difference*, ed. Fredrik Barth, pp. 1–38. Boston: Little, Brown.

Belton, John (1994). *American Cinema/American Culture*. New York: McGraw-Hill.

Bennett, Lance (1998). "The UnCivic Culture: Communication, Identity and the Rise of Lifestyle Politics," *PS: Political Science & Politics*, 31 (4): 741–762.

Bergman, Andrew (1979). *We're in the Money*. New York: Ungar.

Biskind, Peter (1983). *Seeing Is Believing: How Hollywood Taught Us to Stop Worrying and Love the Fifties*. New York: Pantheon.

Black, Gregory D. (1989). "Hollywood Censored: The Production Code Administration and the Hollywood Film Industry, 1930–1940," *Film History*, 3 (1): 167–189.

Blaise, Judd (1994). Review of *Natural Born Killers. allmovie.com.*

Bolter, J. David, and Richard Grusin (1999). *Remediation: Understanding New Media*. Cambridge, MA: MIT Press.

Boulding, Kenneth (1956). *The Image: Knowledge in Life and Society*. Ann Arbor: University of Michigan Press.

Brimelow, Peter (1995). *Alien Nation: Common Sense about America's Immigration Disaster*. New York: Random House.

Brinckmann, Christine Noll (1981). "The Politics of *Force of Evil*: An Analysis of Abraham Polonsky's Preblacklisted Film," *Prospects*, 6 (10): 357–386.

Brockman, Stephen (2010). *A Critical History of German Film*. Rochester, NY: Camden House.

Brown, Jane D., Kelly Ladin L'Engle, Carol J. Pardun, Guang Guo, Kristin Kenneavy, and Christine Jackson (2006). "Sexy Media Matter: Exposure to Sexual Content in Music, Movies, Television, and Magazines Predicts Black and White Adolescents' Sexual Behavior," *Pediatrics*, 117 (4): 1018–1027.

Brownlow, Kevin (1990). *Behind the Mask of Innocence*. New York: Knopf.

Buhle, Paul (2001). *A Very Dangerous Citizen: Abraham Lincoln Polonsky and the Hollywood Left*. Berkeley: University of California Press.

Burnett, Victoria (2014). "Struggling to Film in America's Chokehold," *New York Times*, April 6.

Bushman, Brad J., Patrick E. Jamieson, Ilana Weitz, and Daniel Romer (2013). "Gun Violence Trends in Movies," *Pediatrics*, 132 (6): 1014–1018.

Butler, Lisa D., Cheryl Koopman, and Philip Zimbardo (1999). "The Psychological Impact of Viewing the Film 'JFK': Emotions, Beliefs, and Political Behavioral Intentionism," *Political Psychology*, 16 (1): 237–257.

Camera Three (1976). CBS-TV, June 4.

Cane, Russ (2012). "There Are 32,000+ Gun Deaths a Year in the U.S.—Here Is How We Get That Number to Zero," *www.policymic.com*, December 23.

Chaplin, Charles (1964). *My Autobiography*. New York: Simon & Schuster.

Christensen, Terry (1987). *Reel Politics: American Political Movies from Birth of a Nation to Platoon*. New York: Blackwell.

——— and Peter J. Haas (2005). *Projecting Politics: Political Messages in American Film*. Armonk, NY: Sharpe.

Cocks, Jay (1972). "The Least Hurrah," *Time*, July 17, p. 49.

Combs, James, E. (1990). *American Political Movies: An Annotated Filmography of Feature Films*. New York: Garland.

——— and Combs, Sarah (1994). *Film Propaganda and American Politics: An Analysis and Filmography*. New York: Garland.

Conzen, Kathleen Neils, David A. Gerber, Ewa Morawska, George E. Pozzetta, and Rudolph J. Vecoli (1992). "The Invention of Ethnicity: A Perspective from the U.S.A.," *Journal of American Ethnic History*, 29 (1): 3-41

Crowdus, Gary, ed. (1994). *The Political Companion to American Film*. Chicago: Lake View Press.

Curtiss, Thomas Quinn (1982). "Federico Fellini," *International Herald Tribune*, July 15.

D'Souza, Dinesh (2012). *Obama's America: Unmaking the American Dream*. Washington, DC: Regnery.

Dal, Cin Sonya, Mike Stoolmiller, James D. Sargent (2012). "When Movies Matter: Exposure to Smoking in Movies and Changes in Smoking Behavior," *Journal of Health Communication*, 17 (1): 76–89.

Davis, Curt (1979). "Anatomy of a Play," *Horizon*, October.

De Mille, William (1935). "Mickey versus Popeye," *The Forum* (November): 295–296.

DeSousa, Michael A., and Martin J. Medhurst (1982). "Political Cartoons and American Culture: Significant Symbols of Campaign 1980," *Studies in Visual Communication*, 8 (1): 84–97.

de Toqueville, Alexis (1835). *Democracy in America*. New York: Knopf, 1945.

Derry, Charles (1995). *The Suspense Thriller: Films in the Shadow of Alfred Hitchcock*. Jefferson, NC: McFarland.

Dick, Bernard F. (1989). *Radical Innocence: A Critical Study of the Hollywood Ten*. Lexington: University of Kentucky Press.

Edds, Margaret (1994a). "North Pulls Ad Attacking Robb, But Won't Rule Out Others," *Virginian-Pilot*, October 19.

——— (1994b). "North Says Paper Was Wrong in Flag Report," *Virginian-Pilot*, November 3.

——— (1994c). "What Now for Ollie North?" *Virginian-Pilot*, November 8.

Edelman, Murray (1985). *The Symbolic Uses of Politics*. 2nd edn. Urbana: University of Illinois Press.

—— (1988). *Constructing the Political Spectacle*. Chicago: University of Chicago Press.

Edelman, Rob (1976). "The Politician in Film," *Films in Review* (November): 531.

Eller, Claudia, and Lorenza Muñoz (2002). "The Plots Thicken in Foreign Markets," *Los Angeles Times*, October 6, pp. A1, A26–27.

Everhart, Karen (2002). "Documentary Settles a Hollywood Score from Blacklist Years," *Current*, June 3.

Fearing, Franklin (1947). "Influence of the Movies on Attitudes and Behavior," *Annals of the American Academy of Political and Social Science*, 254 (1): 70–79.

Fayard, Judy (1972). "Would You Vote for This Man?," *Life*, July 28, pp. 45–50.

Feng, Peter X., ed. (2002). *Screening Asian Americans*. New Brunswick, NJ: Rutgers University Press.

Flaum, Marshall (1978). "Foreword" to *Nuclear War Films*, ed. Jack G. Shanhee. Carbondale: Southern Illinois University Press.

Fleishman, Jeffrey (2014). "How U.S. Films Translate Abroad," *Los Angeles Times*, January 19.

Freedman, Carl (2013). *Versions of Hollywood Crime Cinema: Studies in Ford, wilder, Coppola, Scorsese, and Others*. Chicago, IL: University of Chicago Press.

Fuchs, Lawrence (1990). *The American Kaleidoscope: Race, Ethnicity, and the Civic Culture*. Hanover and Boston, MA: University Press of New England.

Ganti, Tejaswini (2012). *Producing Bollywood: Inside the Contemporary Hindi Film Industry*. Durham, NC: Duke University Press.

Gaslin, Glenn, and Rick Porter (1998). *The Complete, Cross-Referenced Guide to the Baby Buster Generation's Collective Unconscious*. New York: Boulevard Books.

Gavin, Patrick (2013). "'The Invisible War' Oscar Film Has D.C. Footprint," *Politico.com*, January 10 (accessed May 15, 2014).

Geertz, Clifford (1973). *The Interpretation of Cultures*. New York: Basic Books

Genovese, Michael A. (1984). "Teaching about Fascism with Films," *NEWS for Teachers of Political Science,* Spring.

—— (1986). *Politics and the Cinema: An Introduction to Political Films*. Lexington, MA: Ginn Press.

—— (1988). "The Politics of the Wizard of Oz," *Los Angeles Times*, March 19.

Gerbner, George (1973). "Cultural Indicators—The Third Voice." In *Communications Technology and Social Policy: Understanding the New "Cultural Revolution,"* eds. George Gerbner, Larry P. Gross, and William H. Melody, pp. 553–573. New York: Wiley.

Giannetti, Louis D. (1996). *Understanding Movies*. Boston: Pearson.

Gianos, Phillip L. (1995). *Politics and Politicians in American Film*. Westport, CT: Praeger.

Giglio, Ernest (2014). *Here's Looking at You: Hollywood, Film and Politics*. 4th edn. New York: Peter Lang.

Gilliatt, Penelope (1972). "The Current Cinema," *The New Yorker* (July 1): 64–65.

Gleason, Philip (1992). *Speaking of Diversity: Language and Ethnicity in Twentieth-Century America*. Baltimore, MD: Johns Hopkins University Press.

Goldberg, Jonah (2014). "Film and Liberal Politics," *Los Angeles Times*, January 28.

Gomery, Douglas (1994). "Conglomerates in the Film Industry." In *The Political Companion to American Film*, ed. Gary Crowdus, pp. 71–74. Chicago: Lake View Press.

Gordon, Milton M. (1964). *Assimilation in American Life*. New York: Oxford University Press.

Grenier, Richard, ed. (1991). *Capturing Culture: Film, Art, and Politics*. Washington, DC: Ethics & Public Policy Center.

Gross, Matthew Barrett, and Mel Gilles (2012). *The Last Myth: What the Rise of Apocalyptic Thinking Tells Us About America*. Amherst, NY: Prometheus.

Guerrero, Ed (1993). *Framing Blackness: The African America Image in Film*. Philadelphia, PA: Temple University Press.

Haas, Michael (1991a). *Cambodia, Pol Pot, and the United States*. New York: Praeger.

———— (1991b). *Genocide by Proxy: Cambodian Pawn on a Superpower Chessboard*. New York: Praeger.

———— (1991c). "Why a Political Film Society?" *PS: Political Science and Politics*, 24 (1): 70–71.

———— , ed. (1998). *The Political Film Today*. New York: Council on Foreign Relations.

———— , ed. (2011). *Barack Obama, The Aloha Zen President: How a Son of the 50th State May Transform America Based on 12 Multicultural Principles*. Santa Barbara, CA: ABC-Clio.

———— (2012a). *Modern Cambodia's Emergence from the Killing Fields: What Happened in the Critical Years?* Los Angeles, CA: Publishinghouse for Scholars.

———— (2012b). *Mr. Calm and Effective: Evaluating the Presidency of Barack Obama*. Los Angeles, CA: Publishinghouse for Scholars.

Harmetz, Aljean (1992). *Round Up the Usual Suspects*. New York: Hyperion.

Harris, Dana (2005). "'Gandhi' in Mideast," *Variety*, April 5.

Hawkins, Robert P., and Suzanne Pingree (1983). "TV's Influence on Social Reality." In *Mass Communication Review Year Book*, eds. Ellen Wartella and D. Charles Whitley, Vol. 4, pp. 53–76. London: Sage

Hayward, Susan, and Ginette Vincendeau, eds. (2000). *French Film: Texts and Contexts*. 2nd edn. New York: Routledge.

Heilemann, John, and Mark Halperin (2010). *Game Change: Obama and the Clintons, McCain and Palin, and the Race of a Lifetime*. New York: HarperCollins.

Higham, John (1955). *Strangers in the Land: Patterns of American Nativism, 1860–1925*. New York: Atheneum, 1975.

———— (1984). Send *These to Me: Immigrants in Urban America*. Rev ed. Baltimore, MD: Johns Hopkins University Press.

Hillier, Jim (1985). *Cahiers du Cinema, the 1950s: New-Realism, Hollywood, New Wave*. Cambridge, MA: Harvard University Press.

Hirsch, Foster (2008). *The Dark Side of the Screen: Film Noir*. Cambridge, MA: Da Capo Press.

Hocking, William (1956). *The Coming World Civilization*. New York: Harper.

Holub, Robert C. (1984). *Reception Theory: A Critical Introduction*. London: Methuen.

Horn, John (2014). "When Movies Stray from Facts," *Los Angeles Times*, January 2.

Hull, David S. (1973). *Film in the Third Reich*. New York: Simon & Schuster.

Hynes, Eric (2010). "We're Living in a Golden Age of Documentary Filmmaking: But You'd Never Know It from Watching the Oscars," *Slate*, February 14.

Ignatiev, Noel (1995). *How the Irish Became White*. New York: Routledge.

Jauss, Hans Robert (1982). *Toward an Aesthetic of Reception*. Minneapolis: University of Minnesota Press.

Kael, Pauline (1965). *I Lost It at the Movies*. Boston: Little, Brown.

———— (1969). *Kiss Kiss. Bang Bang*. New York: Bantam.

———— (1976). *Reeling*. Boston: Little, Brown.

———— (1982). *5001 Nights at the Movies*. New York: Holt, Rinehart, Winston.

Kaplan, Jonathan (2002). Personal communication, November 5.

Kasinitz, Philip, John H. Mollenkopf, Mary C. Waters, and Jennifer Holdaway (2008). *Inheriting the City: The Children of Immigrants Come of Age*. New York: Russell Sage.

Kauffmann, Stanley (1972). "Bob Roberts," *The New Republic*, October 5, pp. 34–35.

Kelley, Beverly M. (1998). *Reel Politik: Political Ideologies in '30s and '40s Films*. Westport, CT: Praeger.

Kibria, Nazli (2002). *Becoming Asian American: Second-Generation Chinese and Korean American Identities*. Baltimore, MD: Johns Hopkins University Press.

Kilpatrick, Neva Jaquelyn (1999). *Celluloid Indians: Native Americans and Film*. Lincoln: University of Nebraska Press.

King, Susan (2014). "Life 30 Years After 'The Killing Fields'," *Los Angeles Times*, January 30.

Kirshner, Jonathan (2012). *Hollywood's Last Golden Age: Politics, Society, and the Seventies Film in America*. Ithaca, NY: Cornell University Press.

Koch, Howard E., Sr. (1992). *Casablanca: Script and Legend*. New York: Overlook Express.

Koh Gui Qing (2013). "China Reports Three New Bird Flu Deaths, Toll Hits 35," *Reuters*, May 13.

Kracauer, Siegfried (1947). *From Caligari to Hitler*. Princeton, NJ: Princeton University Press.

Landy, Marcia (2000). *Italian Film*. New York: Cambridge University Press.

Leach, Jim (2004). *British Film*. New York: Cambridge University Press.

Lee, Jennifer and Frank D. Bean (2010). *The Diversity Paradox: Immigration and the Color Line in 21st Century America*. New York: Russell Sage.

Leiser, Erwin (1974). *Nazi Cinema*. New York: Collier.

Lerner, Max (1957). *America as a Civilization*. New York: Simon & Schuster.

Lefebvre, Henri (1947). *A Critique of Everyday Life*. New York: Verso, 1991.

Lewis, Sinclair (1922). *Babbitt*. New York: Harcourt, Brace.

Litwak, Mark (1994). *Reel Power: The Struggle for Influence in the New Hollywood*. Los Angeles, CA: Silman-James Press.

MacCann, Richard Dyer (1969). *Film and Society*. New York: Scribner's Sons.

Makinen, Julie, and John Horn (2014). "China's Censors Say 'No' to 'Noah'," *Los Angeles Times*, May 9, B1, B3.

Maltin, Leonard (1972). *The Great Movie Shorts*. New York: Crown.

Martin, Philip, and Elizabeth Midgley (1994). *Immigration to the United States: Journey to an Uncertain Destination*. Washington, DC: Population Reference Bureau.

Matthews, Michael F. (2013). "The Untold Story of Military Sexual Assault," *New York Times*, November 24.

May, Larry (2000). *The Big Tomorrow: Hollywood and the Politics of the American Way*. Chicago: University of Chicago Press.

McNally, Victoria (2012). "Movies Banned in Foreign Countries for Weird Reasons," *theatlantic.com*, February 6 (accessed May 15, 2014).

McNary, Dave (2006). "Par Flexes Major Cannes Muscle," *Variety*, May 10.

McQuail, Denis (1994). *Mass Communication Theory*. 3rd edn. Thousand Oaks, CA: Sage.

Medhurst, Martin J., and Michael A. DeSousa (1981). "Political Cartoons as Rhetorical Form: A Taxonomy of Graphic Discourse," *Communication Monographs*, 48: 197–236.

Media Violence Commission, International Society for Research on Aggression (2012). "Report of the Media Violence Commission," *Aggressive Behavior*, 38 (5): 335–341.

Medved, Michael (1992). *Hollywood vs. America: Popular Culture and the War on Traditional Values*. New York: HarperCollins.

Mill, John Stuart (1859). *On Liberty*. Cambridge, MA: Cambridge University Press, 1989.

Miller, Mark Crispin (1990). "Advertising: End of Story." In *Seeing Through Movies*, ed. Mark Crispin Miller, pp. 186–246. New York: Pantheon.

Monaco, James (1976). "The Costa-Gavras Syndrome," *Cineaste*, 8 (2): 20.

——— (1981). *How to Read a Film: The Art, Technology, Language, History and Theory of Film and Media*. 2nd edn. New York: Oxford University Press.

Morgan, Michael, ed. (2002). *Against the Mainstream: The Selected Works of George Gerbner*. New York: Peter Lang.

Morlan, Don B. (1994a). "A Pie in the Face: The Three Stooges Anti-Aristocracy Theme in Depression-Era American Film." Paper presented at the annual meeting of the Popular Culture Association, Chicago, April.

——— (1994b). "Slapstick Contributions to World War II Propaganda: The Three Stooges and Abbott & Costello," *Studies in Popular Culture*, 17 (1): 29–43.

——— (1995). "Pre-World War II Propaganda: Film as Controversy." Paper presented at the annual meeting of the American Political Science Association, Chicago, September.

Muller, Eddie (1998). *Dark City: The Lost World of Film Noir*. New York: St. Martin's Press.

Mulligan, Kenneth, and Philip Habel (2012). "The Implications of Fictional Media for Political Beliefs," *American Politics Research*, 20 (1): 1–25.

Nagel, Joane (1994). "Constructing Ethnicity: Creating and Recreating Ethnic Identity and Culture," *Social Problems*, 41 (1): 152–176.

Nelson, Brent A. (1994). *America Balkanized: Immigration's Challenge to Government*. Monterey, VA: American Immigration Control Foundation.

Nelson, Bryce (1981). "Film's Responsibility as Our 'Central Art'," *Los Angeles Times*, February 9, Section 4, pp. 1–4.

Nimmo, Dan (1993). "Political Propaganda in the Movies: A Typology." In *Movies and Politics*, ed. James E. Combs, pp. 271–294. New York: Garland.

——— and James E. Combs (1983). *Mediated Political Realities*. New York: Longman.

Nornes, Abé Mark, and Aaron Gerow (2009). *Research Guide to Japanese Film Studies*. Ann Arbor: Center for Japanese Studies, University of Michigan.

O'Hagan, Sean (2010). "Camera, Laptop, Action: The New Golden Age of Documentary," *Guardian*, November 6.

Packard, Vance (1957). *The Hidden Persuaders*. New York: McKay.

Parenti, Michael (1992). *Make-Believe Media: The Politics of Entertainment*. New York: St. Martin's Press.

Perry, Tony (2001). "A Joint Exercise," *Los Angeles Times*, May 28, pp. F-1, 8–9.

Phillips, Baxter (1976). *Swastika: Cinema of Oppression*. New York: Warner Books.

Pieper, Gail W., and Marie Clear (1995). "Imagery of Conflict in MacNelly's Editorial Cartoons and the Comic Strip Shoe." Comic Art Section, Popular Culture Association, Philadelphia, PA.

Powdermaker, Hortense (1950). *Hollywood the Dream Factory*. Boston: Little, Brown.

Putnam, Robert (1993). *Making Democracy Work: Civic Traditions in Modern Italy*. Princeton, NJ: Princeton University Press.

——— (1995). "Bowling Alone," *Journal of Democracy*, 6 (1): 65–78.

——— (2000). *Bowling Alone: The Collapse and Revival of American Community*. New York: Simon & Schuster.

Quart, Alissa (2005). "Networked," *Film Comment*, 41 (4): 48–50.

Quart, Leonard, and Albert Oster (1991). *American Film and Society Since 1945*. New York: Praeger.

Reyes, Luis, and Peter Rubie (1994). *Hispanics in Hollywood*. New York: Garland.

Roberts, Randy W. (2010). "You Must Remember This: The Case of Hal Wallis's *Casablanca*." In *Hollywood's America: Twentieth Century America Through Film*, eds. Steven Mintz and Randy W. Roberts, 4th edn., Chap. 10. New York: Blackwell.

Robinson, David (1985). *Chaplin: His Life and Art*. New York: McGraw-Hill.

Robinson, Paul (1978). "TV Can't Educate," *The New Republic*, August 5–12.

Robson, Dave (2012). "Hot Docs 2012: 'The Invisible War' Is Eloquent, Bold, and Devastating," *Sound on Sight*, April 26.

Roddick, Nick (1980). *Aspects of Popular Entertainment in Theatre, Film and Television, 1800–1976*. New York: Cambridge University Press.

Rodriguez, Richard (2004). *Hunger of Memory: The Education of Richard Rodriguez*. New York: Bantam Books.

Rosenberg, Alyssa (2013). "'The Invisible War': How Oscar's Military Rape Documentary Might Change Everything," *Daily Beast*, February 7.

Ross, Steven J. (2011). *Hollywood, Left and Right: How Movie Stars Shaped American Politics*. New York: Oxford University Press.

Sarris, Andrew (1978). *Politics and Cinema*. New York: Columbia University Press.

Schary, Dore (1955). "Motion Pictures and Their Influence on the Modern World." Speech to National Conference of Controllers in Los Angeles, California.

Schickel, Richard (1972). "Politics in the Movies," *Life*, July 7, p. 22.

Schlesinger, Arthur M., Jr. (1979). "Foreword" to John E. O'Connor and Martin A. Jackson, *American History, American Film: Interpreting the Hollywood Image*. New York: Ungar.

Schudson, Michael (1998). *The Good Citizen: A History of American Civic Life*. New York: Martin Kessler.

Scott, A. O. (2010). "Documentaries (in Name Only) of Every Stripe," *New York Times*, October 17.

Shaheen, Jack G. (2009). *Reel Bad Arabs: How Hollywood Vilifies a People*. Rev. edn. Northampton, MA: Olive Branch Press.

Shapiro, Ben (2011). *Prime Time Propaganda: The True Hollywood Story of How the Left Took Over Your TV*. New York: Broadside Books.

Signorielli, Nancy, and Michael Morgan, eds. (1990). *Cultivation Analysis*. Newbury Park, CA: Sage.

Simon, John (1970). *Movies into Film*. New York: Dell.

——— (1981). *Reverse Angle: A Decade of American Films*. New York: Clarkson N. Potter.

Sklar, Robert (1994). *Movie-Made America: A Cultural History of American Movies*. Rev. edn. New York: Vintage.

Slate (2000). "Were the Y2K Preparations in Vain?" *Slate*, January 6 *http://www.slate.com/articles/news_and_politics/explainer/2000/01/were_the_y2k_preparations_in_vain.html* (accessed May 15, 2014).

Sloan, Kay (1988). *The Loud Silents: Origins of the Social Problem Film*. Urbana: University of Illinois Press.

Snider, Eric D. (2010). "What's the Big Deal? *Casablanca* (1942)," June 22, *www.film.com/movies/whats-the-big-deal-casablanca-1942* (accessed October 4, 2012).

Sollors, Werner (1986). *Beyond Ethnicity: Consent and Descent in American Culture*. New York: Oxford University Press.

Solomon, Lewis (2008). *Tech Billionaires: Reshaping Philanthropy in a Quest for a Better World*. New Brunswick, NJ: Transaction Publishers.

Sontag, Susan (1965). "The Imagination of the Disaster," *Commentary*, 21 (10): 42–48.

Stokes, Melvin (2007). *D. W. Griffith's The Birth of a Nation: A History of "The Most Controversial Motion Picture of All Time."* New York: Oxford University Press.

Strong, Edward K., Jr. (1934). *The Second-Generation Japanese Problem*. Stanford, CA: Stanford University Press.

Sunstein, Cass (1992). "Free Speech Now," *University of Chicago Law Review*, 59 (Winter): 255–316.

Suskind, Ron (2011). *Confidence Men: Wall Street, Washington, and the Education of a President*. New York: Harper Collins.

Talbot, David, and Barbara Zheutlin (1978). *Creative Differences: Profiles of Hollywood Dissidents*. Boston: South End Press.

Tan, Amy (1989). *Joy Luck Club*. New York: Putnam.

Tuan, Mia (1998). *Forever Foreigners or Honorary Whites? The Asian Ethnic Experience Today*. New Brunswick, NJ: Rutgers University Press.

Udoff, Yale (1964). "Cinema and Politics," *Film Comment*, 2 (2): 37.

United States, Department of Commerce (2013). *2010–2012 American Community Survey*. Washington, DC: Department of Commerce, Bureau of the Census.

Verrier, Richard (2013). "Making Film Deals with Tax Credits," *Los Angeles Times*, December 26.

Wallace, Chris (2013). "These Days, the End Is Always Near: Disaster Films Plague the Box Office," *New York Times*, July 19.

Walsh, Michael (1998). *As Time Goes By*. Boston: Little, Brown.

Wasser, Frederick (1995). "Is Hollywood America? The Transnationalization of the American Film Industry," *Critical Studies in Mass Communication*, 12 (4): 423–437.

Waters, Mary C. (1990). *Ethnic Options: Choosing Ethnic Identities in America*. Berkeley: University of California Press.

Wellemeyer, Jonathan (2006). "Hollywood and the Spread of Anti-Americanism," *npr.org*, December 20.

Wieland, Chris (nd). "The Nerd Movie." Unpublished manuscript.

Wikipedia (n.d.). *http://en.wikipedia.org/wiki/Political_cinema* (accessed October 4, 2012).

Williams, John W. (1995). "Moles and Clowns: How Editorial Cartoons Portrayed Aldrich Ames and the CIA." Midwest Popular Culture Association, Indianapolis, IN, November.

Willman, Chris (2013). "'Invisible War' Producer Tells How Oscar-Nominated Documentary Is Bringing Change to the Military," *The Wrap*, February 14.

Wills Thomas A., James D. Sargent, Frederick X. Gibbons, Meg Gerrard, and Mike Stoolmiller (2009). "Movie Exposure to Alcohol Cues and Adolescent Alcohol Problems: A Longitudinal Analysis in a National Sample," *Psychologically Addictive Behavior*," 23 (1): 23–35.

Wood, Michael (1975). *America in the Movies*. New York: Basic Books.

———— (1980). "The True Story of 'Star Wars': The Myths Strike Back," *Los Angeles Times*, August 17, Part V, p. 3.

———— (1982). "Living Nightmares," *The New York Review of Books*, 29 (10): 34–36.

Zeitchik, Steven (2013). "Do Films Influence Behavior?" *Los Angeles Times*, November 17

Zimmerman, Paul (1972). "Soft Sell," *Newsweek*, July 17, pp. 78–79.

Film Index

Subject Index

About the Contributors

Editor **Michael Haas** received his college education at Stanford University and Yale University. After teaching at the University of Hawai'i for thirty-five years, he retired to devote his full-time attention to writing. He also serves as President of the Political Film Society in Los Angeles, is a member of the California Senior Assembly, is on the Adjunct Faculty in Political Science of California Polytechnic University, Pomona, and is a member of the International Advisory Council of the University of Cambodia, Phnom Penh. He has edited and written a total of 49 books on government and politics, many of which focus on Asian politics. He maintains three websites related to his activities in regard to film, human rights, and recent publications. *Wikipedia.com* has a fuller biography. Due to his work on behalf of human rights, both through publications and some political activity in regard to American racism and foreign policy misadventures, he was nominated for the 2010 Nobel Peace Prize.

Andrew Aoki is professor and chair of the Political Science Department at Augsburg College (Minneapolis). He is also co-president of the American Political Science Association's Organized Section on Race, Ethnicity, and Politics. His writing has included work on popular culture and politics, and on the battles over multicultural education. Recent publications have examined Asian American politics and the influences of immigration on American politics. His current projects are a study of the role of Asian Americans in the evolving ethnoracial order in the United States and a case study of the evolution of the Japanese American community in Portland, Oregon. He received his Ph.D. at UCLA.

Michael A. Genovese received a Ph.D. from the University of Southern California in 1979. He currently holds the Loyola Chair of Leadership Studies, and is Professor of Political Science, and Director of the Institute for Leadership Studies at Loyola Marymount University. In 2006, he was made a Fellow at the Queens College, Oxford University. Professor Genovese has written over 35 books, and has won over a dozen university and national teaching awards, including the Fritz B. Burns Distinguished Teaching Award (1995), and the Rains Excellence in Research Award (2011). Professor Genovese frequently appears as a commentator on local and national television. He is also Associate Editor of the journal, *White House Studies* and has lectured for the United States Embassy abroad. Professor Genovese has been The Washington Center's "scholar-in-residence" at three Democratic national political conventions, the 2008 presidential inauguration, and the 2012 Republican National Convention. In 2004–05, Professor Genovese served as President of the Presidency Research Group of the American Political Science Association. He is currently on the advisory boards of The Washington Center and The Center for the Study of Los Angeles, and he is the Chair of the Board for the Foundation for International Education.

Ernest D. Giglio holds a doctorate in political science from Syracuse University. He recently retired as Director of International Studies and Professor of Politics and American Studies at Lycoming College. Through his initiative, the Political Film Society briefly became a Related Group of the American Political Science Association and later merged with the Literature and Politics Section. In addition to his book on political film, he is the author of *Rights, Liberties and Public Policy*.

Elizabeth Haas earned her Ph.D. from the University of Michigan and was a Woodrow Wilson Fellow in the Humanities at the University of Texas. She currently teaches at Fairfield University in Fairfield, Connecticut, and is a co-author of the second edition of *Projecting Politics: Political Messages in American Films*. Unrelated to editor Michael Haas, she is the sister of Peter J. Haas.

Hans Noel is an Associate Professor of Government at Georgetown University. He is the author of *Political Ideologies and Political Parties in America*, and a co-author of *The Party Decides: Presidential Nominations Before and After Reform*. Noel was a Robert Wood Johnson Scholar in Health Policy Research at the University of Michigan from 2008 to 2010 and a fellow in the Center for the Study of Democratic Politics in the Woodrow Wilson School of Public and International Affairs at Princeton University from 2005 to 2006. He received his Ph.D. in political science from UCLA in 2006. Noel co-directed and co-produced the award-winning 2001 feature film *The Rest of Your Life*. He completed his doctorate at UCLA.

John W. Williams chairs the Department of Political Science at his baccalaureate Alma Mater, Principia College, while serving as codirector of Asian Studies and Adjunct Faculty at Washington University in St. Louis. A former member of the Civil Rights Division of the U.S. Department of Justice, he holds a J.D. degree from George Washington University and is the author of the *Guide to International Legal Research* and editor of *Career Preparation and Opportunities in International Law*. His ongoing research project is on the lives of African Americans in the county where Principia is located. His professional writings have appeared in such journals as the *International Communications Bulletin, Jersey County Journal, Security Journal, Turkish Journal of Police Studies*, and the *World Intelligence Review*. In 1988, Professor Williams received the Sears-Roebuck Foundation Teaching Excellence and Campus Leadership Award.